20 WAYS TO BREAK FREE FROM TRAUMA

FROM BRAIN HIJACKING TO POST-TRAUMATIC GROWTH

PHILIPPA SMETHURST
Foreword by Sir Terry Waite, KCMG CBE

Jessica Kingsley Publishers
London and Philadelphia

First published in Great Britain in 2025 by Jessica Kingsley Publishers
An imprint of John Murray Press

1

A CIP catalogue record for this title is available from the
British Library and the Library of Congress

ISBN 978 1 80501 310 5
eISBN 978 1 80501 311 2

Printed and bound in Great Britain by TJ Books Limited

Jessica Kingsley Publishers' policy is to use papers that are natural,
renewable and recyclable products and made from wood grown in
sustainable forests. The logging and manufacturing processes are expected
to conform to the environmental regulations of the country of origin.

Jessica Kingsley Publishers
Carmelite House
50 Victoria Embankment
London EC4Y 0DZ

www.jkp.com

John Murray Press
Part of Hodder & Stoughton Ltd
An Hachette Company

Contents

FOREWORD

During the past 30 years or more many books dealing with the subject of trauma have crossed my desk. Some have been highly technical, written for those who are professionally engaged with those experiencing this condition. Others have been written for the general reader. *20 Ways to Break Free From Trauma* is probably one of the clearest expositions of this subject that I have read.

Philippa Smethurst, a practising psychotherapist, has drawn from her long experience and produced a book that will be not only useful for therapists, engaged in this field, but also informative for the general reader.

In 20 clearly and concisely written chapters she begins by defining trauma and explains how it affects those who experience it. She then continues to explore the subject in greater detail through the use of actual case studies with which she has been involved over the years. Following each case study she includes a short poem which she had presented to her patients and which encapsulates something of the experience itself.

Over the years I have known many individuals who have experienced trauma. Some have chosen to deny it and not infrequently paid a high price for this. Others have been successfully helped and have been able to use their experience creatively.

This book should be essential reading, not only for therapists but also for those in high stress occupations and for the general reader who wants a clear and concise exposition of the subject.

Sir Terry Waite, KCMG CBE

INTRODUCTION

Trauma is part of the warp and weft of our lives.

Trauma is our powerful unresolved experience. It can have many faces, it can squeeze out our joy. This book presents 20 different trauma responses, unpacking and illuminating each one and giving ideas and exercises to help release us from trauma's shackles.

This book combines my 30 years of professional experience with the latest research in neuroscience. I began writing the book in the pandemic lockdown when many people were questioning their lives and making changes. Many others felt overwhelmed. To me at that time, unpacking trauma seemed like an appropriate response to a challenge that faced our world.

Based on real-life experience, this book takes us on a 20-point tour of the effects of trauma on both body and mind. One size does not fit all, and we need different approaches to help us. We might imagine the 20 chapters as a 'trauma bookshelf', each slim chapter featuring a different way that trauma manifests and can be responded to. We may recognize ourselves or a loved one somewhere in the 20 responses.

Who am I?

I am a psychotherapist, yet the book is not intended to be an explanation of psychotherapy and I do not suggest that everyone who experiences trauma needs therapy. I do know that trauma can trap us. Through my clinical practice I have learned certain principles about how trauma manifests. Here, I share my understanding and quests for freedom that many have sought and found.

I've known trauma from the inside myself. Those of us who have been traumatized might find ourselves hurt, misunderstood, broken, alone, fragile or judged in the world. As a result of our trauma experiences, we can withdraw or feel permanently stressed, may become numb or disconnected, struggle with feeling alone and depressed, or perhaps frequently respond to other people with suspicion or aggression. We might respond in any one of the ways described in these chapters.

Over many years, I have learned to befriend my trauma. In this book, by separating out particular trauma responses, I show specific ways to help dilute trauma's effects that mitigate its power and bring us more fullness of life. Throughout these pages, I share practical discoveries gleaned from my work with myself and others.

What is trauma?

Trauma is not something big and vague. Brain scans and research in the last couple of decades have shown us what happens to our bodies and minds when we are traumatized. In the Western world, science helps us understand our trauma responses. In addition, we have much to learn from ancient practices and indigenous cultures about healing from trauma.

Trauma comes from the Greek word for wound. The wounds of physical trauma are evident and visible, but the wounds of psychological trauma are often hidden within us: psychological trauma hurts us inside. I try to define what trauma is, not a mysterious bad entity, but a set of responses that happen to us *inside*. Trauma is an inside job. Manifesting in an array of different ways, the tentacles of trauma can work their way into surprising crevices within us. It does not necessarily follow that if we experience bad things we will be traumatized. The opposite is also true: we can be in situations that traumatize us without us even knowing it: some trauma symptoms are hidden within and may feel subtle and confusing.

How can trauma make us feel?

We hear the word trauma used every day in news reports, in conversation, even at the cheese counter at the supermarket. In common parlance, we say we are traumatized when referring to bad things that we don't like. We might be fearful that if we don't examine our past traumas properly, they might trip us up unexpectedly.

Trauma is an injury in our capacity to feel. In trauma's wake, we are easily overwhelmed by feelings, or cannot feel at all. Protective fear dominates our landscape. We no longer trust our capacity to feel properly. We struggle with sorrow, we struggle with joy. We struggle with relationships. Ideally, feelings are our internal compass. If we cannot feel, connect to what we feel or trust our feelings, we have lost our compass. Then we easily lose our direction. We who have been traumatized long to be seen and understood. A client of mine says that those who are traumatized need to carry a card or wear a bracelet to be recognized. Being traumatized doesn't mean we are weak. It is strong to know what is true about our experience. I believe there is a need for trauma's weight to be known and shared.

How we can cause each other trauma

Touching all of us at times, psychological trauma – *woundedness* – is part of the warp and weft of our lives. Part of our fabric but not to be underestimated, trauma can break our connection to ourselves and others. Several chapters in this book (particularly 13–17) examine how people can traumatize each other. When other people traumatize us, we may lose trust in them. That makes us feel isolated and sometimes heartbroken. I examine the seemingly impossible experience of needing someone, being deeply attached to them and also being hurt by that same person. When this happens, we have a dilemma. We need others but we cannot trust them. After such a trauma, we so often cannot trust ourselves either. We may be in pain, yet we plough on with life. We might feel we have no other choice or that it is impossible to feel whole again.

Some things that can happen when we are traumatized

In the face of overwhelming experience, our bodies, from the base of our spine upwards, respond with a volcanic surge of energy, hormones and emotional activation. We often hear of the *flight or fight response* – our hearts race, our palms become sweaty, we get wobbly knees, our pupils constrict to narrow our focus, or we want to run from danger. We may not appreciate that there are so many other trauma responses too. Some of them might be powerful and shocking. Others are less obvious, but we know we just do not feel quite right. Our trauma responses may be a pervading backdrop to our lives, or they might spring up from time to time.

Several chapters in the book discuss the opposite to overwhelm – the 'underwhelm' set of trauma responses (Chapters 6–10). We might physically flop and be unable to move or we might become spacey and zoned out as though we are experiencing the world through plate glass. We may not respond to life as freely and openly as we might want to, or we might feel frozen and tight inside, not able to properly rest and feel safe anywhere. Our brains can get hijacked by trauma's stress surge (see Chapter 8), so we cannot think properly, or we get rigidly convinced of something and hold on to a belief for dear life, with a vice-like grip (see Chapter 9). When we are traumatized, it is so common to only be able to see things in a fixed or binary way.

How trauma can affect the whole of us

One key to understanding trauma is that the body and mind are both involved. Our bodies can hold our trauma responses, even in ways that we don't realize, in our posture, such as hunched shoulders, or in bodily symptoms: maybe a grumbling gut or a clenched jaw. Throughout the book, and particularly in Chapter 12, we will see examples of how, in trauma, our bodies can carry the weight of our experience. A good starting place is to pay attention to our faithful bodies that have helped us survive. One of the book's themes is helping us learn how to use our bodies as guides to tell us what has happened to us. If we pay attention, our bodies can be our barometers for our feelings, letting us know what we might need to do next. There are many exercises and meditations to encourage our bodies to recover and regain our equilibrium – to help us be us.

How trauma changes time

The tricky aspect of trauma is that our trauma responses can so easily return. When we are triggered, our trauma wounds are touched again. Our responses can happen instantly and involuntarily, *as if then were now*. When this happens, then and now can get tangled up. Time-scrambling can be a disturbing, overwhelming and scary experience (Chapter 2). Sometimes our trauma-triggering disturbances diminish over time, leaving no lasting trauma. Sometimes our triggering symptoms get worse. The book examines triggering (Chapter 3), and shows different ways to disempower the debilitating effects of our triggers.

Things that cause trauma, first – event trauma

Trauma can occur when something random or unexpected comes across our path, in an instant changing every moment of our lives from then on, like an accident, assault or sudden loss. Trauma can be caused by large-scale events such as war and natural disaster. At the time of writing there are around 54 countries in the world experiencing war. Trauma may be caused when people are displaced, dispossessed, uprooted or marginalized. When our resources are insufficient to cope with an experience, we cannot thrive.

The second kind – cumulative trauma

Cumulative trauma can occur when our needs are not met over time. Because trauma may be the ongoing reality of our lives, it can be hard to spot. Cumulative trauma could be caused by an experience of ongoing cruelty, neglect and sexual or emotional abuse. Because it is our ongoing situation, we may be hurt inside but do not have space to acknowledge it, so we push the hurt down into an internal chasm inside. We walk around with our wounds unacknowledged, heaping trauma upon trauma. It is important to examine and think about this effect of trauma, and how trauma touches trauma (triggering is focused on in Chapter 3, and destructive cycles in Chapter 18).

What are the effects of trauma and what can be done?

Experiencing trauma may be rather like having too much chilli powder in a bowl of soup. We cannot take the powder out, but we can dilute its effects. I have tried to make this book reader-friendly, with frequent ideas for the dilution of trauma. We can do so much to mitigate trauma, to lessen the chilli effect and help us feel better.

Our minds can be a great help in shedding trauma's load. Finding *words* for our experience can be hugely powerful. Trauma can feel untameable, but if we begin speaking we regain some power. This is often where change starts. The process of using our minds to draw closer to the source of our embodied trauma is a brave thing to do. It entails facing fear and other painful emotions, and this is no easy task. Our overwhelming feelings can make finding the right words extremely difficult, even if we feel safe enough to try. Expressing ourselves may come out piecemeal or in fragments that may not make sense to us – this is the pain of trauma – but words and images can ultimately help us repair and connect us back to ourselves and others.

A note on the stories in the book

All the stories in the book are taken from real life. In many instances, they are composites, woven together from the many people I have worked with over the years. I have taken great care not to make any details identifiable with any specific individuals. In instances where the stories are close, the individuals concerned have given their consent for their stories to be shared.

Explaining the poems at the end of each chapter

Over many years of practice, my clients and I have found that taking time to choose the *right* words can be a powerful way to excavate and sculpt difficult experiences. Mapping confusing thoughts onto a page can be an important tool in untangling what can feel very knotted.

Precise words can show us what is true, even though the process can be painful. In my work, I have tried to encapsulate the 'inside story' of trauma by sometimes writing short impromptu poems immediately after a session, and offering them as a gift. This started as a way of capturing something, an attempt to make something complex and unacknowledged more concrete, to pin something down. I would share an image, a snapshot or a gut feeling, what the poet Louis MacNeice calls 'a splash of words in passing', and this became part of my practice.[1] Naming experience can be hugely relieving and many clients find the words helpful and have started writing too. This is by means of explanation about why, at the end of each chapter, I offer a 'poem' reflecting on themes in the chapter. My recommendation is to use the ending poem as a footnote or as a model for how to do this yourself if you find it helpful.

How understanding trauma can help us relate to each other radically differently

A clarion call for the traumatized: in order to move beyond our trauma responses we need to learn how to treat ourselves with generous understanding. We need to move from *reacting*, to understanding what our reactions are about and *responding* to them kindly. Urie Bronfenbrenner says: 'Every child needs at least one adult who is irrationally crazy about him or her.'[2] Historically, we may not all have experienced this, and those who have adverse experiences in childhood will have less ability to manage that missing experience and will face its lasting legacy. Childhood or developmental trauma is explored throughout the book. This subject needs our sensitivity as its roots can be deep, hidden and painful.

---

1   MacNeice, L. (1979). 'Entirely' from *The Collected Poems of Louis MacNeice*. E.R. Dodds (ed.). London: Faber and Faber.

2   Urie Bronfenbrenner (1917–2005) was Professor of Human Development and Psychology at Cornell University. His most basic belief states in scientific terms how trusting bonds with children are the most powerful force in young people's development. This sentence is a summary of one of the necessary propositions that he cited, as outlined in Bronfenbrenner, U. (ed.) (2005). *Making Human Beings Human: Bioecological Perspectives on Human Development*. Thousand Oaks, CA: Sage Publications.

Quality matters

A call for compassion – a dollop of loving kindness in response to pain – is demonstrated in the ideas and stories throughout this book. Even a little good quality connection can begin to heal our trauma and make us feel much better. If we live with someone who is traumatized, there are many ideas here about what might help and why. I believe that gaining information and knowledge is the starting place to finding ways to heal. So equipped, we can then learn to treat ourselves and others with informed kindness.

A recommendation to go lightly with the book

This *quality* of responsiveness to ourselves and others is the strongest ingredient in building resilience to stress and trauma. With this in mind, it is important to say that some of the stories here may touch your own traumas at an emotional level. If this happens, reach out to someone you trust, if you can. Or skip over a section and come back to it, or look ahead for the ideas that can help with our trauma responses at the end of each chapter.

What help is possible at any one time

Part of my plea is for understanding of the traumatized. For many who are in ongoing traumatic situations, healing and recovery may not be possible right now. We may not immediately be able to break free. If we or others are living in an ongoing traumatic situation, we need support to just keep going on the journey. A little support goes a long way. It helps relieve the burden and may make all the difference. In supporting individuals, we must never lose sight of the systems and conditions that cause trauma and find ways to speak out about injustice and the systems that wound us.

How the book works

Chapter by chapter, I investigate the following trauma responses in depth. Feel free to pick whichever chapter seems most relevant to you.

We are taken over by a sense of urgency (Chapter 1); we lose our usual flow of time (Chapter 2); we are susceptible to further mini-traumas – 'triggers' (Chapter 3); we have a compulsion to fight (Chapter 4); we attempt to escape in some way (Chapter 5); we freeze (Chapter 6); we withdraw under the radar (Chapter 7); our brains are so hijacked that we cannot process information properly and we latch on to ideas with fixed certainty (Chapters 8 and 9); we disconnect, becoming numb or fragmented (Chapters 10 and 11); we feel trauma in our bodies (Chapter 12); our trust in others can be affected (Chapters 13 and 14); we become ashamed (Chapter 15); we guard our wounded and painful hearts (Chapter 16); we feel deeply alone (Chapter 17); we become caught up in destructive patterns (Chapter 18); we pick up trauma from those around us (Chapter 19); and find ourselves building resilience (Chapter 20) – new strength and purpose – as a result of our trauma. The final chapter draws together ten threads towards post-trauma growth in the final chapter, distilling resources for healing and offering tools to assist our journeying on with confidence.

My hope is that by showing the inner workings of trauma, its power can be transformed. I hope that you will see trauma responses mitigated and the threads of inner tapestries reconnected in the following chapters. I believe that we can find ways to sew goodness around the painful holes that have wounded us. We can learn to weave ourselves back together.

Where I am
I begin here
Breathing in
The good air
Exhaling
Pausing
My out-breath
Love in this rhythm
This song
Peeping out daring to
Look with hope
Even from here

You can find an introductory video at https://
www.youtube.com/watch?v=k5ssTIQWMlE
or by scanning the QR code. Links and QR
codes for further videos can be found at the
end of each chapter.

— Chapter 1 —

TRAUMA TAKES US OVER

Trauma is being overwhelmed by too much stress.

In response to 'too much', a flooding of fear that overwhelms our nervous system can feel like being taken on a whitewater raft without having control of the currents.

A person in the throes of a traumatic response to a life event may *know* deep down that something is wrong, yet can still feel trapped and unable to do anything to change it.

Trauma is a word that is often used and is sometimes misunderstood. Many people think that trauma relates to an event that is experienced but in fact *trauma is not the event itself. Rather, it is the imprint of an experience that leaves its mark on our minds and bodies.* Definitions matter. Peter Levine said that trauma is 'a highly activated incomplete biological response to threat, frozen in time'.[1]

Trauma is what is left inside. We may not experience extreme events traumatically, while we can experience less extreme events as trauma.

As outlined in the introduction to this book, there are two kinds of trauma. The first is a response to a single event, such as a sudden illness, a terrorist attack, a fire or someone becoming unexpectedly scary – big T trauma. The second is the sort of cumulative trauma that perhaps is more a part of our lives than we might imagine. We can become traumatized when we live in an environment that abuses, disregards or neglects us on an ongoing basis, when we have to endure something, when someone gives us the message that we need to be a certain way

---

1   Peter A. Levine PhD made this statement in a class he taught and its origin is unsure. It is reproduced with permission from his office in California.

to be loved, when we feel a sense of dereliction or desolation, when we do not get our needs met. The effects of these small t, cumulative, repetitive micro-traumas are not always so easily recognized but their tentacles are far-reaching, eliciting powerful responses.

The overwhelm of trauma

Trauma involves both our bodies and our minds – all the 'fire alarms' in the 'citadel' of our bodies and minds are on high alert and we can feel as if anything can happen. When our safety is threatened, our biological survival is imperative. Understanding this is our starting point. Respecting the physiology of trauma can help us to find ways to navigate through it. Trauma marks our bodies and the effects can be long lasting.

Let's think about specifically what happens to our bodies and brains. In trauma (overwhelming experience), a volcano of fear erupts from the base of our spine upwards, sending a whoosh of alarm through our emotional (limbic) brains and activating the almond-shaped *amygdala* that is situated near our temple – *the brain's smoke detector* – and raising the alarm.[2, 3]

After the amygdala signals danger, the vagus (meaning vagabond or wandering) cranial nerve, that runs down our entire body from the brain through the heart and lungs to the digestive system, sends messages to our organs. They release powerful stress hormones that help us narrow our focus on the danger or predator and survive whatever challenge faces us. In a more sustained situation, the hormone cortisol keeps the amygdala activated over a period of time and keeps us alert to danger.[4]

---

2   The amygdala can be enlarged as a response to us being overwhelmed in trauma and is then less likely to respond in a nuanced way to uncertainty or unpredictability. We perceive everything as danger. For an interesting exploration of the amygdala, listen on BBC Sounds to the Radio 4 programme *Amygdala Made of Stronger Stuff* with Dr Xand Van Tulleken and Kimberley Wilson, first broadcast on 27 October 2022.

3   'The brain's smoke detector' referring to the amygdala is a term first used by Bessel van der Kolk in *The Body Keeps the Score* (2014) London: Penguin, p.69.

4   Sherman, C. (2019). The Quest to Cure PTSD. *Psychology Today* (November/December), p.64. This article states that this hormonal response arises from the hypothalamic-pituitary-adrenal axis 'swinging into gear, tripping off a cascade of hormones and culminating in the release of cortisol, which extends the mobilization reaction'.

The activation or physiological *arousal* of our nervous system can lead us to experience phenomena such as an increased heart rate, tunnel vision, dilation of pupils, sweating and wobbly knees. When this happens in our bodies, our brains try to make sense of the arousal by looking around for evidence of the threat, narrowing our field of attention and causing us to either go into battle or flee – the fight or flight response. We might call this heightened activation our 'red-zone' response.[5] Fight and flight responses are examined more thoroughly in Chapters 4 and 5.

The underwhelm of trauma

Another response to the overwhelm of trauma is to dip under the radar into underwhelm – the 'blue zone'. To save us from an unbearable experience, our parasympathetic nervous system cuts in like a corrective brake, our blood pressure drops and we temporarily feel too little rather than too much: we zone out. Something terrible might be happening, but when observing a person in the blue zone you would never know. Their bodies have responded to the overwhelm by not engaging, like an animal under attack that might feign dead. This feature of our nervous system has only been fully understood in recent years.[6] We will look at blue-zone responses in Chapter 7.

Hyper and hypo responses as trauma solutions

The red- and blue-zone responses are both solutions produced by our bodies/minds to the problem of *too much* (*trauma*). They are solutions for our 'dysregulated' (out-of-control emotionally and stressed out) nervous system because they take us away from an experience that is unbearable for us, by fighting or fleeing (in red-zone responses)

---

5   For more information on zones of arousal, red, blue and green/yellow, see the National Institute for the Clinical Application of Behavioral Medicine (NICABM) worksheet infographic at www.nicabm.com and search for Window of Tolerance, accessed 26/11/23. Also see the diagram in Chapter 20.

6   In 1994, Professor Stephen Porges proposed the Polyvagal Theory. This theory focuses on the autonomic nervous system's arousal levels, and particularly the way that the parasympathetic branch of the vagal nerve collapses in an involuntary way in the face of overwhelming stress, which has a protective function for mammals.

or disengaging, not knowing about and escaping (as in blue-zone responses). Of course, it is quite normal for humans to be disturbed by adverse events and these symptoms often fade naturally over time: equilibrium is found and there is no lasting trauma. For some of us, however, these trauma responses can become frozen in time and linger after the event. Then they eclipse our capacity for joy and love and reduce our ability to cope with life.

Restoring well-being in the green zone

The good news is that these effects can be mitigated. Depending on the severity of the trauma and the existing resources we have, restoring well-being can take time and various types of help. One size does not fit all and we need to be creative to determine what works for each individual. If we pause, we can find things that can enrich our humanity and mitigate trauma's overwhelm.

For us to feel better, our nervous system needs to find its way into the green/yellow zone. When we are in the green zone, we have a sense of well-being and safety in the world and with other people. Trauma temporarily annihilates the safety of our body's and mind's green zone.[7] We get stuck in either red or blue. Later in the chapter and throughout this book are ideas and tools to help return to a green-zone sense of safety but first let's look at how this works in real life.[8]

---

7   Daniel Siegel, Clinical Professor of Psychiatry, developed the idea of the Window of Tolerance to describe the best state of arousal in which we are able to function and thrive in everyday life. For further explanation see his book *Mindsight* (2011) London: Oneworld. See Chapter 20 for a diagram and further explanation of the Window of Tolerance.

8   There are some chemical and non-invasive brain treatments on the horizon that may increasingly be used to bring down the level of activation in the brain and nervous system and increase psychological safety. For example, neuropeptides block PTSD responses, ketamine mitigates stress, and therapeutic use of MDMA (Ecstasy) and Psilocybin may increase our ability to tolerate emotion. Neurofeedback and Transcranial Magnetic Stimulation are non-invasive ways of altering brain states that are being used. MDMA is already approved in Israel and Australia and is likely to be so in the US and UK before long. Catherine Jackson writes that psychedelics allow a trauma sufferer to understand the powerful feelings that come up without overwhelm and help us get out of the thought loops that are so prevalent in trauma (Is working with psychedelics the future of therapy? *Therapy Today*, July/August 2023, pp.19–22). We do not fully know how some of these treatment options will be developed and integrated with existing treatments and the picture is changing all the time.

Trauma shakes us to the core and this chapter's focus is on one of its primary effects – a powerful sense of urgency that propels us forward. As Keisha's story shows, it is by learning to slowly build trust in ourselves, the world and other people again, step by step, that we can begin to return to the fullness of life in the green zone of well-being.

TRAUMA STORY: Keisha's night walks

Keisha's adored father dies in a car crash when she is 11. Afterwards, her mother emotionally collapses and is unable to function for over ten years. For Keisha, her mum's mental illness has always dominated. There is never much space for young Keisha's feelings and because of this she never feels properly safe. Mum is unpredictable, full of worries, eruptions and cruel accusations. But their relationship gets much worse after the crash. Deep down, Keisha suspects her mother blames her for being noisy in the car at the time of the accident. The only person who properly believed in her was her dad. Since his death she feels as if she is holding on to the world by a thread.

Adult Keisha works in a bank, a job where she excels. She loves being there. Keisha is popular but careful never to tell colleagues about herself. At night, the things that Keisha feels often bubble to the surface. Without the distraction of her daily tasks, she feels a pressurizing energy, her agitated thoughts torment her with an urgency that is overwhelming. She becomes terrified, her heart pounds, her muscles twitch. She experiences intrusive thoughts telling her she is not safe in the house and that she urgently needs to get out, so she leaps into action. She takes long walks, striding in the dark through the populated areas. Always alone, she sometimes meets lone men, but she doesn't feel afraid. She ignores them and presses on. Keisha is compelled to keep taking her night-time walks. The more danger she is in while outside, the better: it matches what she is feeling inside.

One night Keisha happens to be spotted by one of her co-workers, who is an unusually lovely person. Fran is alarmed by how vulnerable and exposed Keisha appears. Concerned for Keisha's safety, Fran talks to her line manager. The manager does not want to intrude into Keisha's private life, but gently enquires about her well-being, using open questions and looking Keisha in the eye kindly and calmly. Keisha is defensive at first, repeating that she is fine, but her line manager's patient, kind and non-intrusive enquiries have an effect. She finds herself explaining that she has not been coping well on her own at home lately. The line manager's listening skills and open, non-judgemental demeanour help Keisha feel safe and open up a little. The manager makes it clear that Keisha does not have to say or do anything that she is not ready for. Together, they think about options that might help her feel safer at home. Could she consider taking on a lodger? Or a dog? Might it help to take self-defence lessons or attend a restorative yoga class to help unwind and relax after work? Keisha feels she has finally landed on a rock of safety. She is no longer quite so alone.

Keisha feels as if she is on an express train that she can't get off because there are no stops. Sometimes, feeling so out of control can be scary, but it can sometimes also be strangely addictive and exhilarating: trauma fear is the only answer we know. 'We must protect ourselves from more harm,' says fear. The difficulty is that we can become imprisoned by these fear responses and fear grows like a snowball going down a hill.

Other physical aspects of trauma arousal

Let's think about Keisha's body-mind responses some more. When we are experiencing trauma, our nervous system gets dysregulated. This means we have too much stress in our system that we are then unable to control. It may seem strange that seeking thrills is the trauma solution Keisha comes to, but this is a very common response. There are two reasons for this.

One reason is that the hormones released in trauma, such as adrenalin and cortisol, can be addictive. Another is that trauma can affect our capacity to think properly about consequences. In the overwhelm of trauma, the whoosh of fear that surges upwards through our limbic brain affects linkages in the pre-frontal and frontal cortex. This causes our brain functions to be temporarily disabled: we cannot think strategically or logically. We cannot think and we cannot *link*. (We will explore trauma's brain hijacking effects, and our inability to process information, in Chapter 8.)

Keisha's red-zone activation, and her misfiring amygdala and short-circuited brain functions, lead her to come up with a solution – to leave the house and walk alone at night. The walking activity both releases and expresses the trauma charge but danger begets danger. At the same time, Keisha is operating in the disconnected blue zone, cut off from understanding the danger she is in. This is typical of trauma: the parts of Keisha's brain that can think properly, helping her to reflect, assess a situation and care for herself properly, are taken over by the overwhelming trauma reaction that eclipses everything else. What helps is the calm line manager's intervention. Her unflappable kindness is a starting point for Keisha to access her green zone once again, at least for some moments to start with. The part of Keisha that dominates – the exaggerated stress response of her trauma – is challenged by the caring of another person. She can begin to let go of her fear.

Be led by the traumatized person

The wise manager is led by Keisha and takes her cue from her. This is an important principle when we are alongside someone who has suffered trauma. When we feel supported and not pushed, we quickly relax and our rational thinking can be restored. In the safe space of her line manager's office, the part of Keisha that knows she has been taking risks comes back online. Now, she can begin to take care of herself once more. She knows she needs to calm down and it is an enormous relief to do so. Putting the first piece of a support framework in place is important for trauma mitigation, but not always easy.

Raphael's story has some similarities to Keisha's, though the way his trauma expresses itself is more elaborate and tangled up with his vocation as a journalist.

TRAUMA STORY: Raphael, the war reporter

Raphael has early exposure to danger. He is physically and sexually abused as a young child, and is later treated cruelly in foster care and children's homes. As a result, Raphael's young mind and body is wired for threat and has become red-zone central. As a teenager, he becomes feral, takes risks and seeks thrills. Through his experiences, he develops an extraordinary ability to master tricky situations, which, together with his acute intelligence, makes him determined to work his way up from a basic print-room job to eventually becoming a journalist. Raphael is drawn to reporting on conflict situations, and excels at keeping a clear head and capturing the essence of complicated situations in words. When he moves into broadcast journalism, his two-minute summaries filmed close to gunfire and shelling are sought after by television companies. Raphael becomes known as an expert and has an international reputation. He starts to take more risks on each trip. Like Keisha, he only feels fully alive when he is in acute danger.

Long before this, Raphael fell in love with Maria when they worked in the print room together, and they have now been happily married for many years. She is supportive of his vocation as a journalist, but suffers terribly with worries when Raphael is away. Then when he returns home, he alternately becomes obsessed – anything can be a candidate for his next fixation – and remote, unreachable and depressed. Raphael is unable to cope with ordinary life: the calmer life is, the more unhappy he is. Being in danger draws him irresistibly. When he survives danger and understands difficult things he feels a sense of power in doing something useful and this power inures him to danger. Danger excites and compels him. Feeling a hero at work is intoxicating and intense. There is another aspect at play for Raphael. Being a success is a ticket out of trauma; it is very different to his traumatic past when he was utterly helpless, unable to stop terrible things happening to him.

Maria realizes Raphael is seriously out of balance and needs a reboot. She is unsure what to do for the best. Without consulting Raphael, she decides to book a break for them at a spa hotel. She instinctively knows Raphael needs to slow down, but how will he react to her intervention? At first, Raphael strongly resists and tells her flatly he is not going to the hotel. She stands up to him, telling him firmly that he has been frenetic and weird and needs space to sort things out. Somewhere, Raphael knows this to be true.

The determined constancy of his wife's love reminds him of what he most needs to do: calm down.

It is important to note that the reboot is not a magic solution but a start. It takes several repetitions of this story for Raphael to see and accept his pattern of behaviour when trauma takes him over. First, he seeks danger, then becomes in thrall to fear-fuelled obsessions, before falling into a collapse. With each repetition things get worse. At the same time, Raphael needs the repetitions because on each circuit he sees things more clearly. Awareness of his trauma response is like slowly focusing a camera, helping Raphael to take himself more seriously and chip away at his compulsive behaviour. When he is able to calm down, Raphael can think more objectively about what is happening to him and begin to set appropriate limits. With some psychological help, he comes to recognize his trauma fear as a powerful force compelling him to act. He begins to befriend this force and learn its ways. His employers also start taking his trauma seriously. They refer him for a psychological assessment before they allow him to get on the next plane.

Trauma logic in risk-taking

The risk-taking inherent in both Keisha and Raphael has a kind of trauma logic. Expression of intensity following trauma can sometimes be a healthy arc for us to follow. What this means is that the intensity of red-zone activation sometimes seeks full expression before we find a calm on the other side. There are some treatments for trauma that recreate the intensity of the red zone, enabling parasympathetic restoration and equilibrium to be found. For example, cold-water swimming, sweating in a sauna or pushing ourselves to an edge physically can help our bodies to express and discharge trauma, be in the present moment and find our equilibrium.

How trauma's power eclipses safety

However, while in thrall to the raw power of their trauma, Keisha and Raphael are not safe. Their trauma responses have temporarily cut them off from their needs and their ability to think properly, though both are fortunate to have another person step in. The existing trust Raphael has in Maria allows her to temporarily 'take charge' by organizing the break for him to reboot. Using the trust you have established with a traumatized person can be important. When someone is lost, it may be important to authoritatively and kindly present them with what they need, even if they are not in a position to see it or take it up immediately. It is a good use of the power you have.

How to approach trauma

A first question you might ask is not 'Why are Keisha and Raphael behaving like this?' but 'What happened to them?' And second, as Maria did, you might ask, 'What might they need?' Using your imagination to consider this question and looking beyond any tricky behaviour is another important rule of thumb: give them the benefit of the doubt because something is likely to have happened to them that is outside their (and maybe your) experience. If someone's life has changed them by trauma, they need others to imagine the enormity of their experiences. Any attempt by others to do this for them may make all the difference.

Let's think about the science here. When Keisha loses her beloved father, she experiences the withdrawal of the hormone dopamine, which produces a warm feeling of safety that comes from being closely attached to another person. This may have been as severe for her as the withdrawal symptoms experienced by an addict coming off an opioid drug. For the abused young Raphael, the repeated invasion of his body against his will and the chaos at home sends the stress hormone cortisol surging through his body, leading him to feel constantly and profoundly unsafe. Repeatedly placing himself in a dangerous environment paradoxically makes Raphael feel 'safe' because it feels normal. Sexual trauma has disabled Raphael's ability to trust his instincts because he had to accept things he knew were wrong. His amygdala has lost its capacity for clear messaging and is misfiring all over the place, telling him that profound danger is 'normal' and is what he needs. His trauma responses are ruling the roost.

With this in mind what helps?

For the moment, let us assume that all of us at some time or another have been affected by trauma. When we humans are emotionally disturbed, we need empathy and connection to soothe the volcano in our stomachs or guts, calm our wired and buzzing nerves, regulate our stress and access the green zone. Trauma cannot be turned off like a tap but we can work on empathy and connection. This can be done in the following ways. We need to counteract *the 'bottom-up' body to brain activation in trauma by sending messages of safety from our minds to our bodies.* This is the work of regulation.

Regulation central

Regulation means finding ways to bring our activation down, much like the water level is brought down in a glass that is overflowing. This is likely to make us feel vulnerable. This is a problem if we have rarely or ever felt properly safe in our lives. Keisha and Raphael were lucky to find trusted others with whom they could risk being vulnerable. Though feeling uncomfortable and uncertain, they both take the risk of slowing down and facing their trauma. This is not easy. Why? Becoming vulnerable can feel as if we are putting ourselves in more danger, and out of control. How do we know we will not be judged, hurt or rejected all over again? How can we risk being 'seen' even if this is what we most need?

Both Keisha and Raphael are lucky to have enough trust to risk being seen in this way and this calms them. This seeing has a particular quality: *it is emotionally connected.* Sadly, other people's responses to us when we are traumatized may not be so helpful or connected. As we have already examined, a dysregulated person is no longer open to logic. In fact, logic can trigger us further. As Sally Donovan writes: 'The Gun of Logic has a barrel that bends back on itself.'[9] If we are dysregulated, a logical, reasoning response from someone may aggravate us. This is because when we are traumatized, we easily feel cut off from others and we don't trust them. Their logic

---

9   Donovan, S. (2019). *The Unofficial Guide to Therapeutic Parenting: The Teen Years.* London: Jessica Kingsley Publishers, p.46.

may only further confirm our aloneness and exacerbate our internal lack of safety.

We may not be fortunate enough to have another to emotionally see us when we are dysregulated. Even if we do, they may not get it 'right' and help us. They may not know what to say or they may say the wrong thing. What can we do then? Our primary and immediate need when panicked and flipping our lids with trauma is finding *safety inside*. We may need to find ways to put on our brakes to promote inner balance.[10] Where can we start? We may or may not have a calm and trusted person to see and soothe us. But we can use our breath to calm ourselves.

Breathing out as trauma first aid

Breathing out is a simple 'first aid' antidote for trauma, as it calms our panic, helps us feel safe inside and lowers our heart rate. In our breath is our life and we can use breath to soothe ourselves and reduce our arousal levels. I will outline some breathing exercises at the end of this chapter. This is basic physiology. A repeated exhale massages our vagus nerve and allows our bodies to lead us to a place of greater tranquility again and again. When we literally give ourselves *breathing space*, we are recognizing that our body has become aroused and stressed. It is only doing its job: something new and unpredictable or uncertain has happened and touched our trauma. Can we thank our body and mind for alerting us and then find ways to soothe ourselves and let the stress go? Another thought: can we ask someone for a 30-second hug to reduce our and their cortisol

---

10 Living in times of chronic uncertainty or high arousal in this particular time in history, with reduced access to resources to combat stress, we may be helped to develop our own daily 'tool box' of self-care, to enhance our capacity to bring our minds and bodies into greater balance. Our autonomic nervous system can be so revved up in the red-zone activation of the sympathetic nervous system that we do not easily access the brake of the blue-zone parasympathetic branch. Sometimes, we need help to do this. Techniques offered by autogenic training, started by the German physician Johannes Schulz in the 1920s, have recently been offered in the form of six standard exercises that can be learned alone, including heaviness, warmth, cardiac regulation, respiration, abdominal warmth and cooling of the forehead (Tudhope, G. and Draper, R. (2023). *Achieving Equilibrium: A Simple Way to Balance Body and Mind*. London: Aeon Books). If we suffer severe trauma, we may need a skilled practitioner to help us use these.

levels? A simple act can help restore our confidence. (This may not always feel easy or possible.)

Regular use of meditation for just a couple of minutes to start with or going for a walk and becoming aware of our senses helps with regulation. Meditation can physically shrink our stressed amygdala.[11, 12] Learning to focus on something that captures us completely in the present moment will soothe the charge of trauma. We can find a myriad of ways to ground ourselves in the moment, such as deliberately pressing our feet into the floor as we breathe out or finding a place to be where we can feel our back is supported. We can hold a meaningful object in our palm to access a memory of safety or security, or return to a familiar activity or place. When finding a place of warmth and safety, we can slowly adjust our position, deliberately taking time to find maximum comfort. These techniques can lower the activation of our nervous system in just a few seconds.

Self-soothing

Just as babies feel safe when they are soothed, we can soothe ourselves as adults. For example, we might feel soothed by gazing at the sky and allowing ourselves to hear birdsong or the wind in the trees. As humans, we are soothed by being social, so making contact with someone we love and feeling safe in proximity with them can also help regulate us, promoting an increase in the feel-good-by-being-connected

---

11 There are many forms of meditation, some of which originate from the Buddhist tradition such as Vipassana, which means 'insight'. By turning inwards, practitioners turn inwards to their mind and body. By focusing on one thing and 'dropping' thoughts and distractions over time, meditators sharpen their focus and calm their bodies and minds.

For other mindfulness-based meditations see the work of Mark Williams, Emeritus Professor of Psychology at Oxford University: *Mindfulness: Finding Peace in a Frantic World*, https://franticworld.com, accessed 26/11/23.

12 Sara Lazar PhD is an associate researcher in the psychiatry department of Massachusetts General Hospital and Harvard Medical School. On the Radio 4 programme *Amygdala: Made of Stronger Stuff*, on 27 October 2022 (accessed on BBC Sounds 26/11/23), she speaks about her research and explains that, with regular practice, meditation may 'rewire' the amygdala due to the neuroplasticity of the brain and, in *some people*, the amygdala can become reshaped to a smaller size. Activities such as yoga may not have this specific effect on the brain but nevertheless bring powerful body-mind regulation of the nervous system, making people less irritable and more forgiving towards themselves and others.

hormone oxytocin. However, our trauma might have given us a different message, making us fear that contact with others is really not a good idea. Though we might profoundly need it, closeness with others may feel like taking a risk: a double bind. We will consider this aspect more in Chapter 13.

Frameworks of support

In addition to regulation, both Keisha and Raphael need a framework of support, practically and emotionally. Keisha is fortunate in having a supportive line manager and Raphael a loving partner. This is not the case for all of us. Trauma isolates us and some of us are isolated already – a double whammy. There are no easy solutions to this, but the evidence of isolation is everywhere. My goal in these chapters is to highlight the inside job of trauma, and awareness must be part of the answer, at an individual, societal and global level.

Community matters. For instance, a man who has experienced a pile-up on the motorway and is unable to drive his car as a result might find that his neighbours have organized a rota of people to drive him around. Others might cook his favourite food and leave it on the doorstep. Making someone feel special often involves attention to detail. This sort of framework and cocoon of support is essential for reversing the immediate effects of trauma and strengthening resilience. Like Raphael, some traumatized individuals may be fortunate in having a pre-existing framework of support they can draw on. Support structures are a determining factor in recovery. If we know someone who has been traumatized, we could consider their support structures first. If we are a part of a structure for someone, we may need to remember to keep physically and emotionally close and in regular contact with them. Our non-pressurizing care will soothe them. We can remind them that nurturing activities are kind to stressed-out vagal nerves. Like Raphael, it is not always easy for traumatized individuals to self-soothe or accept help. Such recovery can be a marathon, not a sprint. We can practise remaining hopeful that creative new possibilities for self-care can be found and patiently allow time for this to happen.

How can I help?

A great question for anyone traumatized to ask is: *Even though I feel stressed, anxious and overwhelmed, what can I do/focus on right now that might help?* There may be things that we already have in our tool box of resilience. *What resources do I already know/have to help me 'be me'?* In physics, resilience refers to a substance that remains essentially unchanged after an experience. What activities help us calm down because they are already familiar, natural or instinctive to us? Slotting into a groove of *what is known or interesting/distracting* can be one way to help regulation and contribute to resilience-building after trauma. For some, it may be cooking; for others, music, yoga or competitive sport. In trauma's stress surge, 'then' becomes 'now'. By finding strategies to soothe ourselves, we mitigate the stress, put on our brakes, and learn to claim our 'now'. Are we *now* in an environment of safety or beauty? Being more aware in the safe or beautiful present reduces the stress hormone cortisol in our systems.

There is an expression in the West Indies: 'They that feel it, know it.'[13] A trauma arousal surge makes us lose our centre, our equilibrium. The starting place for trauma mitigation is to know fully, to acknowledge the experience of overwhelm and what it does to us and why; to pay proper attention; to admit the truth that trauma that has happened to us has led us to feel fearful and estranged. Then we can take it seriously, properly weigh it, sit with it and take stock. Can we ask ourselves: what support and attention do I need right now to harness and begin to soothe my body and mind? How can I find safety?

As I wrote in the Introduction, the right words can help to give shape, form and safety to experience. This 'poem' was given to Raphael after I had been with him, as an attempt to instantly capture his experience of trauma:

Frightened jumping
This way that way
Only knowing my fragmented terrified
Beyond twitchy self I

---

13   France-Williams, A. (2020). *The Ghost Ship*. London: SCM Press, p.55.

Bump off edges
Jarring jangled
Ricocheting
At the mercy of life
At the mercy of me
My pinball self
Let me rest
I long for a kinder way

BREAKING-FREE POINTERS WHEN TRAUMA TAKES US OVER

▸ Understand that trauma has power and can take us on a stress ride.
▸ Understand that trauma has the capacity to disable our capacity to think.
▸ Learn ways to regulate through developing empathy for our traumatized selves and use our minds to help our bodies feel safe through the work of regulation.
▸ Learn to approach a traumatized person with caution: logic may backfire! Look beyond logic to the emotional story, to hear the drumbeat of pain or fear.
▸ Be led by the traumatized person and take cues from them.
▸ Remember to use power wisely if helping a person experiencing trauma, and be hopeful – even a small gust of wind can help change the direction of the sail.
▸ Reboot – making a significant, even temporary, change in our environment can be an important start to mitigate overwhelm.
▸ Fear grows like a snowball. Breathing out is a simple first aid and helps regulation.
▸ Community matters – we can do so much to relieve trauma's weight with awareness and proper systems of care.

QUESTIONS FOR FURTHER REFLECTION

1. If I am 'swept away' by trauma reactivity, does it help to wonder what happened to cause it? What do I need when I feel 'swept

away' and out of balance? What helps to anchor myself in 'now', to 'safety', to 'good things' that I know nourish me?

2. What framework of support do I have in place to be able to do this? Who do I trust to be safe, kind and accepting?

BREATH PRACTICE

▸ 7/9 breathing: Breathe in on a count of 7 and out on a count of 9, and repeat.[14]

▸ Child's slide: Imagine ascending the steps of a slide as you take in regular repeated sips of breath. When you have filled your lungs at the top of the 'slide', allow yourself a very long exhale while imagining your descent, and push the breath as far as you can along the flat slide to reach right to the end.

SURRENDER TO GRAVITY EXERCISE[15]

Rest your whole body on the ground, with your legs stretched out. If more comfortable, bend your knees with the soles of your feet touching the ground. Find exactly the right way for you. Take a little time to properly arrive in your body for a moment. Adjust your position carefully to make yourself super comfortable.

Imagine that your body is making an imprint in the warm sand. What would it look like? Would there be any difference on one side or the other? As you imagine this, feel the weight of your body sinking lower, really being supported from underneath.

Gently roll your head from one side to the other, taking time to stop in the middle. Really feel the weight of your head and the muscles working as you do this.

Let your knees fall just a little from side to side. As you do this, really feel the weight of your pelvis and allow your pelvis and your glutes to get a little massage from the ground.

---

14 CAUTION: Those suffering with chest complaints such as asthma or low blood pressure only breathe in for as long as is comfortable.
15 Drawn from yoga: shavasana; Feldenkrais.

Surrender to Gravity
Gravity is my best friend
Always present
Always available
Always ready to respond
Gravity is holding me
Letting me sink and
Absorbing all my stress
Downwards[16]

You can find a short video that highlights some points from this chapter at https://www.youtube.com/watch?v=ddl7M5Kho7o or by scanning the QR code.

---

16 Adapted from Sabatini, S. (2006). *Breath the Essence of Yoga – A Guide to Inner Stillness*. London: Pinter & Martin Ltd and Fannen, L. (2021). *Warp and Weft: Psycho-Emotional Health Politics and Experiences*. Bristol: Active Distribution Publishing.

— Chapter 2 —

TRAUMA TAKES US OUT OF TIME

Too much fear can arrest and distort our sense of time.

Normally, we experience the momentum of life having flow. We have a sense of progression from moment to moment. However, when a sudden loss or unexpected scary event cuts across our everyday lives, our bodies and minds can experience it as if we have been caught up in a flood that sweeps away our perspective on time. Vera Brittain (1933) used this metaphor in *Testament of Youth* to describe the devastating impact of the First World War on society: 'It was the one perfect summer that I ever experienced, as well my last care-free entertainment before the Flood.'[1]

When we suddenly experience a shocking event, we can have no idea of its meaning or implications. Such events can change everything. Living in 'trauma time' can mean many things. For some, the arresting of flow or time distortion occurs at the moment of trauma, lingers in its aftermath, and then eventually wears off. For others, depending on the severity of the trauma, the effects can last longer. If such symptoms persist in a person, this may be an indication of PTSD and professional help is likely to be needed.

Annabel's experience is an example of trauma's sudden arresting of time and its aftermath.

---

1   Brittain, V. (1933). *Testament of Youth*. London: Victor Gollancz Ltd, Part One, Chapter II, section 9.

TRAUMA STORY: Annabel and her husband

Annabel loses the love of her life, her husband Sean, in a hit-and-run road traffic accident. On waking that morning, she feels his warmth beside her in bed, then he pops out to the shop for some milk. Next, a policeman stands on her doorstep and tells her that Sean is dead. Life utterly changes in that instant. The event defines everything: her thoughts, her moment-to-moment confidence in the world, all her hopes for the future. Everything simply stops, changing Annabel's perception of time and its flow.

Annabel now lives in another reality, out of time, trapped in the moment that Sean stopped living. She is fixated and obsessed by repeated images and thoughts about every detail of what she imagines happened. Her mind plays with time – looping to snapshots of the last moments she was with him, as well as memories of when they first met years ago. The recent past assumes an extraordinary intensity. Sean is so vivid to her – she has him, she holds him, he is as close as her breath, then he is taken from her embrace and she falls into an abyss. The terrifying separation from Sean is written on her body. She trembles, twitches and shakes when required to report his death to the coroner or tell her son what has happened. Her breath stops, her throat blocks, she has no words. She feels a charge of electricity through her body, taking her over. Unable to accept the enormity of the truth, her mind works in overdrive, running back through time, erasing the catastrophic event, expecting with every ring of the doorbell that Sean will walk into her living room.

The freeze frame of trauma

There are a number of time-related trauma features in Annabel's story. First, her mind repeatedly creates visual miniatures, or *flashbacks* – trauma's creative mix of truth, imagination, memory and reality (for further exploration of flashbacks see Chapter 3). Not knowing the exact details of how her husband has died fuels her imagination with a relentless and desperate search for facts and details. This freeze framing of trauma is her mind's way of coming to terms with a violent, hideous and terrifying reality, and can also rob the future of meaning, destroying hope and joy.

Trauma disturbs our confidence

Second, in usual times, we have a bodily confidence in time unfolding moment to moment (Chapter 12 has a fuller exploration of this). The shocking flood of trauma stops body confidence in life. Though the initial shaking wears off, Annabel's experience of this life-changing event continues to be deeply physical. She feels destroyed, broken and shattered into pieces. Her bodily sense of annihilation is what dominates: she fears she or her son might die. The shock and flood of trauma can be so devastating to the body and the mind that usual competencies are obliterated. Annabel stutters. She is unable to find words that before would have flowed effortlessly. It does not allow her to function in everyday ways or speak the truth of what has happened. Such powerful body experiences are more convincing than our logical processing. Our bodies stop us in our tracks.

Trauma destroys our ability to predict

Third, Annabel has a *new relationship to life itself*. Her trauma – the sudden and violent death of her husband – is more real to her than her current life and becomes her life's dominating background canvas. Though the initial dominance of the event and her emotional response does fade over time, her relationship with the world is profoundly changed by the trauma. Annabel feels as though she can now no longer predict anything: her confidence is shattered because the world no longer feels safe or stable. She does not trust that the thread of her life will flow forward. She can't make decisions or think strategically. Annabel exists now in a provisional and uncertain state: she feels she has become another person. It takes many months before she can re-engage with current life. For a long time, she seems to live in another place, as if experiencing the world through plate glass. Trauma doctor Gabor Maté describes this state as 'a physio-emotional time warp'.[2]

---

2   Bramley, E.V. (2023). The trauma doctor: Gabor Maté on happiness, and how to heal our deepest wounds. *The Guardian* (Health and wellbeing), 12 April 2023, accessed 26/12/23.

Time travel of trauma

Trauma plays with our minds. It can make us *time travel* in a variety of ways. Our minds can powerfully attempt to erase the traumatic event: we can 'forget' what happened for periods of time, and then suddenly remember, with stomach-wrenching horror. When taken over by a trauma memory our 'now' is erased, our bodies and minds are back when it happened.

In the moment of crisis, we can feel sharply alive or, like Annabel, we continue to live in a state of perpetual suspension. We might speak of time slowing or speeding up, or of seeing our life passing before our eyes. The surge of trauma can make our life's difficulties and priorities suddenly seem very different. Sometimes we are fuelled by trauma fear – imperatives that may not be good for us or others. This is very different from longer-term priorities and perspectives gained through trauma that can bring positive outcomes.

In these ways, trauma 'plays' with our minds, yet this word does not convey the suffering that can be experienced by such time distortions. The psychoanalyst Robert Stolorow writes: 'Trauma destroys time.'[3] He says these three powerful words to someone he worked with who is in a highly distressed and triggered state, lost in the time of trauma. Her response is to smile and say: 'I just came together again.' Speaking this truth helped mitigate trauma's power. Although words are frequently lost at the time of trauma, as they were for Annabel, finding words and speaking about our experience over time can help us cohere once again.

Trauma time versus clock time

Our standard perception of time is chronological. Trauma scrambles this. For Annabel, the very roots of her sense of security about the way that the world works are disturbed by a terrible event. This manifests in her ongoing difficulty in understanding or coping with 'clock' time. Individuals who have been traumatized early in life may have altered brain functioning, the trauma arresting the development

---

3   Stolorow, R.D. (2007). *Trauma and Human Existence*. New York, NY: The Analytic Press, p.17.

of their frontal lobes and disturbing the cognitive functioning that makes links between behaviours and consequences. This is one reason why children in care who have had a variety of unreliable attachment figures in early life may have particular and severe and profound difficulties dealing with deadlines or organizing their time.

The arresting of time is our trauma response's attempt *to protect us from pain*. We humans find it hard to accept a huge flood of terrible reality. There can be a powerful disparity between our protective halt of trauma and the unwelcome inevitability that time carries on regardless. This juxtaposition is expressed in W.H. Auden's poem 'Stop all the clocks'.[4]

> *Stop all the clocks, cut off the telephone*
> *Prevent the dog from barking with a juicy bone*
> *Pour away the ocean and sweep up the wood*
> *For nothing now can ever come to any good*

In the following case, Freya's life is shattered by the terminal illness of her child. What is striking is her trauma mind's attempt to stop what is happening in real time.

TRAUMA STORY: Freya and her locking trauma mind

When Freya's ten-year-old daughter is taken into hospital, Freya packs their bags in a relaxed way. Elsa has a chronic lung condition. Hospitals are home from home. Freya calmly drives Elsa to A&E, then thinks about whether she needs to cancel her work engagements for the day. After being in the waiting room for a couple of hours, Freya is surprised when a senior medic approaches with a name badge and asks if she can sit down beside her. Gently, she explains that Elsa has had a bleed. 'We couldn't stop the flow,' she tells her, 'and she has lost too much blood. I'm afraid we can't operate. We have put her on a ventilator and we are about to take her to ICU [intensive care unit]. Would you like to see her?' 'Is she

---

4   'Funeral Blues', or 'Stop all the clocks', is a poem by W.H. Auden which first appeared in the 1936 play *The Ascent of F6* (Faber). The first two and last two lines are quoted here.

going to die?' asks Freya. 'I'm so sorry, but yes, she is. It's just a question of time.'

Freya is deeply confused by the doctor's words. She is convinced she must have made a mistake. Her trauma mind locks in. 'You can't take her to ICU!' she repeats over and over again. When she sees Elsa on the hospital trolley, she grips hold of it, refusing to let the medics take her. It is an imperative just to stop this action: every part of her mind and body refuses to accept the truth of what the doctor is saying. What she focuses on with all her might is her desperate attempt to stop time going forward. Going to ICU must not happen. Time, she has been told, is about to steal her daughter from her.

Elsa is taken to ICU, of course. And, eventually, with her closest friend with her, Freya is able to enter the ward and spend long hours keeping vigil beside her daughter, touching her body and letting her tears flow. When she first wakes each morning, she is at first unaware that Elsa is dying, before the reality crashes into her mind. She moves in and out of acceptance of this reality. Death has become an interloper in her mind. On a practical level, it surprises her how quickly she and other close relatives adjust to their new roles, scurrying in and out of the ICU on a rota, attending to the repertoire of ordinary tasks in usual time. She takes strange comfort in thinking of everyday things and the ritual of going home to feed her cat twice a day. However, making other decisions feels completely impossible when her mind is locked into repeating the death-bed scenario. It is an enormous relief when her boss rings her, assuring her that nothing is required of her – her work has been covered. Right now, a part of her is flailing about and collapsing inside and she needs others to hold her up like tent poles.

After Elsa's death, Freya faces the acute pain of grief at the same time as her mind endlessly revisiting the trauma of the hospital. Some months later, when talking to a friend, Freya casually mentions her old love of skating. The following morning, she wakes early, finds her old skates and makes her way to the ice rink. When it opens, she soon finds her skating legs and does not stop for several hours. She cannot believe her body slips so easily into the right rhythm. It feels great to move her body in this old familiar way. It gives her a glorious sense of freedom. The focus needed for the activity quietens her mind and it broadens out. Old thoughts return, along with comforting memories. She looks on the beauty of the world differently. Freya returns to the ice rink every day and skates for the love of Elsa. That love, her skating says, continues on like a golden thread, despite Elsa's death, and despite the terrible trauma of the hospital experience. Skating is a great consolation. It carries her forward in time, towards hope and a sense of peace.

Trauma time is protective

It may be hard to see Freya's gripping of the hospital trolley as protective, yet it is her mind's attempt to prevent and survive the hurt of an overwhelming situation. Her mind's repeated recalling of traumatic events is a clarion call for her to pay attention – an attempt to begin to bear something unbearable. Our minds will continue to highlight and repeat miniatures of an event until we assimilate and integrate it. This triggering feature of trauma we will explore further in the following chapter.

The preventative device of the arrest of time is at the heart of this feature of trauma. It is the mind and body's best attempt to save us from experiencing something unbearable that we have already experienced, at the same time as keeping our attention on it. *It is our mind's lockdown.*

A striking example of this is found in Charles Dickens' novel *Great Expectations*, where Miss Havisham is jilted before her wedding and afterwards remains forever in her wedding dress. Though her behaviour could partly express hope that Compeyson will one day return, and is therefore a denial of reality, it can partly be seen as her shock and trauma reaction after being jilted. In her stuck place, Miss Havisham is arrested in time, locked in a preventative measure that stops her in her tracks. The 'highlight' or marker of her terrible humiliation and pain is the wedding dress, always worn, a kind of physical flashback.

More subtle examples of trauma time

Being 'out of time' may manifest in less dramatic ways than it did for Annabel, Freya or Miss Havisham. We might find ourselves not quite being able to feel properly engaged with our present lives, as if we belong to another time and place altogether. In relationships, we can have difficulties in relating to someone in our lives and not under-stand why. You may have had the experience, as I have, of meeting someone to whom you feel an uncanny connection or aversion and not know why. On reflection, it later occurs to us that our response is elicited by some kind of similarity between the current person and someone else we have encountered. Our inner responses come from another place or time.

Ways to reclaim life's flow post-trauma

Freya reclaims her equilibrium through movement and the passage of time itself. Reminders of the goodness in the world may gently, in time, persuade us to return to it. We might consider what may be important in helping us or someone else regain flow after trauma. The piecing together of memories and the truth of what happened may or may not be possible. Past trauma memories may or may not return and neatly cohere into a complete narrative. We might never complete the jigsaw and know what really happened or precisely why we respond and feel the way we do. The power of trauma can eclipse the brain's time-keeper function so that we can sometimes no longer be sure whether our responses are related to then or now.

However, when we are arrested by memory or emotion that feels as though it clouds our present, we can consider returning to focus on something that grounds us in the present. We need to touch base. If trauma destroys time, what can we focus on right now that gives us a sense of life's flow? What is soothing or life-giving for us? When we are stuck can we consider what may gently assist our moving through time once more?

Freya's skating is a creative act that helps the flow of her life return post trauma. Meditative practices such as the one at the end of the chapter can also help achieve the inner stillness we crave if our peace and sense of the flow of time have been shattered by turbulence. There are many ways to regain our flow but it may take us time to find what helps us personally to break free from our own mind's lockdown.

Reflections on the pandemic

We might think of the Covid-19 pandemic as an example of an abnormal event distorting time. People have reported an elasticity of time during this period. Many of us will recognize the concertina effect of multiple lockdowns, noticing that we cannot quite remember what happened when. Sometimes, time has been experienced as very slow or rushing past, and we have lost a sense of the progression of events that we would have experienced over a period of time. At times of strangeness and turbulence, many people write journals or find some other ways of keeping their chronology ordered and this may be enormously consoling. Repetitive acts help us move from right brain overwhelm to finding words – the domain of the left brain (Chapter 8 explores this further). Freya discovers consolation in the repetition of attending to her cats. When trauma time distorts our minds and bodies, simply taking time to look at the same view or notice a particular tree, perhaps to regularly connect with the land where we live, can help reinstate our temporal markers.

In the global pandemic, the temporal markers changed for all of us and some may have experienced this as trauma. In the aftermath of the imposed halt of flow, we may notice a tendency to 'pandemic amnesia', or a tendency to minimize the experience. These are both possible responses to trauma. Maybe we observed in ourselves a reluctance to hug or kiss acquaintances after the pandemic. Some people have continued to be fearful about emerging fully into life once more, behaving in a Miss Havisham-like manner, as if they are still in lockdown.

Whether or not we recognize any of these lingering pandemic responses in ourselves, it can be argued that the universal experience of the change in our temporal markers through the pandemic gave us insight into what it is like to be suspended in trauma. That when trauma comes crashing in on chronological time, it takes us over, disorientates us and unseats our flow.

The following words were written for Freya.

Flood terror
Takes me by the scruff
Mind trapped in now
Horror
Arrested
Me befuddled
No signposts
Can't think, respond, predict
My ducks are all over the place
I need love
No demands
Rest to breathe again
And flow like a river

BREAKING-FREE POINTERS TO HELP WITH TIME SCRAMBLING AFTER TRAUMA

▸ Trauma's scrambling of time can mean we lose our temporal markers.
▸ Trauma lockdown can result in flashbacks – trauma's creative mix of truth, imagination, memory and reality – or in us losing confidence in our ability to predict life's flow.
▸ What can help? Finding ways to 'touch base' with ourselves after trauma, through repetitive acts that ground us, console us and free us. These are likely to involve our bodies through soothing or moving practices.
▸ Trauma's preventative lockdown responses can mean we exaggerate or minimize reality. Ways to break free can be found through finding our own 'golden thread of continuity' like Freya did. This might mean being diligent in searching for what most matters to us deep down, taking time to connect with and trust this intuition, and being open to whether following it might help us reclaim time's flow.

QUESTIONS FOR FURTHER REFLECTION

1. Do I recognize that my mind and body are sometimes taken to another place in a way that halts the flow of my life? Are there ways that I can practise claiming *now* when I am stimulated or overtaken by a scary *then* in sensation or thought?
2. Can I use my mind to find a safe space of relaxation in the present? What things, maybe creative, or physical, anchor me to now, expand my appreciation of now? What helps me, or someone I'm close to, feel safe in a place where trauma has less power to overwhelm or harm me?
3. Can I remember a time when everything changed for me, like a watershed moment? Is the change wrought on me or others integrated and accepted, or do I have some work to do to understand its implications, accept its reality and begin to let it go?

WATERFALL MEDITATION

Find a place where you are private and your body feels safe, supported and comfortable. Notice your breathing, as you move your attention from the outside world to your inner world. Pay focused attention on breathing in and then out, noticing any details, such as the expansion of your ribs on the in-breath and the swelling of your belly on the out-breath.

As you do this, you may notice that thoughts come into your mind. Think of them as a waterfall that will keep flowing. Imagine that waterfall and that you are swimming in the pool at the bottom. The power of the waterfall is strong, but you are able to find a ledge behind the waterfall where you can sit. From there you can feel the energy of the waterfall but you are not caught up in it, you are observing it. You are not trying to stop the flow of the waterfall, you are focusing on the stillness of the pool and the riverbed underneath.

From that still place, you observe the power of your thoughts. Whatever they 'say', you are responding 'Aha, that is a thought' from the observing position on your ledge. You are letting the power of any thoughts about past or future, memories, impulses or sensations that emerge to be noticed. You are finding a still place that does not react to your thoughts from your comfortable ledge, a place 'underneath' the turbulence of your thoughts. Enjoy any peace or clarity or energy that comes as a result of this practice.

You can find a short video that highlights some points from this chapter at https://www.youtube.com/watch?v=fBjɪVkYGPio or by scanning the QR code.

Chapter 3

TRAUMA REPEATS UNTIL IT IS RESOLVED

Trauma can shatter our world view like an explosion. Our minds sift and sort through the wreckage, hoping for healing and recovery.

In Chapter 1, we learned how the overwhelming surge of trauma takes us over. Here we focus on the repetitive nature of trauma. The wreckage of what remains can include intrusive images of the trauma in the form of dreams and re-enactments. On one level, repetition is our mind's way of struggling with the reality of overwhelming experience, highlighting it so we pay attention. Sometimes we need to visit the wreckage many times to find healing after trauma. The following story of Earl is an example of how elements of trauma can return, form patterns and sometimes gather momentum and escalate out of control.

TRAUMA STORY: Earl's bad luck repetitions

Earl is treated badly, picked on by his peers because he doesn't quite fit in at school.[1] His family are poor, his brother has been (wrongfully) convicted of a crime, then to cap it all, his father loses his job. Earl feels enormous pressure to be the breadwinner for his mother and sisters. Determined, he enters the army and trains to be an engineer. Earl hopes to learn a trade and find a sense of belonging, but instead he is shunned and victimized for being different.

Things get worse a few months later when a piece of machinery

---

1   See https://mhanational.org for statistics on incidence of mental health difficulties in black populations in the US, accessed 26/11/23.

falls on his hip at work. Earl is pensioned out on disability. He applies for many jobs, but his disability is a barrier to getting physical work. He goes for desk jobs but still doesn't get hired. Quite often, people are not kind to him. Getting by on a small allowance, Earl feels alone and desperate. He reinvents himself again, making component parts for machinery and selling them on the internet. One day, his hand slips on a lathe and he cuts himself badly. He becomes dizzy, his breathing is shallow, his heart beats fast and his mind replays snapshots of memories from his humiliations at school, being spat at in the army and discriminated against for his disability. Later when he calms down, he becomes numb. With a start, he realizes it is exactly one year after his army accident. His mind spins back through all the traumatic memories of his life in ·a fragmented way, going over and over them...

Earl does his best to make good choices and suffers bad luck with the accident, but the trauma thread running through his story is in the wounding bad treatment by others due to him being in an ethnic minority. This treatment leaves him feeling profoundly got at, vulnerable and alone. It becomes expected and familiar: a pattern develops. Sensitized and expecting more bad treatment, his nervous system is hyper-aroused much of the time, like a pressure cooker. Trigger touches trigger as trauma's power cascades and is released.

What is triggering and how does it happen?

We have probably all had the experience of one thing going wrong, then another, in a spiral. Here is what can happen, from a physiological perspective. As we learned in Chapter 1, when something frightening crosses our path, our bodies become activated, ready for mobilization. When Earl is victimized, his threat system is activated. The hormone cortisol circulates in a loop around his body and mind, sending messages to his brain to focus and act protectively in crisis. Adrenalin levels are heightened, bringing arousal, telling him to be vigilant, expect the worse or do something. As the hormones surge, so the emotional responses get replayed. When triggered like this we may feel irresistibly compelled to repeat behaviours that we know, like a moth to a flame. With the hormonal surge, we have less control of our actions. Around an anniversary of an event, memories can resurface and emotions can surge again, sometimes leading to 'mysterious' repeated accidents. Flashbacks and the reliving of past events and bodily reactions can lead us on a horrible repetitive dance that gathers speed, frequency, reaches a crescendo and eventually spins out of control. This dance can be worse than the trauma itself.

Triggering – being overwhelmed by feelings and impulses – happens in a moment, like a gunshot. Triggering means a present moment response to an event or situation that is associated with something in the past. As we learned in Chapter 1, our amygdala is our brain's signal box, alerting us to something that might be dangerous, new, ambiguous or unknown. In an experience that is too much for us, our amygdala loses its capacity for clear messaging and fires up to max, with whiplash reactivity, even if the event or stimulus is relatively small. So, a response that was appropriate to a past event or situation but is not appropriate in our current lives can become a big problem. For example, we need to be alert to danger so that if there is an explosion we will run to safety, but if we are startled every time a door bangs, our lives can feel horribly out of control.

A repetitive trauma cycle can become an unwelcome gift that keeps on giving. Imagine being trapped in a maze where we can find no exit. The experience of repetitive looping can be terrifying and wretched. The intense repetitions can make us feel as if we have no control over our minds and are going mad. We may have no conscious understanding of why we respond to a minor irritation as if we are about to be attacked.

Triggers can be dramatic or more subtle. We may wonder why we feel no joy at our child's birthday party, but just numbness. Or we may have an uncanny fear that intrudes whenever the light fades. We may have a vague knowledge that we do not feel right and perhaps experience guilt about somehow not feeling fully part of the human race. Fearful responses are like water – they find their way through cracks and appear in all kinds of places. Maybe our response to trauma activation is towards risk-taking like shop-lifting. This may have a strange logic: if we feel dead, doing something like this can make us temporarily feel more alive. We can observe triggers, repeated traumas, in our feelings, thoughts, body sensations, memories and behaviours.

Ultimately, there is hope, however, because, as the following story suggests, even sufferers of chronic PTSD with elaborate trauma symptoms can discover ways to ease their symptoms and find meaning in life again.

TRAUMA STORY: Joe, the mountaineer[2]

Joe loves the mountains. He lives for climbing. One April, he and his best friend Steve take a trip to the Alaskan peaks, in avalanche territory. On the second day, they hear what sounds like an explosion. Suddenly, a huge weight of moving snow drags Joe miles down the mountain. Injured, Joe pulls himself free, his mouth full of snow. He is horrified to see Steve's body a hundred yards away. The avalanche has killed his best friend.

Joe is rescued and, in time, his body mends. His mind takes much longer to recover. Springing up like red flags in his mind, flashbacks highlight danger everywhere. At first, Joe tries to avoid them by keeping away from mountains, but they can happen anyway, even when he is just walking down the street. Later, Joe is irresistibly drawn back to the danger, becoming part of a mountain rescue team, but adrenalin surges only serve to further fuel his fear.

As time goes on, Joe develops full-blown PTSD. His flashbacks become elaborate hallucinations. Disasters unfold that seem utterly real, unravelling him with their intense sounds, smells and sensations. It is as if his mind keeps taking him to horror movies. When this happens, Joe loses touch with his present moment experience and is incapacitated. He is getting worse, seeing the world according to his fear. His triggered mind shows up in Joe's actions: he checks and cleans random things obsessively, he is moody and unpredictable with his family and friends. He is emotionally exhausted.

---

2   Joe Yelverton told his story called 'I survived an avalanche, but the real challenge came after' on the BBC Radio 4 *Outlook* programme on 22 March 2022, on BBC Sounds, and it is available to download from the archive (accessed 26/12/23). He has given his permission for me to adapt his story here.

Desperate, Joe seeks help from a therapist. He has been running from his trauma for 15 years, frightened that facing it will make things worse. The therapist helps him to begin to observe his flashbacks and thoughts from a distance, helping him to understand: 'your thoughts are not you'. In this way, the therapist is helping him to distance himself from the story that the flashbacks and the traumatized part of himself are telling him.

This perspective is a revelation for Joe and almost immediately his body starts to relax and his flashbacks become less frequent. In a place of safety with his therapist, he is gradually taught how to find safety in his mind. Joe is amazed that the experience of being listened to also helps him feel so much better.

Joe meets a tattoo artist, Bill, who often listens to people's stories as he inks their skin. Bill tells Joe how his clients feel much better when they have their stories properly heard. Joe decides to have the word 'listen' tattooed on his forearm, and dedicates his life to being curious about and helping others with their difficult stories and life experiences. Helping others helps him.

The repetitive loop of Joe's trauma is arrested when he is literally brought to his knees by the severity of his PTSD symptoms. He is helped by giving spacious understanding to his triggering, widening the tight concertina. Trauma often tells us to hide from pain, but life often does offer us opportunities to live more fully and more honestly. Our triggers point us to painful truths. As Vadhana discovers in the following example, with the right support, we can find ways and means to claim our triggering truths and dissolve the power of our repetitive patterns.

TRAUMA STORY: Vadhana illness

Vadhana, aged 15, is diagnosed with a congenital condition affecting her sexual development and involving painful surgeries on her reproductive organs.[3] She has little emotional support as her family do not know what to say or how to help, so they generally

---

3   MRKH (Mayer Rokitansky Küster Hauser) syndrome is a congenital (born with) abnormality, characterized by the absence of the vagina, cervix and uterus (womb), which affects one in every 5000 women.

stay silent. The doctor tells her not to mention her condition to anyone. As a consequence, Vadhana feels deeply ashamed and alone inside. On the outside, she can be brittle and defensive.

Later she marries Suni and they are happy together. Secretive by nature, Vadhana tells her husband nothing about her painful history, on the outside always pretending she is fine and smoothing over difficulties. However, her inner world tells her something else. Vadhana frequently has a dream in which she survives a plane crash and walks clear of the wreckage. In the dream, she meets a member of her family, and when she mentions the crash, she is met with the response: 'Never mind!' She tries hard in her waking world not to mind by telling no one about her history, but the repeated dream keeps reminding her that something bad did indeed happen.

One morning after waking with a particularly vivid version of her dream, Vadhana is rushed into hospital with a 'mysterious illness' – she is very anxious and her breath is shallow. Back again in another hospital, her panic is so severe that she thinks she is having a heart attack. Having examined her, the doctors tell Vadhana and Suni that her symptoms seem to be a panic attack as a result of psychological trauma. During a physical examination, one of the doctors reads her notes and asks Vadhana about her surgeries long ago. Cornered, Vadhana finally shares with Suni the story of her painful medical past. Suni is shocked and appalled that his beloved has suffered so much in her early life and has never mentioned it. He has always felt shut out by her secretive smoothing of everything. He worries about what else she hasn't told him. The turning point for Vadhana comes when she allows the truth to be known, trusting she will not be judged for the disclosure of her secret. It is a bold step for her. She is facing the unknown, which is difficult for a person with trauma.

Vadhana's next step is to join a support group recommended by the hospital. Tentatively at first, she decides to speak about her scary dream; she reflects that the plane crash in her dream has kept on showing her what was so terrifying for her when she was 15. At the centre of it all, she was devastated and alone in that hospital long ago. A part of her still is. To mitigate her fear and to soothe her broken heart, Vadhana learns to visualize a safe place, imagining what it feels and smells like. She then practises lengthening her out-breath to relax and let the trigger go (see the exercise at the end of Chapter 1). She reminds herself she is no longer in danger: the turbo-charged panic was a repeat of the panic she'd felt in the hospital all those years ago and is not her present reality. She is encouraged to tell someone when she is triggered and to get to know the signs in her body. When her breath becomes shallow, she takes a walk and also uses running to regulate her overall stress levels. These skills give Vadhana a sense of power and agency when she gets scared. She learns to befriend her fear rather than run from it. As she does this, fear gradually loosens its hold over her and she feels calmer.

Vadhana decides that the time is right for her to go back to the hospital where she had been so ill and alone as a child. Until this moment, her mind has banished its memory. When she first thinks of it again she becomes hot and sweaty. She knows she is ready to actively conquer the repetition and triggering, though she hates the thought of it. With Suni by her side, she visits her childhood home and then, slowly and gently, retraces the journey to the hospital, unshackling her mind from the painful past. She reminds herself that she is brave, she was brave and that she did survive those dreadful surgeries all those years ago. Vadhana feels a sense of achievement in deciding to make this difficult journey. She walks into the hospital with minimal activation and her head held high. She feels brave and powerful in her chosen pilgrimage. She finds being actively thankful helps her regulate herself and prevent a return to the old fear and panic. Finally, she changes the end of the story by giving a donation to the hospital to help future treatment of children suffering with the same condition she has.

Changing a repetitive pattern often requires much perseverance and courage. We are unlikely to find this process easy without the patient support of others. Freud was the first to theorize the human capacity for 'repetition compulsion': things repeat until they are understood. This is tricky, as we have seen, because triggered patterns and emotions are often under the surface so it is hard for us to be fully aware.[4] Behaviours can be more complex to unravel when repetitive sequences become ingrained and entwined with our view of ourselves. This is one reason why a person may find difficulty in escaping an abusive relationship. (Chapter 18 will explore in more depth how destructive cycles can develop and become entrenched.)

What can help with triggering and loops?
We can learn to spot and examine our own repetitions

It can be a relief for a person in the throes of trauma repetition to be told that when they are triggered they will think and respond in the same old ways: *trauma creates trigger central in our minds and bodies.* Sometimes we keep making life choices that are bad for us because we are locked in a trauma cycle. Although painful, the reality of understanding our particular triggering cycles can bring clarification and understanding. Can we ask the question: if this is what *trauma* does, what can *I* do differently? If I don't know where to start, can I talk with someone who might be able to support and encourage me? How can I find spacious understanding?

We can pay attention to our dreams

For Vadhana, her plane crash dream was like a talisman, pointing to the truth of her painful experience. Dreams can be a gift as they continue to play out what has not been assimilated. When we have bad dreams, it can help to imagine other endings for them. It can also be helpful to write our dreams down and ponder their meaning, maybe with someone else.

We can carefully consider our support

Repetition compulsion is like being caught up in a powerful whirl-pool of thoughts, sensations and actions. In order to withstand its

---

4   Sigmund Freud's use of the concept of 'repetition compulsion' was first defined in an article of 1914 ('Remembering, repeating and working-through'). He notes how the patient does not remember anything of what he has forgotten or repressed, he acts it out, without, of course, knowing that he is repeating it. Quoted in Malcolm, J. (2018). *Psychoanalysis: The Impossible Profession.* London: Granta Books.

powers, we may need to be determined to think and act differently, if we have enough support to do so. We might divide support into three kinds.[5] At the most basic level are our physical needs. Next is safety and security, and then comes our need to belong and to feel accepted by others. Only then can we properly begin to thrive, not just survive. With this framework in mind, we can ask: do I have enough of the basics in place to truly change my cycle of repetition? Am I ready to and do I want to?

We can practise bringing ourselves to a place of safety in our minds

Joe and Vadhana were greatly helped by learning these skills. Being overtaken by trauma repetitions can leave us feeling horribly out of control. Finding a sense of safety in our minds and bodies is a mighty skill to develop. It leaves us feeling in charge once again. There is a space-clearing exercise at the end of this chapter that might assist with this.

We can face our painful experience slowly

At the centre of our repetitive cycles is painful experience that we can maybe learn to face bit by bit. When we attempt to tolerate our triggers and fears, it can sometimes feel too much to face the painful truth of our experience directly. It is all too human to fearfully turn away, but it can be illuminating to own the truth of our experience, perhaps with the unflinching and loving support of another person. The poet Rumi wrote:

> Don't turn your head.
> Keep looking at the bandaged place.
> That's where
> The light enters you.[6]

We may have too much on our plate right now to work on assimilating

---

5   As American psychologist Abraham Maslow outlined diagrammatically in his paper 'A theory of human motivation', published in the journal *Psychological Review* (1943), there are basic kinds of support that are needed for us to not only survive but thrive. They have been called our human Hierarchy of Needs.
6   https://enlightenedrumi.wordpress.com/2013/03/22/wound-is-the-place-by-rumi, accessed 07/01/24.

our trauma experience, so our best trauma work at the moment may be regulation (self-soothing) and self-care.

If we have space and support to face a part of our painful experience directly, we may need to consider how much and when

Facing and assimilating painful experience can be a difficult thing to do and it may not be possible without professional support. Like Vadhana, if we are leaning into our pain, we are very likely to need a companion to support us. This is important, though trauma so often tells us to go it alone. Tolerating our painful truths in bite-sized chunks may be the right course, but it is important to go at our own pace and at the right time. This kind of reclaiming can bring us a sense of mastery and control once more. For those of us alongside someone with trauma, *we need to be led by them* in the journey of exploration and assimilation of their experience. Like Vadhana, it can be healing and therapeutic to create a different ending, or be determined to make something good come from the trauma.

When we are in the throes of trauma cycles, it can feel impossible to calm down, protect ourselves and think properly. Perhaps, like Joe and Vadhana, the place to begin is to pause and recognize that where we are right now is not working. Then courageously consider how to break out of our trauma cycle. We may need to be determined to risk doing something new, if only in small moments to begin with. These are the words written after being with Vadhana:

> *St Vitus repetition*
> *Shattered glass*
> *Shards of fearful reminiscence*
> *I dance on the edge of myself*
> *Fever pitch horror movie ramps up*
> *Showing me my*
> *Wreckage inside*
> *Afraid of what's there and*
> *Doing anything different*
> *A glimmering truth:*
> *Safe is what I need*

BREAKING-FREE POINTERS TO ASSIST WITH TRIGGERING

▸ Things stack up in trauma: external bad treatment, unintended consequences, bad luck, body-mind responses, and memories can all become part of repetitive patterns or habitual loops that we and others expect to happen, so they can easily be reinforced.

▸ Trigger responses can be dramatic and as quick as gunshot, or more subtle like a strange numbness, unease or deadness that we may not understand.

▸ Triggers can be feelings, thoughts, body sensations, memories or behaviours.

▸ We can 'face' our triggers, becoming curious about what they signify and the pain that may lie underneath (like Vadhana). If we do this we are advised to take this slowly, with support, in order to maintain our equilibrium as we go, as this may be a painful journey. We will therefore need oodles of self-compassion. Sometimes, over time, our wounds can be transformed to our strengths.

▸ We may decide it is not right for us to investigate the roots of our trauma directly, but instead consider what support we need (when triggered) to regain our sense of well-being and foothold in life.

QUESTIONS FOR FURTHER REFLECTION

1. When I find myself in a repetitive cycle of triggering, what might help me halt and understand this? How might I clear a space and where might I find spaciousness, like the opening of a concertina?

2. Do I have the basics in place to thrive and not just survive? What choices can I make to increase my sense of inner and outer safety?

3. When looping, can I tolerate knowing that I am doing this? Can I, like Joe, observe my thoughts and know they are not me, or not the whole of me? Can I use out-breath practice (outlined at the end of Chapter 1) to notice my arousal and let it go?

4. Can I face knowing and admitting how scared I may be of doing anything different? Is there anyone I admire, who might not reject or judge me for my fears, who might be a safe person for me to be honest with right now?

MEDITATION: CLEARING THE SPACE

(Trauma triggering can lead to a space of internal clutter and reactivity. This exercise can be repeated when we feel overburdened by 'too much'.)

Imagine yourself on the edge of a room with a huge pile of parcels and boxes in the middle. They are all connected with you. As you take stock, notice how many there are and any feelings you have about this. Choose one parcel to look at, slowly and deliberately, then get up, approach the parcel, bend down and pick it up and take it to the very edge of the room. As you lay it down, acknowledge that the parcel is important and you will return to it later. Repeat the same process with all the parcels in the room until you have cleared the space in the centre. Notice any changes in your physical sensations or breathing as you do so and reflect on what is important now.

OPENING-UP MEDITATION[7]

Trauma triggering leads us to close down our breadth of focus because our attention is purely on survival. When we broaden our focus in a place that we know is safe, we quickly counter the effects of trauma.

First, ground yourself with some long out-breaths and get into a rhythm. Then, lengthen your backbone, open your chest and begin to orientate yourself in the space you are in, noticing details about it. Then, choose an object in the scene or room that attracts you. Without judging your process, notice any sensations in your body or thoughts in response to the object that you have chosen. If a memory, feeling, thought or sensation that is triggering returns, simply return to your breath. You could let yourself know: 'That was then (trigger/ fear/memory). This is now (your safe space and your chosen object).'

---

7   This meditation has been adapted from many sources and for my own use. It draws on the idea of the body scan 'invented' by Jon Kabat-Zinn and written about in his book *Full Catastrophe Living* (2013) London: Piatkus. I have also drawn on Holmes, J. (2022) *Families and Individuals with Trauma*. London: Palgrave.

You can find a short video that highlights some points from this chapter at https://www.youtube.com/watch?v=FDFhWsoRSts or by scanning the QR code.

— Chapter 4 —

WHEN ANGER DOMINATES

Fear and stress can make us want to fight.

The part of us that gets easily riled, bad tempered and cross can become dominant in trauma. When we are overwhelmed, our capacity to deal with stress may be diminished and our fuse shorter than usual. When I feel threatened in a situation (even subtly), a pressurized tension ramps up inside which can quickly become horribly urgent for me and I easily show others around me an unreasonable impatience, if I'm not careful. Trauma anger is often turbo-charged, out of proportion and sometimes shocking.

We may never remember a time when anger was not a strong feature, in ourselves, or someone else. If our trauma comes from a history of abuse and neglect, we will know what it means to be living in a scary and unpredictable world, and to have no power. In recent years adverse childhood experience (ACE) studies have researched the effects of feeling profoundly unsafe when we are small.[1] After childhood is over, the legacy of such experiences continues. As a response to fear, 'fight' tells us to defend ourselves for survival. Over time, fight can develop into a dominant solution, easy to turn to but not so easy to stop: anger, aggression and suspicion becoming our habitual responses to the world.

---

1   The CDC-Kaiser Permanente adverse childhood experiences (ACE) study was conducted between 1995 and 1997. It is one of the largest investigations of childhood abuse and neglect and its effects on health and well-being later in life.

Fight in the brain and body

As mentioned in Chapter 1, neuroscience studies show that, in trauma, our limbic brains flood, our amygdala fires off and the frontal lobes of our brains are temporarily disabled and we cannot think properly. From this place of imbalance, trauma responses can so easily eclipse other parts of us. We might approach the world as if everyone is an enemy. We fight in order to feel powerful. We fight to feel safe, perhaps fuelled by a desire to put something right that was wrong long ago. Finella is such a good example of this truth.

TRAUMA STORY: Finella the angry lawyer

Finella is under tremendous stress in her work as a lawyer. She is the subject of an investigation after a complaint is made against her for professional negligence. Anger is imprinted on her face. She is easily provoked and regularly barks instructions at her co-workers.

When Finella was a young child, her father was in chronic pain, living with a progressive disability that increasingly eroded his equilibrium. He was often lovely with his family but then his temper could erupt violently and unpredictably. He offloaded his frustration by shouting in their faces. He often made unreasonable demands. Finella loved him, but felt helpless, terrified and stunned by his violence and rampages. There was not much respite with Finella's stoic and sacrificial mother because her attention and care was completely swallowed up with caring for and tiptoeing around her husband. Finella could not help feeling alone and painfully in the way, a wound she carried deep inside.

In the present day, Finella is fired up by injustice and derives much satisfaction from being able to make a difference in her work as a lawyer. It is so much better than the powerlessness long ago. Though she is very controlled and professional most of the time, her tolerance and control start to become eroded under extreme pressure, especially when someone complains.

Things ramp up. Finella becomes highly critical of the administrative staff in her office, who begin to bristle when she comes in. The final straw happens when someone cuts her up in heavy traffic on the way home and stops in front of her. Finella sees red and, before she knows what she is doing, she pulls over and bangs her hands aggressively on their windscreen. Thankfully, the motorist is so shocked that the situation does not escalate.

However, Finella finds her own road rage alarming and sees it as a wake-up call. She rings a close friend and tells her what has happened, and they take a long walk together. Finella tells her friend how miserable and angry she is. She knows that she is driving others away. As they talk, it becomes clear to Finella why this is. She explains that it is really hard for her to tolerate being wrong. It makes her ashamed and that is painful. She cannot bear the feeling of being 'in the dock', or under pressure. She realizes that she felt this pressure – to make something better – at home long ago but never could. Her emotionally sensitive friend suggests that it is when Finella feels blamed, under pressure or in the wrong that she lashes out. Finella weeps painful tears, because she knows this is true. Since the complaint at work, she has felt like a coiled spring inside. She knows this tightness comes from this shame – a deep sense of culpability.

This knowledge makes all the difference. Finella starts to notice when the blame feeling is activated and then does a variety of things to calm herself down and stop her anger taking over. She begins taking regular breaks. She concentrates on her breathing, and goes to a couple of anger management classes. Finella is helped by understanding that her present anger is really located elsewhere. It belongs to the unbearable family situation long ago. She realizes that this angry way of being has dominated everything and she has lost her edge at work. She begins to develop some self-compassion for the part of her that still feels vulnerable, scared, hurt and powerless. When she does this, she is surprised to notice she feels less need to lash out.

The instinct to fight is an important survival strategy. But when our reactions are governed by trauma, anger can become our only mode. When we are in survival mode, we cannot avoid lashing out. We are wound up by perceived injustice and see it everywhere. The first step when we are caught up in fight is to de-escalate and regulate, so we are free to think once again. One person thought of his anger as a vicious dog. In his imagination, he put it in a box with a strong lid. This resource helped him over time to regulate and put safety between him and his rage. With much practice, he could control his vicious dog rage and even call on 'him' when needed to fight injustice. (More on the positive uses of anger later in the chapter.)

Rage may be fired when boundaries or territory are threatened

When I was working with a project supporting a group of asylum seekers and refugees in Central London, we noticed how anger was often provoked when volunteers crossed boundaries, such as touching guests' (asylum seekers and refugees') possessions. These possessions had a charged importance for those living on the streets, as they were all they had. Guests would sometimes react sharply to such boundary violations, painfully reminding them of the bad treatment they had experienced. In training volunteers to work with guests' angry trauma responses, we invited them to take time to be objective and stand back, noticing their own emotional responses to being around anger, so that they might best support the guests when a red mist erupted. Mindful breathing and counting, for example, were useful to de-escalate a situation and 'win time' before reacting.[2]

Fight's protective function

The guests' bodily instinct to fight was a protective defence. Fight instinct works at a defence level but it also works at a psychological level. One of its purposes is to protect us from acknowledging our own pain. The second step in changing the pattern is to consider the hidden pain below the fight. This is not so easy to do because fight has real power. Fight needs this power because it may be protecting some painful truth, like a feeling of helplessness which was unbearable and *still feels unbearable*. We could think of denial as being a form of fight response – saying 'no' to the truth of things is like a defensive punch, stopping us from having to deal with what feels too much for us to

---

2   Smethurst, P. (2017, June). Borders and boundaries. *Therapy Today*, p.31.

bear and tolerate. If we are traumatized, we can feel that 'attack is the best form of defence', so we flip into controlling behaviour and being intolerant towards those around us. We are quick to blame others but less ready to accept any portion of blame for ourselves. Blame may not immediately seem like fighting but it pushes our own responsibility outwards, so it is a kind of violence.

Fight impulses can lurk inside, buried deep but sometimes can leak out in unexpected and unwanted places in maybe passive aggressive ways. Blame can be like passing a hot potato – it saves us having to own our own feelings and culpability.

Fight and fear

In trauma, anger is frequently tangled up with having been afraid, so pulling fear and anger apart may sometimes need time and help. Anger and fear are often pretty close, one protecting the other. Finella's trauma was rooted in the denial of her vulnerable feelings: she feared them. When we feel attacked something *ramps up inside*. It is so *human* that we touch the trampoline of trauma-induced fear, and we naturally spring up into anger. But we must approach these things with caution. It is complicated, delicate work to begin to acknowledge and harness fight when it is rooted close to fear.

Respecting fight's purpose

Our fight response may have helped us survive a painful reality, and therefore deserves respect. Anger alerts us to injustice; if we have felt powerless, beginning to feel and claim anger on our own behalf can bring inner power and agency. Part of this can be the experience of having another person hear our anger without judging it, which can be enormously relieving. It helps us tolerate our own anger and begin to use it effectively.

Using anger effectively means being able to be assertive when we need to be – we are finally on our own side rather than at the mercy of ourselves and the world. One role of anger is to let us know if something does not feel right for us. If we listen to anger's protective voice, we can then consider our choices and think about setting a boundary. An important purpose of anger is to keep us safe.

Becoming angry at injustice can be a creative force – good for the world. We can be inspired by individuals and leaders who use anger in awe-inspiring ways – to rouse others and drive change. Others, in extreme situations such as incarceration, use the power of anger as passive resistance to defy another's aggression, not permitting it to humiliate them.

Our relationship to anger

Anger is a powerful force and, depending on our experience, we may understandably fear that our anger might damage another person, especially if we have been hurt by another's anger. Like Finella, we may have been in an agonizingly out of control situation long ago. We may believe that being vulnerable or soft is a weakness so we defend ourselves by blaming another person. Our journey may be to learn to study and to tolerate our angry feelings and be open to being thoughtful about other feelings we may encounter on the way.

On such a journey, we will inevitably face our fears. As the famous Chinese philosopher Lao Tzu wrote: 'The softest things in the world overcome the hardest things in the world.'[3] It is a paradox that ultimately our vulnerability is where much of our strength lies.

I believe there are three principles for dealing healthily with trauma anger.

1. Own and understand trauma anger as an interrupting force in our lives

Understanding anger as a legacy of our trauma can allow us to take steps to mitigate its power. If there is space for us to own it, we can again be opened to a full palette of our feelings in a creative way, as is shown in Mike's story.

---

3   https://libquotes.com/lao-tzu/quote/lbm4f4b, accessed 07/01/24. Lao Tzu lived in 6th century BC in China and was the founder of Taoism. He may have been the author of the *Tao Te China*, a seminal Daoist text that influenced Chinese folk and national belief.

TRAUMA STORY: Mike, the marine

Mike is a marine who served in Afghanistan and Iraq. He was injured a number of times and lost close colleagues in the same platoon. Some of his friends died in unspeakable ways right next to him as shells screamed past his ears. The images of their last moments are etched on his brain. When Mike comes home to his young family, he is a different person, no longer able to freely play with his children or enjoy their company. He irritably flies off the handle at the smallest difficulty. He has zero tolerance for domestic life, is highly critical of them all and on a short fuse with anything that does not run smoothly. When the whole family get together for a summer barbecue, Mike becomes immediately upset by the excited squealing of the children at play. When someone says something he does not like, he erupts in rage and storms off, leaving everyone in a state of shock.

Mike is diagnosed with PTSD[4] and referred for post-combat trauma counselling, where he is offered a variety of strategies to help soothe his agitated nervous system. He begins to tell the story that is being relived in his nightmares. He learns that the out-of-control rage is a direct result of his mind and body experiencing unimaginable terror and horrors in the war zones. The specialists refer Mike to a range of therapeutic options to assist him with dissipating the stress charge in his body over time. Not all of them fit, but Mike finds dance does. He has always loved dance and finds that moving his body in time with others helps him release deeply held emotions through the repetition and rhythm. His body sweats as it moves. It feels good. Mike feels free there and never misses a class. Through his regular

---

4   Post-traumatic stress disorder (PTSD) is a psychiatric diagnosis first added to the third edition of the *Diagnostic and Statistical Manual of Mental Disorders* (*DSM-III*) in 1980 in the wake of the Vietnam War. The diagnosis recognizes the significance of an outside event – the stressor – on a person, that overwhelms our ability to cope. The term disorder means symptoms that do not recede but can increase over time. As time has gone on the term has been critiqued and is problematic in two ways. First, I would say that trauma, even when full-blown and severe, is a *response* to experience and not a disorder. Second, often overwhelming stress is ongoing for individuals and communities, so trauma is not 'post'.

5Rhythms dance,[5] the charge of his long-held rage decreases and the dance brings him greater peace and equilibrium. Over time, his guilt decreases and his passion and gratitude for life increases. Through moving, he lets his body know that now he is safe. The passion he finds for dancing makes all the difference.

2. Manage anger by containing it

Mike learns to harness his anger and uses his dance practice to do this. As we have said, fight is felt physically, so it follows that the way to discharge and release it is to use our bodies. Another person might flush out their trauma response through taking up a new sport or a stimulating activity that engages and challenges them. Over centuries, humans have found a multitude of ways to discharge, carry, contain and express powerful emotions. Rituals can help with this. We can be helped by forms of words that can carry the 'freight' of our emotions, at significant milestones such as weddings or funerals. We may think of rites of passage evolved by indigenous peoples, tug-of-war contests or the emotions released in football. There is a multitude of creative ways to physically move, have agency, express and contain our fight energy.

3. Witness and accept the anger of others

If we accept our own anger and take responsibility for it, then we can allow another the right to be angry too, and not allow it to diminish us or them. Our anger means something. A colleague described the way he would contain his young child who was having an angry tantrum. He formed a huge circle with his arms around the young child, not touching but providing the child with a sense of safety through his physical proximity. He would say, 'I know you are angry and scared, but I am right here and not going anywhere.' Sometimes, of course, it is right to touch and hug a child or adult. That can be profoundly soothing. Yet, at other times, we may feel we need to simply have another person unflinchingly acknowledge our feelings without them

---

5   5Rhythms is a group dance practice that was developed in the 1970s by Gabrielle Roth. It draws on spiritual practices, Eastern philosophy and Gestalt therapy. Central to it is the idea of using movement as expression, through patterns and rhythms.

necessarily touching or intruding on us, but just remaining close and calm. Witnessing another's feelings can help them to feel safe. Invariably, when my colleague's child felt safe and witnessed, her distress and frustration eased: her emotions were contained helpfully and not squashed. There was space for them.

These words were written for Finella, the lawyer who had no one to witness her feelings long ago but is enlightened to discover and learn from them later in life:

Rage ramps up
Rampages red
Hot screams
Spring from pain
Flying in all directions
How to tame the lion
Claim more colours

BREAKING-FREE POINTERS FOR TRAUMA FIGHT

▸ Trauma anger or rage can be scary to be on the receiving end of, and can become our mode of response when we are triggered.

▸ Trauma anger springs from fear and often from pain and having been out of control in our trauma experience.

▸ When in fight mode, we can feel justified and powerful in the moment, but we don't always feel good afterwards, especially if we hurt others.

▸ One way to change this pattern is to locate the fight response as belonging in the 'engine room' of our trauma and separate 'then' from 'now' in our minds.

▸ We can learn to de-escalate the volcano of fight in the moment through the discipline of mindfulness, learning to speak our truth, taking regular breaks, breathing and counting (to name a few).

▸ Caution: Fear and anger are often close, so handle them with care!

▸ Working with our anger rather than being at its mercy involves:
  - claiming its power while developing self-discipline and restraint (not easy and achieved only through repetition and practice)

- turning anger around to be a force for good
- respecting and listening to anger's message (i.e. something is wrong!)
- being prepared to investigate the meaning of the anger and where it is held in the body
- being curious about the vulnerability that anger tries to protect and making space to nurture that vulnerability
- widening our tolerance to our own anger and being more prepared to accept the anger of others.

▸ Breaking free from our trauma anger might mean learning to tolerate other feelings in ourselves, such as the pain underbelly of an angry defence.

▸ There are a multitude of wider ways to contain anger, such as rituals, art and sport, that help us dissipate anger naturally. We may find some extra 'turbo-charged' fight emerging while engaging in one of these that may be an indication of unfinished trauma.

QUESTIONS FOR FURTHER REFLECTION[6]

1. What are the things that make me angry? Do I or someone else ever use my anger in a powerful or a destructive way?

2. Does my anger or another's anger do damage to relationships in my life?

3. What is my own relationship to anger? Maybe I have mixed feelings at different times. Do I generally respect it? Do I fear it? Do I avoid it? Does it sometimes dominate me or another person?

4. What is my response when someone is angry with me? If it makes me feel small and frightened, can I befriend and be kind to that vulnerable part?

5. When I get really angry, is there some truth inside that I may be unwilling to tolerate? Can I honour that truth?

6. Do I notice how the narrative of fear and anger dominates in less obvious ways?

---

6 CAUTION: These questions may be very difficult to face alone. You may need to take time with a trusted other or professional to consider them and their implications carefully.

7. Can I dig down into being safe at the level of my roots to maybe find my hurting vulnerable self, to become less of a stranger in my world when I feel angry, alone or out of control?

KNOW YOUR ROOTS EXERCISE

▸ Just for five minutes, allow yourself to be still.
▸ Become aware of your breathing and focus on its rhythm.
▸ Allow your body to be in alignment, so that your backbone is straight and your shoulders back.
▸ Then gently bring your attention to your legs and your feet, pushing them into the ground.
▸ Imagine they are your roots.
▸ Like a tree, imagine your roots extend beyond your feet and go under the floor, anchoring you more deeply to the place you are right now.
▸ Take some more breaths as you do this and notice any effect of this practice on your nervous system.

You can find a short video that highlights some points from this chapter at https://www.youtube.com/watch?v=HfAZZ5iwMfg or by scanning the QR code.

Chapter 5

OUR NEED TO ESCAPE PAIN

One solution or response to trauma pain is to dampen it or run from it.

Flight is a very common trauma 'solution' and we humans are endlessly inventive in our ways of escaping. The difficulty is that the solution can become addictive. We might increase our alcohol consumption or lose ourselves in a particular behaviour more and more – so it becomes irresistible. When flight takes hold, our brains themselves change their story and perspective. Our amygdala is hijacked, giving us the message that something – our flight solution – is our priority, necessary for survival. The cost is that we can exchange one kind of pain for another.

TRAUMA STORY: Tom's flight

Tom spends most of his adult life being professionally successful and high-powered as an investment banker. Outside work, he plays hard, abusing drugs and alcohol, behaviours that very nearly derail his functioning.

As a child of six, Tom lost both his parents in a traffic accident and after that he was brought up by a kind uncle. When he is 28, his uncle dies and Tom's substance using intensifies. The wheels really start to fall off when Tom takes more and more time off work. He misses his uncle's funeral and throws wild parties with friends that last for days, finding ever more inventive and elaborate ways to distract himself. Alcohol places a film over the chasm of loss inside.

Each addiction holds its own particular charm. For Tom, alcohol consumption becomes the best show in town. The light on the fridge door can so entrance a binge eater they cannot resist opening the door. We may rely on smoking pot 'to hide in plain sight', as a client once put it. Body-building can bring a temporary hormonal relief to our emotions, giving us a pseudo-strength that stops us confronting what we feel underneath – maybe weak, empty and small.

What addiction does to our bodies and minds

Our addiction of choice is likely to bring a feel-good flood of the hormone oxytocin, the sense of reward afforded by dopamine, or affect our mood regulator serotonin. Taking drugs such as opioids can feel like a blessed temporary relief from a brain that is consumed with whirring anxiety. Drugs and alcohol change the chemicals in our brains, flooding us with pleasure. They also numb us from anxiety and pain. We temporarily feel in control and the promise is compelling. It can work temporarily but, of course, the 'solution' brings profound problems in its wake (including in the case of prolonged drug and alcohol use, brain and other physical damage). In the longer term, an addictive trauma solution does not relieve us so easily, demanding more and more for the same effect. Our body-mind gets wired for an addiction that can become compulsive. When our flight runs the show, lives can be destroyed.

TRAUMA STORY: Nikko is captured by fantasy

Nikko's family collapses when he is 17 after his father dies. There is no insurance or savings and the family falls apart soon after. Always solitary and sensitive, Nikko feels ill-equipped to cope with the world. His mother and siblings appear to have more resources to manage than him. When Nikko struggles, they have little time for him. He flees to another country where he hopes he will have more luck with money. Nikko feels worthless and is socially awkward, but excels with numbers and gets a job in an accountant's office. This is low paid, so Nikko supplements his earnings by buying and selling on the internet. He likes gaming, and develops 'friends' online. Each night he enters into virtual worlds, pitting himself against others and losing himself in elaborate and complex feats of survival. It is exciting and gradually becomes more real than his waking world. In his everyday life, Nikko becomes distracted and agitated. Increasingly, he cannot bear being still. He loses interest in food, and orders fast food on the internet, many deliveries arriving on his doorstep each day, the boxes piling up in his living room. He orders more than he needs because he is scared of not having enough to fill the aching emptiness inside.

Nikko is now addicted to gaming. The internet becomes the world he is in thrall to. He is completely alone and trapped in flight behaviour. (Go to Chapter 20 to find out what happens to Nikko later.)

How our addictions work as 'solutions'

There are many isolated Nikkos in the world. When one solution does not work anymore, flight may tell us to fix things in other ways – change our job, our partner, our location – in the hope that we will gain control of what feels very much out of control inside. Desperately fixing things or trying new things is one aspect of flight. Avoiding or running from things is another.

Flight can be far more powerful than logic, and when it is dominant it can feel as though we are stuck in high gear at speed. In the stories of Nikko and Tom, we can see escalation of pain and how flight solutions emerge. The devastating loss Tom feels on losing his uncle touches the earlier trauma of suddenly losing both parents, completely unseating him emotionally. It is at this point that his flight solution (alcohol and avoidance) really comes into its own. Once we become used to a solution that numbs us from pain, we are compelled to perpetuate it. We can become manic and full of cravings, engaging in activities that feel like imperatives. Another reason we stay with our flight solution, as with Nikko, is that flight and addiction can actually co-opt our brains.

Addictions can change how our brains work

Addictions can actually change the way our neurotransmitters work, forming new tracks in our brains. Like a magnetic sequence, the way that flight attracts and captures us can be supremely hard to resist and easily be reinforced – we can lose control of ourselves. The repetitive loop of habit, trigger and addiction is so powerful that our flight part may be highly persuasive. Our best intentions may easily be short-circuited by an addictive loop that tells us to 'go on, just do it'. In addition, we may be light years away from being able and willing to admit that our addictive behaviour is any kind of problem. One person I spoke with calls this defence her 'wolf in sheep's clothing'. In the throes of his flight solution, Nikko increasingly struggles to bear being still and reflective, yet that slowing down is necessary in order to properly attend to his needs and reach out to others for help. We might fear being vulnerable for all kinds of reasons. To become open can be an enormous and sometimes impossible journey to make.

Losing control through addiction

Our addiction is an attempt to save ourselves from pain. It shouts a message that we need it. Its loud voice can drown out any worry we might have that our addiction is in charge of us, rather than the other way round – we are out of control. A client described their addiction to me: 'I just hold on, hoping I will come out the other side.' When we are in flight mode, we might be going so fast that we cannot hear things that we do not want to hear. Metaphorically, we have our hands over our ears. Flight offers us the illusion that *if I keep going like this, I will feel as if I have control over my world* (which is preferable to feeling that I actually have no control).

Flight becomes so powerful because of its capacity to shield us: we flee from painful truths about how we really feel inside. Flight excels at covering pain and can make us do anything rather than risk being vulnerable. Facing ourselves honestly can feel like a very scary thing to do.

We are adept at ignoring our vulnerable selves, and not acknowledging what we most need. When we are operating in flight mode, someone close to us may notice that we are not quite standing on solid ground: we may sometimes act in unpredictable, secretive or scary ways. Or we may create a storm around us that might cover truthful things and confuse everyone. It can be virtually impossible to live with and support us in this predicament, but even small gestures can be a lifeline, as they were for Conor.

TRAUMA STORY: Conor's chaos and his mother's faithfulness

Seventeen-year-old Conor is in a whirlwind of chaos. He seems to be acting out his very turbulent early years before he was adopted. He hooks up with 'friends' online who are on the edge of criminal behaviour. He keeps seeking out danger. He goes on frequent rampages if challenged. The disarray of his bedroom reflects the whirlwind of his emotions. As he gets older, his mum has increasingly less ability to protect him from being preyed on or getting into trouble. She is consumed by anxiety, but she knows she needs to keep faith with him, despite his choices.

Once a week, she goes into Conor's room, strips his bed and washes the bed linen with a fragrant detergent. The day after, Conor always hugs and thanks her for the loving act. It is one way she can reach through the chaos of his life with the fragrance of her care and show him her love.

Flight covers vulnerability

Conor's mother and Conor have a dilemma in the throes of flight. Changing things feels difficult or impossible because the 'cover' or 'running' solution *almost* works, and we can become extremely attached to it. Yet there are ways that can help us find our vulnerability, and help us risk letting flight's messages go. Both the fact that Conor's mum shows her love and that he can recognize and acknowledge her support are hopeful signs. On some level, she reaches his vulnerability this way. It is important to keep faith with loved ones trapped in flight and trust they will find a way through, even if it is not clear how they might. Small things can be catalysts of change. For some people, these may come through creativity or a closer relationship to nature. The power of art to move us can find the crack in our brittle shell, a way into our soft centre.

At the beginning of the chapter, we met Tom who was addicted to wild parties to avoid the chasm inside. As was the case for him, sometimes life offers us opportunities to stop, reflect and change direction.

TRAUMA STORY: Tom is captured by art (continuation)

One day, Tom goes to the cinema with a friend to see a film about a family who have become fractured and disconnected after a tragedy but find their way back through working together to save their farm. Over a pizza beforehand, Tom's friend tells him she is worried about him, as he seems more agitated than usual. In the cinema, Tom is swept away by the emotional intensity and artistic beauty of the film. The family's losses touch his. Afterwards, he cannot leave the cinema, weeping way past the credits. The evening becomes a turning point in his life. He is finally able to openly and honestly face his grief for his lost parents and uncle, the only people he has ever felt properly safe with. He trusted their love and now he feels broken and unveiled. In this moment, he chooses to face the truth of what he feels inside.

Unable to function or sleep, Tom visits his GP who signs him off work and recommends he joins a group bereavement process at Cruse and also attends Alcoholics Anonymous (AA) meetings to address his relationship with alcohol. Slowly and courageously, he begins to talk about his painful losses. Tom feels as if he is opening a vault deep inside, a place that he has fiercely guarded and defended.

Some time later, Tom begins attending classes in nature drawing at night school. He is quietly amazed he can do this so easily. He likes the part of him that feels so alive when doing his art. Through becoming absorbed in the mindful activity of his drawing, Tom finds a new way to be himself – it is a revelation and a calm oasis, so different from the frenetic banker's lifestyle. He thinks about his uncle and parents when he draws. He nurtures his drawing gift and excels at it. A breakthrough comes when Tom dedicates his first book of illustrated prints to his deeply loved and missed uncle and parents. At the launch, Tom speaks about his uncle publicly in a beautiful and emotionally connected way. He has come a long way.

Finding something that becomes more important

Tom's route out of addiction was finding something else – his art – that was attractive and powerful enough to draw him away. The word 'addiction' is derived from a Latin term for 'enslaved by' or 'bound to'. If we have struggled to overcome an addiction – or have tried to help someone else to do so and seen the consequences of its trap – we will understand what this really means. The power and magnetism of addiction makes it a very thorny problem to solve. Not everyone is able to free themselves from its slavery. To be trapped like this causes untold suffering. We leave trauma in our wake.

Yet, deep down, we may know that our flight, though compelling, does not fully convince us or bring happiness or true connection to all of who we are. The film helps Tom touch his painful loss and his art becomes part of his new identity. However, it is sometimes easier to stick with flight rather than face the terror we feel about being brutally honest with ourselves and others.

When caught up in trauma flight, we are desperate for the soothing of our beleaguered nervous systems. On some level, we are desperate for the safety of being immersed in the beauty of nature or that a relationship with a trusted other might bring us. We might long to let go of flight's messages and impulses, and risk doing something different. How do we begin to do this? It helps Tom to find space to talk about his compulsions in a trusted group. Many of us who struggle with addiction find that rigorous, repeated and transparent honesty, even with strangers through groups such as Twelve-Step programmes,[1] is ultimately what helps us stay free of flight's addictive powers to capture us.

What can we do for someone who is in flight, running, covering, deflecting, minimizing, hiding, wearing a mask, creating chaos, struggling for control yet being out of control? We might remember they are emotionally overwhelmed and fragile. We might remember that they need us to keep faith with them, however hard this is to do. We might find ways to try to nurture them kindly, setting attentive boundaries to help keep us and them safe, when they are lost and hurting themselves. A little goes a long way.

Flight is a solution to the problem of our pain, yet in order to fully live, we may need to be ready to hear a question and reflect on it: *What am I hiding and running from?*

---

1   Twelve-Step programmes support recovery from substance abuse. One principle is the idea of a repeated return to 'powerlessness' and open honesty in the face of the addiction and risking rigorous and open honesty about ourselves within the safety of a group and through the support of a trusted confidant called a sponsor.

These are words about Nikko. They might equally apply to Conor.

The hermit crab
Was actually a Coke can
Which caused you more problems
Didn't protect you at all
Inside your shell
Your painful vulnerability
It is all you have
Perhaps one day this may be your strength

BREAKING-FREE POINTERS FOR TRAUMA FLIGHT

▸ A flight solution can be a thorny problem to solve. Its addictive 'go on, just do it' persuasive inner voice along with hormonal and brain change take much hard work, discipline and support for us to turn around.

▸ Our addictive 'solution' almost works, which is why it can become compelling. For example, drugs bring blessed relief from unbearable anxiety.

▸ Ultimately, addiction is likely to derail us and be destructive as it captures and enslaves us, demanding more and more.

▸ Being around addiction is often traumatizing.

▸ Small things can be a catalyst for change; sometimes, like Tom, we need to be 'brought low' to see the emotional truth that we are running from.

▸ It can feel terrifying to face who we really are, honestly. But it can be liberating to face it, understand it and, in so doing, discover our worth. This is a step-by-step choice that many addicts worldwide take daily with the help of their chosen 'tribe' (e.g. AA, NA or Al-Anon or Alateen meetings).[2]

▸ If we know someone who is lost in fixing, escaping, changing,

---

2 AA (Alcoholics Anonymous) and NA (Narcotics Anonymous) are groups within the 12-step recovery movement started by Bill Wilson and Bob Smith in 1935 and Al-Anon and Alateen are groups for family members who have experienced the addiction of someone close to them.

avoiding or covering or creating chaos in their lives, we need to remember what they are likely to feel deep down inside (frightened, vulnerable, alone and lost) and, like Conor's mum, find ways to keep faith with them, hoping that, even perhaps from the place of their broken heart, they will ultimately find ways to break free.

QUESTIONS FOR FURTHER REFLECTION

1. Do I recognize the urge to run and keep going rather than face what feels too difficult to face?
2. Do I have an addiction solution that I wish I had a handle on?
3. Do feelings of discomfort let me know the truth of this?
4. Am I ready to begin to make a decision to make a change? Am I ready to say only truthful things, however difficult and however much I would rather do something else?
5. In flight, individuals become solo operators. The truth is that we cannot heal alone: 'no man is an island'.[3] Am I open to challenging myself to learn to trust others with my vulnerability in order to heal myself?
6. Might I be open to considering seeking out a regular place of support I can return to, a place to be honest and vulnerable, step by step? Am I ready for such a long and difficult journey?

SPEAKING THE TRUTH MEDITATION[4]

With a trusted friend or partner, find a safe space. One person in a calm, neutral voice asks the other, 'Who are you?' The second person says the first thing that comes into their mind: 'I am a person who likes dogs... I am a gardener... I am tired.' The questioner waits for the response and simply asks the question again and waits for the next response. Allow several minutes. Then reverse roles. Be curious about

---

3   Donne, J. (1923). *Devotions Upon Emergent Occasions*. Cambridge: The University Press.
4   This exercise can be done in twos as described or within a group who form pairs and then report the experience back to the wider group.

how you each respond to the question. Notice whether you answer about your identity, your preferences or your feelings.

You can find a short video that highlights some points from this chapter at https://www.youtube.com/watch?v=FcD2nYLvlvs or by scanning the QR code.

Chapter 6

WHEN WE FREEZE INSIDE

We freeze to keep safe, so that nothing bad happens.

A deer caught in the headlights of an approaching car will be terrified but unable to move. This trauma response has a purpose: if the frozen deer blends into the background, it may remain unobserved by a predator.

In humans, the freeze response to crisis can linger in the body and mind well after the event. This is important to understand, for two reasons. First, when we are in a frozen state, little that is new can enter our brains. We cannot take in information or anything else we might need. Second, if left vulnerable and unprotected, we are unable to stop things impacting us negatively. We are vulnerable. We are in a holding position to protect ourselves from harm but the problem is that nothing good happens either.

TRAUMA STORY: Frozen Pete

When Pete is 11, he loses his beloved mother to cancer and his world changes. The ground he walks on no longer feels solid or safe. Mum understood him, unlike his father, who seems to find him an embarrassment. When dad remarries, it becomes painfully clear to Pete that his father has no real interest in him. When they meet, he is critical of Pete, comparing him negatively to his more confident brother.

Pete pours his energies into becoming technologically brilliant. A highly sensitive person, Pete feels safe at work and is capable of standing his ground knowledgeably, but in personal relationships he develops a stutter and struggles to find his voice. He finds it easier to agree to things he doesn't want to do. His friends sometimes call him Passive Pete in jest, but he secretly hates the nickname. He feels got at and attacked, even when his friends are just being lively with banter. He feels they don't really know him at all.

When someone asks Pete's opinion on anything, he panics and almost forgets to breathe. He is only confident when talking about computers. He deflects things with embarrassed laughter, but it is agony for him to be put on the spot. He has no idea what he really thinks and feels about things and is amazed when others confidently express their opinions. Sometimes, Pete secretly wishes other people would just go away. In company, he goes to a dark, precarious place inside. He doesn't want to be known, not really. He is terrified of what people might find.

Pete's fundamental security had been rocked when his mum died and, as a result, deep inside a part of him remains a frightened and stiff 11-year-old. He is only able to experience feelings with a couple of friends and his brother, George, whom he trusts. They are like islands of safety for Pete. Being in their company brings him a rare sense of ease. Reminiscing with George about their mum together brings Pete enormous solace.

One day, when they are making a cup of tea in the kitchen, George, usually a quiet taciturn man, hugs Pete out of the blue. Pete gasps with amazement. Later, when they talk about it, they remember their mother hugging them both really tightly as youngsters and jokingly insistent, asking: 'Can you feel me hugging you?!' Through George's touch that day, Pete can somehow feel his mother's hug once more. His muscles release a little and he breathes more deeply than he has for a long time.

Freeze is so physical

After an overwhelming experience like Pete's, we might notice in ourselves a feeling of paralysis, a sense that we are not able to decide anything or achieve much, and therefore we don't quite have a sense of completion or satisfaction. We are frozen and stuck, like a computer locked and unable to update. We might want to move but our bodies and minds just don't let us flow and respond fully. It can be easy to underestimate the power of a body freeze; even if we tell our body to move it may not let us. Freeze is a device that can protect us – a device that can become an embodied state of being.

In frozen mode, we might clench, hold our breath or hold tension in our lower belly rather than allowing it to flow out with ease and easy rhythm. Like Pete, we may feel like we don't have solid ground under our feet. We go through the motions, like treading water. Living this way can mean we are cut off from our own inner emotions and body messages. They are too scary for us to connect with. We do not trust our own experience. Our bodies can hold so much freeze that we do not feel sensations: the freeze dominates. I have met traumatized individuals whose faces have a perpetual startled expression that has become habitual. For such people, the world feels scary, both inside and outside. Freeze's signs can be quite subtle and so they are hard to spot. Like Pete, we may find ourselves deferring to others' perceptions rather than voicing our own, we may not take risks, and are just 'getting through' life, rather than feeling comfortable in our own skin.

Freezing in relationships

Freeze can have a big impact on our close relationships. We may function pretty well in many areas, but some habits or parts of us feel blocked off and impossible to change, rather like inner 'no go' areas.

Perhaps you know someone who keeps secrets and has difficulty trusting their opinions. They may hide their vulnerability, even from those closest to them, freezing them out rather than being open. It may be easy to get frustrated with someone who appears to be non-responsive, when actually they are in a freeze. That is all they can do. Trauma needs a solution and freeze is one such response.

A person in freeze may be helped to dig down into a deeper truth about their experience. While fearful of it, on some level they have a wish for their painful truth to be told.

What a person in freeze might need and want

Someone who is frozen really needs the people around them, even if they do not show it. Like the roots of trees that search for water, we have parts of ourselves that need to be safe and secure on the ground that we stand on. To deeply acknowledge what has hurt us can become a liberation. However, it is important also to acknowledge the danger inherent in such an excavation: if we can bear to go deeper, we may find pain as well as riches and truth. In the following case, Daniela finds some solace in the physical warming of her feet in the newfound gift of sisterly love and care.

TRAUMA STORY: Daniela out in the cold

Daniela is terribly and consistently abused within and outside her birth family, and is often neglected and left alone to cope with no care. No one protects her. Terrified, she leaves home, sleeping in cars and living on the streets as a feral teenager. To survive, she learns to duck and dive, not always telling the truth, in case it backfires on her. She becomes a street fighter. She tends to chronically neglect her body, which often feels numb and cold. As others have violated her, she sometimes hurts herself just to feel something in her frozen body.

When Daniela finally finds a stable foster family, they set ground rules, firmly demanding honesty and straightforward communication from her. They are kind. They tell her they are not going anywhere. Daniela finds this hard to believe and tests it in many ways.

Daniela's hands and feet are always cold, and yet she often forgets to put gloves and socks on. She is amazed when her foster family notice her red hands and feet and gently encourage her to cover them. She notices that when her feet are warm, her breathing flows more smoothly and she feels a bit safer. After some time, one of Daniela's new sisters buys her a foot spa. Her sister has wrapped the gift in blue tissue paper. Daniela unwraps it carefully, noticing the soft feel of the paper. It is unbelievable. She squirrels it away and later, by herself, she carefully heats the spa, noticing the steam on the water, dipping in her fingers with excitement. Can she bear it? Gingerly, she places first one cold toe, then two, in the delicious soothing warmth of the hot water. It is a revelation to Daniela that anyone should notice her needs, care about her feet or indeed any part of her. It is so painfully shocking for her to feel the enormity of the lack of care she experienced that Daniela suddenly wells up, weeping hot bitter tears. Her tears are also a release. As her feet are warmed, her senses are activated and her spirits lift in response to the beautiful care shown in the gift.

A variety of ways to work with freeze

Daniela's sister was spot on in her targeted care, as emotional freeze is so often held physically. She feels her emotions – she unfreezes – through attention to the body. After freeze, we can practise awakening our senses. A first step, as for Daniela, may be to try to tolerate a tiny amount of warmth and closely observe its effects. We might experiment with self-touch to see if it soothes us or deepens our breathing. We can practise grounding ourselves by feeling our feet on the floor or tolerating the warmth of a bath or a soft garment, and noticing whether it feels good (see the sensory grounding exercise at the end of this chapter). The deep pressure touch of weighted blankets can help calm the sensory arousal of anxiety. Oxygen levels drop in freeze, so experimenting with our breath can increase our sense of vitality at a physical level. Freeze may cause our breath to become punctuated, rather than flowing in natural rhythm. Conscious work can mitigate this tendency: a long out-breath will bring us to a more regulated green zone in our nervous system, ground us and calm our fear.

Movement after freeze

We can also work to mobilize our bodies post trauma and raise our oxygen levels. Moving gives them the message we are safe. After acknowledging the trauma has passed, we might mobilize ourselves by stamping our feet, crossing our arms and tapping our shoulders rhythmically, or push ourselves through our moment of freeze by getting up and having a dance to get our bodies moving. Getting our blood flowing can activate our brains, bringing more energy and a sense of power or agency. We can take tiny steps towards relaxing our freeze's hold by reconnecting with ourselves from the inside out. Psychotherapist and trauma specialist Carolyn Spring tells us that people in traditional societies, after recounting their trauma stories around a fire (about, for example, surviving a bear attack on their compound), would then deliberately mobilize themselves by barricading their compound and then attending to the daily business of life. First, they acknowledged the trauma, then they took steps to protect themselves, then they moved on. Physical movement is often a helpful antidote to freeze.[1] We can ask ourselves, what can I do now?

After experiencing trauma, many have found solace in walking and being part of nature. I am reminded of the idea of pilgrimage, where richness is found not in the destination but in the experience of journeying. An example would be Raynor Winn's autobiographical book *The Salt Path*, which describes how, after a series of cruel life setbacks, she and her husband found that the only thing that made sense was to walk the Cornish coastal path.[2] Though they partly walked because they lost their home, they came to value walking for its own sake, without a known goal or defined outcome. Walking itself brings insights and healing.

Ways to work with freeze are as varied as we are. Soothing can come from as simple an act as stroking an animal or soft fabric. In the early 2000s, Japan suffered economic downturn, terrorist attacks, an earthquake and later a nuclear leak in 2011. Soon after, a number of cat cafes sprang up in the metropolitan area around Tokyo and in other urban centres, and they are still popular. The comforting and healing qualities of cats come from their physical warmth. The visceral, pleasurable texture of their fur allows individuals, many of whom live alone or are stressed, to be soothed and relax. Cafe owners work hard to create an ambience that is highly domesticated – a soft, comfortable and gentle environment for all the senses – and it is not unusual to see people in the cafe sleeping with a blanket covering them, as if they are in their own bed at home.

Giving our time uncluttered by demands

Softening an inner freeze may need gentle, repeated, patient and slow attention. Where are the places we can go that help us unknot and

---

1   Carolyn Spring, Trauma Needs a Solution. Available at: www.carolynspring.com/podcast/trauma-needs-a-solution, accessed 07/01/24.
2   Winn, R. (2019). *The Salt Path*. London: Penguin.

untwist the held tightness in our muscles? How can we allow our bodies to let go their freeze? Depending on how sustained or intense it is, working to soften our bodies may a slow job, like turning around a large ship. If the body is frozen, it may freeze all the more if too much mitigation is given too quickly. Freeze is a trauma defence that becomes habitual, so relaxing it does not always feel easy to do.

Being in a relationship with a person who is frozen may require a slow, subtle, kind and patient approach, like Daniela's foster family. Trauma can feel so cold and stiff. If you know someone who feels like this, a little human warmth may make all the difference to them, even though they may never give you feedback. You may need to give them time that is not cluttered by demand. It may be hard at first to trust that this will make any difference. It is unlikely that explanations, instructions or content will assist a frozen body to feel safe. Simple, caring communication, even in tiny ways, may act to thaw and soften it. A small gesture of kindness or a touch on the shoulder can communicate more than many words. Art and music can also be a way in to soften a frozen soul. Earlier in the chapter, we met Pete who lost his mum aged 11 and finds people hard to trust. Later, life presents him with an opportunity for something new to happen in an entirely unexpected way, as we will see in the follow-up below.

TRAUMA STORY: Pete (continued)

Some time later, a colleague invites Pete to an opera about a man who is perceived as being different in his community. He is treated cruelly and scapegoated. As the closing notes of the opera die away, to his great surprise, Pete finds himself weeping bitter tears. Even though usually so controlled and anxious around others, the power and beauty of the music unlocks a grief in Pete's lonely, fearfully frozen heart. The colleague is deeply moved by Pete's tears. He does not know what to do, but then remembers Pete always gets hot chocolate from the vending machine in the office. He takes him to the cafe and places a mug of hot chocolate in front of him. Pete finds himself beginning to trust in his friend's gentle care and kindness. This is the beginning of a lifelong friendship for Pete, which gives him much quiet joy. He also develops a life-giving passion for opera.

Life and warmth can return even to the coldest parts of us. These words were written for Pete, expressing his inner austerity and the beginnings of his inner thaw:

Frozen cold
Locked in
Frozen in fear
If I tell them
I'm a frightened child
Cold moon in my chest
Hard to give words even to
This painful core
Yet as I do I thaw
Just a little

BREAKING-FREE POINTERS FOR TRAUMA FREEZE

▸ The freeze response of trauma is a biological survival response to blend into the background when in danger. It is a protective device that can become embodied.

▸ When in freeze, we tread water. We cannot easily take in new information, like a computer that is full and cannot receive updates.

▸ We may need warmth, comfort and safety in order to soothe our inner freeze. We may also need to raise our oxygen levels through movement.

▸ In a relationship with someone who is frozen and maybe finds trust difficult, it is important to be slow, consistent, subtle, kind and patient, like Pete's work colleague and friend. There is pain underneath freeze.

▸ If we have a tendency to freeze we may easily feel overloaded by instruction or too much content. Like a person parched in a desert, we most need drops of water – that is, the precious gift of patience and minimal demand in order to feel safe enough to relax our freeze.

QUESTIONS FOR FURTHER REFLECTION

1. Do I recognize a part of me that may have responded to life fearfully, by becoming stiff and cold?
2. What activities or cultural/social/sporting events might help me to feel more alive?
3. Does attending to my needs spaciously and slowly, in the moment, at the level of my senses, bring solace, stilling and thawing? Can I assimilate and repeat these things as part of my essential self-care?
4. Are there individuals in my life whom I trust and who warm me inside, helping me feel at greater ease with myself? Can I reach out to them?

EXERCISE TO ENGAGE THE SENSES

Look around you and bring your attention to:

- ▸ 5 things you can see
- ▸ 4 things you can hear
- ▸ 3 things you can touch
- ▸ 2 things you can smell
- ▸ 1 thing you can taste.

This technique directs you back to the here and now and brings you back to your senses and into the calming part of your brain. You can do it anywhere – when you're boiling the kettle, when you're out for a walk, when you're waiting for a meeting you are nervous about, or when you are in the bathroom – it's quick, easy to remember and always to hand when you need it.

You can find a short video that highlights some points from this chapter at https:// www.youtube.com/watch?v=32p4YKjyBtw or by scanning the QR code.

— Chapter 7 —

GOING UNDER THE RADAR

A post-trauma slump of exhaustion is an involuntary
survival mechanism after something unbearable.

In this chapter, we explore feelings of low mood, depression and
hopelessness as a physiological reaction to trauma. Nearly a third
of us who experience trauma have this kind of shut-down response.

What are its signs? We might be exhausted beyond measure, have
difficulties engaging with life, or motivating ourselves to make decisions. I referred to this 'blue-zone' response in Chapter 1.

Starting from our biology

It may be helpful to think how this response works physiologically.
When a gazelle meets a lion in the savannah, its best bet for survival
may be to feign dead rather than fight or flee, so its body tries to save
it. Part of the animal's vagal nerve moves the animal into a shut-down
state.[1] As a result, the gazelle's muscles then become flaccid and inert
and it may defecate. This mechanism in mammals is there to help
them survive; the lion, when denied the thrill of the chase, may move
on elsewhere.

We are mammals too. We might remember a time when we
received bad news and our legs gave way and we felt like collapsing.
Research by Stephen Porges has shown that when trauma activation
is high in humans, the same dorsal branch of our vagal nerve, linked

---

1   The dorsal branch of the vagus nerve shuts down a mammal's body, moving to
immobility when in danger.

to the organs below the diaphragm, kicks in to save us.[2] When our minds sense danger and are overwhelmed, our bodies flop, and we become hopeless, slumped, depressed or collapsed. Our bodies put us into a survival state. Using a defence mechanism related to how we have evolved, we become like a reptile that is able to stop breathing under water to reduce metabolic activity – we shut down.

TRAUMA STORY: Jon's collapse

When Jon is 11, his dad becomes suddenly and seriously ill. No one has time to talk to Jon, who is deeply shocked when he is taken to see his dad dying in great pain in a hospital bed. Jon has had no preparation for the horror that is unfolding. In the face of a terrifying reality, his body and mind find immediate escape and he shuts down and becomes unconscious. The family are panic-stricken, wondering whether Jon has also become physically ill. The nurses reassure them that Jon is in shock and they have seen such reactions before. Jon isn't sick; this is his body and mind's response to trauma. Having this information really helps Jon and his family. Later, Jon tells them he feels guilty that he missed the moment of his dad's death. The rest of the family remember what the nurses said about the zoning-out response in a crisis situation and they reassure him. They tell him that, in extremis, his body tried to protect him from something that was too much for him to cope with. This knowledge is a strange kind of solace to them all.

Why do we slump and does understanding it matter?

The slump mechanism is a gift, a defence of last resort when fight/flight and freeze are not possible. Young Jon detected life threat as his father died in front of him, and in response, his body underwent a rapid drop in blood pressure and he shut down. After a traumatic event such as a violent attack, it is common for survivors to feel guilt or shame about not fighting their adversary (shame is explored further

---

2   Neuroscientist Stephen Porges introduced Polyvagal Theory in 1995. It has been instrumental in transforming our understanding of trauma, particularly the defensive immobilization or shutdown response of the nervous system in the face of threat.

in Chapter 15). The truth is that our bodies act for our benefit to minimize injury. We survive the best way we know how and there are circumstances when, if we fight, we might be killed. This can be important information for those who have been traumatized. Victims of rape, for example, can be hugely helped to know that they were physically unable to do anything other than passively submit. Understanding this has helped victims of violent crimes and sexual offences from developing shame – that is, believing that they are bad or wrong because they did not fight their adversary. Instead, they can be helped to find a new personal narrative of self-compassion, and learn to see their bodies as heroic. As Porges says, this may be challenging in societies that 'treat people who don't fight or effectively mobilize as if there is something wrong with them'.[3]

Some wider effects of going under the radar

This defence may show up in more subtle ways. After a painful or overwhelming life event or situation, we may find ourselves simply not being able to get out of bed in the morning, thinking 'What is the point?' We can physically feel as if a dead weight is pressing us down, passive, hopeless or defeated. Nothing puts a spring into our step. We go through the motions. Someone I heard of felt so dead she could not feel the heat in her shower.

As humans, we are wired for connection. A state of powerlessness, though protective, can become a prolonged response, keeping us disconnected and isolating us from others. This understanding may help us become more compassionate towards ourselves and others when we feel hopeless in the face of huge and complex life difficulties.

After the prolonged lockdown imposed due to Covid-19, we may have noticed, in ourselves or others, some fearfulness when we emerged from our enforced hibernation. In this case, a reluctance to re-engage with the world is less likely to be a fear of contracting the virus and more of a trauma response, having been cut off from the world and other people for so long. We may have noticed one legacy

---

3   Porges, S.W. (2017). *The Pocket Guide to Polyvagal Theory*. New York, NY: Norton & Co, p.177.

of this in some reports of low numbers of volunteers who returned to help with community projects. Fewer participants in live events is perhaps an indication of a process of recovery after the pandemic. As a global society, warfare and economic uncertainty have followed in the pandemic's wake. If we add into our contemporary challenges the real and existential fears about climate change and wars in Europe and the Middle East, it is hardly surprising if we notice a tendency to slump into helplessness or despair. Without this understanding, it is easy to become critical of our own or another person's slump. This happened to Jon's mum Kay after the death of her husband.

TRAUMA STORY: Kay on the sofa

During her husband Graham's painful and traumatic illness, Jon's mum Kay had been a stalwart tower of strength for everyone. Now, she finds herself responding to life in a new way. She has always been an active and highly resourceful person. During the pandemic, she home-schooled her children as well as working long hours from home. Now, her beloved husband is dead. Kay pushes herself to do what is absolutely necessary, but increasingly she feels like a zombie, and is hardly able to move from her sofa. She vaguely worries that she has not wept for Graham and, during a row, one of her children lashes out, accusing Kay of being heartless and uncaring. She wonders if this is true but she knows she cannot do anything different.

The cost of being in a slump

Kay's slump is an involuntary physical response to an overwhelming experience. There are emotional effects too. Our bodies produce endorphins that numb our experience so we do not feel pain; but this comes at a cost, because in our collapse state, we cannot think, respond or feel properly. In her slump, Kay is cut off from her grief. Another issue is, that in this shut-down dorsal vagal state, we cannot easily activate our more active survival responses when we may need them to get us out of danger. In our slump, we can therefore be unaware of danger and unresponsive to social signals, so our vulnerability can put us at risk. Our slump response may also lead us to submit to things that are not good for us. This is the case with people who are sexually violated and abused and tolerate bad treatment rather than being able to protect themselves from it.

When a slump becomes a longer-term state

A chronic slump can develop into a way of being. We can feel such disconnection and helplessness that our belief that 'I can't' can grow and become established as a defence, developing to a prolonged state over time. As we have seen, in an impossible situation, it may have been our nervous system's best strategy to slump, accept and go along with things. These responses may have long roots; research has shown that individuals who have experienced trauma in childhood may have dampened responses to pain and therefore have a tendency to put up with and become numb to discomfort.[4] The shut-down defence may also disrupt things physically. The connection between the vagal nerve and the organs beneath the diaphragm can link individuals with trauma histories to certain health consequences, such as irritable bowel syndrome, fibromyalgia and other gut issues.

The kind of chronic depression that can be associated with a slump trauma response can sometimes be (unkindly) labelled or diagnosed as 'resistant depression', as it may not easily respond to treatment. Depression often comes in trauma's wake. You may know someone who appears stuck in a perpetually negative or hopeless response to the world and find them difficult to be around. It may be helpful to identify the 'I can't' as a facet of trauma. It is not always easy to be with someone who is in a state of hopeless defeat. It may be increasingly irritating when they respond to everything with a different version of 'I can't!' You may find your own nervous system responding powerfully, maybe wanting to kick-start them to make them just do something! If so, bracketing your judgements can be a skill to develop. It is important to remember that from a position of defensive slump it is extremely difficult to trust engaging with the

---

4   Dr Molly Carlyle from the University of Queensland's School of Psychology (2021) in *Addiction Biology* (doi: 10.111/adb.13047) writes: 'Childhood trauma affects the development of the endogenous opioid system – a pain-relieving system that is sensitive to chemicals including endorphins, our natural opioids.'

world again, both physically and psychologically. From a place of understanding, you are more likely to begin to move to a more loving response that gently supports them. Inside, they may be an ignored child in whom no one has ever properly taken pleasure.

Approaches that might help

It is quite amazing to know what can happen when we smile. Smiling has powerful neurological effects, releasing neuropeptide chemical messengers that help combat stress and activating a number of feel-good neurotransmitters that help us. *Serotonin* raises our mood, *endorphins* reduce our pain, and *dopamine* stimulates the reward centre of our brains. When we see the crinkling of the facial muscles at the corner of someone's eyes, their ocular nerve may be soothing their nervous system. Smiling is also infectious: try it when next around a person in a slump, and you may be doing more than you realize!

Slump is a trauma response that needs particular care and patience. The primary gift to offer someone in this condition is empathy and connection. It is hard to come out of shutdown. It can feel risky. It therefore takes time and courage. Conscious gratitude practice may help us re-engage when we are ready (there is a gratitude exercise at the end of the chapter).

Empathy matters as it connects to the heart of the trauma. We end up feeling hopeless and defeated when we do not feel seen or valued for the enormity of what we have experienced. This may be the original source of our trauma. It will help us enormously if another person knows its weight. Most importantly, it helps us to know trauma's weight and to be empathic with ourselves.

What causes hopelessness in our individual histories

Common trauma triggers to hopelessness and slump are: not being taken seriously, being marginalized or degraded, never being hugged, not having our feelings or situation acknowledged, not being emotionally engaged with, and feeling attacked and dominated. Our capacity to experience pleasure will be affected by someone taking pleasure in us long ago. If we did not have this intense interest in our thoughts and feelings, we may not have learned to respect our own desires and impulses, so we slump instead. In the next example, Gemma's trauma is caused by prolonged emotional neglect. Slump is her protective trauma solution: if she slumps she is less likely to be ignored and hurt all over again.

TRAUMA STORY: Neglected Gemma

Gemma is the youngest in her large family. Her parents are chaotic, and traumatized themselves, so they do not properly focus on their children's needs. Sensitive and quiet, Gemma's need for attention always seems to go unnoticed: there is never enough care to go round. Gemma does not feel properly safe and secure, but perpetually hurt, misunderstood and ignored. A consequence of this over time is a difficulty in organizing her thoughts and her belongings. Under-achieving at school, Gemma is negatively compared to her sisters and does not pass her exams; her employment prospects are minimal. On leaving school, she works in a drive-through restaurant, taking money from customers in their cars.

One day, while serving, a customer's mobile phone goes off. After 30 seconds, the customer completes the call to her child, smiles at Gemma and apologizes. Gemma's eyes well up with tears of surprise and she says: 'Thank you so much. At least you apologized. No one even looks at us.' The customer is surprised and moved. She comes back to the restaurant later that evening to speak with Gemma. At the end of the conversation, the customer, who turns out to be an adult education teacher, offers Gemma a place at an open day for mature students interested in returning to education.

This act of kindness is a turning point for Gemma, who is amazed that such possibilities are open to a failed school leaver. The fact that the customer takes the trouble to seek her out profoundly challenges her opinion of herself. Maybe she has some worth after all? As she signs up for her first class, Gemma feels terrified and, at the same time, the stirrings of a new and surprising excitement inside. She wonders if she will meet others like her and what they will be like. With this thought comes a new spark. *I can and I will*, she says to herself. *Dare I...?*

Being noticed and having her experience acknowledged is a powerful antidote to Gemma's trauma slump. Being paid attention is a catalyst for change. She starts to feel a vitality awakening in her through the connection with someone who cares. The possibility of studying gives her a glimmer of self-worth. A little goes a long way. The everyday hero in the drive-through sows a seed of hope in her life.[5]

These are the words written for Gemma:

Powerlessness
Put up and shut up
Be passive, don't fight bad treatment
Submit was best
But where's the power gone?
Can I grieve for my powerless self?
Can I find shafts of light within the dank cloud?

BREAKING-FREE POINTERS FOR TRAUMA SLUMP

▶ Going under the radar in a slump is another survival mechanism – think of the gazelle meeting the lion. It is our body acting in our best interests to minimize injury.

▶ Like Jon, our slump may be dramatic, or our powerless response may be a more subtle and prolonged response to life.

▶ It is easy to be critical of our own or another's person's slump or perpetual 'I can't' or depressed hopeless response to life. We need to remember it can feel very risky to come out of a protective shutdown response.

▶ To break free from powerlessness we need empathy and connection.

▶ Giving someone attention is a powerful act that can change so much!

---

5   See the YouTube video, *The Power of Everyday Heroes*, by Jaz Ampaw-Farr for an inspiring exposition of how believing in someone, like Gemma's adult education teacher did, can make a huge difference to someone's life.

QUESTIONS FOR FURTHER REFLECTION

1. Do I recognize a powerless response in myself or others I am close to? Does it help to think of 'I can't' as a fear response? Can I practise changing my language to: I can, I want, I am willing, I choose, I am? Maybe I can notice if my posture changes when I open up to possibilities.

2. What might help me become more compassionate towards myself or another person when I or they are immobilized by fear and in a slump? Might they need my protection or some other kind of care? Can I take the risk of engaging with them in a strong and loving way?

3. Do I recognize a habitual low mood part of myself that may have its roots in a non-affirming situation over which I feel powerless? What do I most need when I feel like this?

4. What are the things that bring me to life, like the sparks in a fire? Can I take time to fan the flames? Do I notice any feelings when I engage with them? Any impulses in my body?

GRATITUDE EXERCISES

Begin by looking around your immediate environment and gently noticing something that pleases you. Hold your attention on this pleasing object as you consider how wonderful, beautiful or useful it is. Notice every detail about the scene carefully and maybe try taking a picture memory of the scene that you can recall later. And as you focus on its qualities for longer, notice if your positive feelings about it increase.

Though you may feel down, dull and colourless, try using your imagination to connect to brightness, beauty and power. Imagine the sun is hiding behind a cloud and allow your mind to connect to that idea while taking some mindful breaths in and out. Practise trusting its power for good and enjoy connecting with it. Imagine that flow of sunshine coming right into you.

Sometimes we get so used to the good things in our life that we stop feeling appreciation for them. Sometimes beauty is invisible and needs seeking out. It can help to see things, people and places that you love through the eyes of another. For example, you can share something with a friend and notice their response and how it affects you:

- Take them to your favourite coffee shop.
- Lend them a book that you love or recommend a film that you have seen and like.
- Share something that makes you laugh.
- Notice the effects of small connections on your mood.

DRAWING EXERCISE TO ASSIST EMBODIMENT POST-TRAUMA

In a seated position, with both feet firmly planted on the floor, take a few seconds to come inside, focusing on your breath. Then, starting from one foot, trace round the outline of your shape, imagining you are drawing round the edges of you. Taking time, carefully 'draw' in your mind, tracing your shape up your leg, torso, arm, shoulders and down the other side. As you draw, become as aware as possible of any sensations in the nerve endings of your skin. When you have completed your 'drawing' come back to your inner sensations and your breath once again. Notice if tracing your body helps you feel more 'here'. You might like to repeat this exercise a couple of times.

You can find a short video that highlights some points from this chapter at https://www.youtube.com/watch?v=kN2F2Ec_tcQ or by scanning the QR code.

Chapter 8

BRAIN HIJACKING – AN INABILITY TO PROCESS INFORMATION

Trauma hijacks our brains, like a cartoon explosion that fills the square of a comic strip.

Trauma can take up most of our internal space. As a result, our ability to think and process information is compromised. When in danger, we do not need these top-level functions, in fact they would get in the way of our instinctive survival. In this chapter, we examine how this works.

Again, starting from biology

The origins of hijacking are found in our neurobiology. Trauma danger activates our brain stem and instinctive body responses, the 'bottom-up processes' that are responsible for survival reflexes and automatic survival. Our middle brain is then flooded by fearful feelings, our amygdala is hijacked and we are overtaken by emotional reactivity. When we are so captured by an experience, we can only respond to the world in a way that is biased by that experience.

The difficulty arises when our instinctive survival processes continue to dominate after the scary situation or event is over. Depending on the severity of our trauma, our higher cognitive functioning may continue to be blocked or inaccessible or quickly go 'offline' when we are triggered. This may affect our ability to make sense of new information, or understand what something means based on the evidence in front of us.

Trauma responses are cruel because they prevent us from experiencing fullness of life. It is a particular kind of misery to be locked into our own hall of mirrors or not able to think or organize our thoughts properly.

When Kay is in an immediate trauma overwhelm, she needs other people to help her function.

TRAUMA STORY: Kay revisited

In Chapter 7 we met Kay, who loses her husband to cancer in a traumatic way. This is partly caused by a catalogue of mis-managements by the over-stretched medical professionals who underestimate how ill he is. When Kay is in shock after his death, she can't make decisions or think straight. When her friends ask her 'What do you need?' and 'What are you going to do?' she finds it impossible to answer. She just keeps saying 'I don't know'. She can just about stand up, but she can't move forward. Sometimes she finds a few minutes of fast gear, perhaps when she has to do what some bereaved people call 'sadmin', but then all energy and focus drain out of her and she sits staring blankly at paperwork for hours.[1] When her best friend comes over and offers to go through Graham's workroom and accounts, she is inordinately grateful. Thinking about things is just beyond her right now. She says, 'My brain isn't working properly right now, can I borrow yours?!'

Hijacking may involve the left/right brain

In addition to these 'bottom-up' processes there may also be left/right brain processes going on in trauma. The psychiatrist, neuroscientist and philosopher Iain McGilchrist's research culminating in his weighty book, *The Master and his Emissary*,[2] traces how Western culture over many centuries has been shaped by a dominance of the brain's left hemisphere approach to the world.

---

1   'Sadmin' is a term often used to describe the tying up of the affairs of someone who has died.
2   McGilchrist, I. (2009). *The Master and his Emissary*. New Haven, CT: Yale University Press.

What does this mean? We might recognize our contemporary world in the following description of the left hemisphere. Its preference is to nail things down and be concrete about things. The tendency is to shout out its certainties, to reduce complex ideas to sound bites, to mechanistically repeat goals and operate from a pressing need for outcomes and quantifiable evidence. Left-hemisphere dominance can lead us to react defensively to danger. We might obsess about details, seeing things partially and not from the perspective of the whole or bigger picture. This preference for the left hemisphere and neglect of the right may be seen in a *lack of balance* that is a hallmark of trauma, in a lack of trust in our ability to properly consider things and reflect calmly.

Some psychiatrists argue that left-hemisphere dominance appears to be similar to certain features seen in autism. Those who understand the world from a neurodiverse perspective may well be traumatized by the constant experience of not being understood or not fitting in to the 'way of the world'. Different kinds of help may be needed to help access our thinking processes when we are traumatized, as is illustrated in the following story of Michael, who had a chaotic and scary start to life.

TRAUMA STORY: Michael's alarms

Michael's body is wired for danger from his earliest days as a baby, when he is repeatedly left alone in his car seat in the cold for hours. Michael is passed from foster home to children's home with little consistent care and attention. As an adolescent, he is safe in his adopted family but does not feel it. His fear dominance does not allow him to trust even good attention. He frequently absconds from school. Michael is bright but struggles to think logically, concentrate, remember things or process information. He believes he is stupid, but as a result of his early trauma his brain is often simply 'full up'. His adoptive parents and teachers know when he is 'full' as he loses eye contact and can often seem 'somewhere else'. He is labelled naughty and difficult because he is often unable to do what someone tells him to. Michael's jumpiness affects his ability to be receptive and take things in; he is like a cat on hot bricks and does not feel quite at home in his body. In his hypervigilance, he is attracted to danger, and perceives threat everywhere. He often lashes out in temper and hurts other people with his words.

A teacher in the pastoral support team suggests Michael goes to a lunchtime visualization class. The idea is presented in assembly. One of the school's coolest teachers explains that visualization helps relaxation and can even rewire the brain. He surprises Michael by talking about how visualization helps him de-stress at the end of every day. He is funny. Michael likes this teacher and feels safe with him. Michael is curious about the idea of rewiring his brain. He doesn't know if he can do it, but he trusts the teacher enough to try.

The teacher invites Michael to place his mat close to him as together as a group they close their eyes, imagining themselves on a beach, the waves coming in and the warmth of the sun on their faces. Michael likes the fact the teacher is doing the visualization too. They all giggle at first, but quite soon they are able to imagine getting up and walking to the sea and collecting shells. The teacher invites the class to focus on any small body sensations they notice when they do their visualization. Michael is a bit self-conscious and finds it hard to focus at first but is surprised to find he likes it and can use his imagination to feel and enjoy the sensation of warmth on his face. It feels calming. Back in class in the afternoon he notices he can hear what the teachers say a little more than before. He is amazed to discover he can concentrate better and even colours seem brighter. The next day Michael asks the pastoral support teacher if there are going to be more visualization classes.

Michael's trauma body was full of alarms. Unsurprisingly, even though now in a safe situation, his body continues to insist on him surviving and his alarms are easily triggered, alerting his stress hormones, adrenalin and cortisol. He has to calm down to release their charge, and the visualization class is a 'way in' to help him begin to do this. The safety of the trusted teacher and proximity to other 'cool' friends are also important in soothing his nervous system.

The cognitive part of our brain can also be compromised by incident trauma, as in the following case of Trevor.

TRAUMA STORY: Trevor's experience at rehab[3]

Trevor loses a leg and an arm in an accident with the machinery on his farm. He is fitted with prosthetics and attends a rehabilitation centre, where there are other amputees who have lost limbs for a variety of reasons. On the first night, when they all meet together. Trevor thinks he has come to some kind of madhouse. Someone starts speaking but then stops abruptly. Another says something completely unrelated and bizarre. It is really strange and sometimes comical. It is as if they have lost not only limbs but also brain connections! On the first day, it makes Trevor want to run away (his flight response) but as he gets to know these quirky folk one by one, he begins to like them. They all have such stories to tell. It is amazing they are here at all with all they have been through, and hardly surprising that their words do not flow in an orderly manner.

Rebuilding our fragmented selves post-trauma

The amputees' ways of organizing and linking their thoughts have been temporarily and dramatically disrupted by the startle effect of trauma. We might think of the multitude of skills and abilities we rely on in our minds and bodies as being like building blocks. Our emotions, five senses (smell, taste, sight, touch and hearing), movements and inner awareness and judgement can all be fragmented by trauma (this aspect is considered further in Chapter 11). We then experience them in a disorganized or piecemeal fashion. Depending on its severity, trauma can also cut across the signals and information we receive from our bodies and we continue to neglect our most basic bodily needs. Learning to reclaim our bodies' messages can be a route to transforming our trauma, reconnecting our building blocks and finding pathways of care to ourselves.

Whether our difficulties are caused by developmental or incident trauma, a process of paying careful attention to the neglected mind and body, with the help of trusted others, can enable new neural

---

3   Trevor is inspired and adapted from GB Paralympic athlete Martine Wright's story: *Unbroken* (2017) London: Penguin Random House. Used with her permission.

pathways in the brain to open up. As more of the brain's functionality is reclaimed, it is literally 'rebooted'.

Such regeneration is rather like Antony Gormley's sculpture, Matrix lll, which was displayed at the Royal Academy of Art in London in 2019.[4] The whole room was filled with interconnected steel rods. The size and scope of the matrix was humbling, reminding us of the sheer enormity of our human capacity to restore through making connections.

Matrix
Mind stress hijacked until
Brain reconnects
Humbled my
Matrix repairs
Regenerates
I'm arriving on earth
For the first time

BREAKING-FREE POINTERS AFTER BRAIN HIJACKING

▶ 'Top-level' brain functions are not needed for survival, so one legacy of trauma is not being able to think, process or link our thoughts properly as we are still somewhere in survival mode.

▶ Trauma's effects can be far-reaching, making us lose connection with ourselves in many dimensions. The very basic building blocks of our perception and brain-body messaging and transmission circuits can be awry.

▶ Children who have experienced trauma often have difficulty with concentration and focus, for example. Such children (and sometimes those who have neurodiversity which can sometimes

---

4   Antony Gormley's Matrix was an installation l saw in London at the Royal Academy of Arts and gave a postcard of it to a traumatized client. It consisted of a mass of interpenetrating space frames, rectangular volumes delineated by their edges of thin steel reinforcing mesh – the invisible skeleton of concrete architecture reminded the client of her disconnection within her brain of messages to look after herself, for example. At the same time, the interconnected rods were a symbol of the new neural pathways that opened up for this client through the therapeutic process.

overlap with trauma) can be easily judged as 'naughty' without a full understanding of their processing difficulties.

▸ Finding safe spaces to calm down, like Michael did with the visualization class, can help dissipate stress hormones and increase thinking capacity as well as improve a person's ability to enjoy and appreciate life more fully.

▸ In a place of regular safety, learning to pay attention carefully (through the example of another's patient attention) can work wonders. Neural pathways can regenerate and be restored over time.

QUESTIONS FOR FURTHER REFLECTION

1. Do I recognize myself or someone I know in Kay's description of herself, being able to stand up but not move forward? Might this be a response to overload?
2. Do I need to take steps to regroup and rewire? Might grounding, stabilization, visualization and mindfulness, and/or more active rebalancing, help me?

EXERCISE TO HELP STABILIZATION[5]

(This exercise may also be helpful for disconnection – see Chapter 10.)

▸ Sit with your arms and legs uncrossed with your hands in your lap and your back straight and supported by the back of your chair.

▸ Focus on breathing in and out, slowly and deeply. It can be helpful to count your breaths up to ten, speaking the number out loud on your out-breath. When other thoughts and feelings come in, imagine them going past you like a cloud in the sky, then return to your breath.

---

5   The stabilization exercise is adapted from a number of sources, including Psychological First Aid promoted by the National Child Traumatic Stress Network (2021) in the US; Pearson, M. (2004). *Emotional Healing and Self-Esteem*. London: Jessica Kingsley Publishers; and Woodcock, J. (2022). *Families and Individuals Living with Trauma*. London: Palgrave Macmillan.

▶ Look around you and choose four ordinary things you can see. Name each in turn and notice every detail of them in as much detail as possible. For instance, 'picture of tree, windswept leaves, Autumn colours' and 'light switch, rectangular, grey, shiny, four buttons, three up, one down'.

▶ Return to your breathing and breathe four more times, as deeply and slowly as you can.

▶ Name four sounds you can hear and describe them in detail. For instance, 'I hear the hum of traffic in the distance, I hear the tick of a clock, I hear a child shouting and another one squealing.'

▶ Return to your breathing and breathe in and out, deeply and slowly, four more times.

▶ Now name four objects you can feel. For instance, 'I feel the touch of my hair on the back of the chair, I feel my tongue moving in my mouth, I feel the softness of my slippers, I feel my back muscles slightly aching.'

▶ Return to your breathing and breathe in and out again, slowly and deeply. Count your breaths up to ten, and speak the number on a long out-breath. When other thoughts and feelings come in, let them go, like the clouds passing across the sky.

BODY SCAN RELAXATION EXERCISE[6]

▶ Lie or sit somewhere comfortable.

▶ Close your eyes if you wish.

▶ Breathe in deeply and slowly. Breathe in, notice your belly rising, then let your breath go, like deflating a balloon, breathing out long, slow breaths on a count of five or six.

▶ Then scan your body. Notice any areas that draw your attention. Maybe an area feels tight, uncomfortable, heavy or sore – focus on it in your mind. Might this area have a sound or vibration? Can you describe a particular sensation? Does it have a colour? If so, imagine those areas are bathed in the most intense shade of that colour.

---

6 This meditation has been adapted from many sources for my own use. It draws on the idea of the body scan 'invented' by Jon Kabat-Zinn and written about in *Full Catastrophe Living* (2013) London: Piatkus.

▸ Imagine your breath is a favourite colour. Breathe in your colour. As you breathe out, visualize the breath going right down into your left foot, filling your left foot with colour. Wiggle your toes and notice any sensations.

▸ As your warm coloured breath encounters any area of discomfort, imagine it filling it up and changing its colour to your favourite colour.

▸ Breathe in your favourite colour again. As you breathe out, visualize the breath going right down into your left leg below the knee, filling your left calf with colour. Feel its warmth filling you. Notice the sensations.

▸ Breathe in your favourite colour again. As you breathe out, visualize the breath going right down into your left leg from hip to toe, completely filling your left leg with colour. Feel your breath filling you and making your leg full and warm. Notice the sensations.

▸ In the same way, slowly work through each section of your body: right leg, pelvis, lower abdomen, stomach, chest, shoulders, left hand, below the elbow, left arm, neck, back of head, face, forehand, crown of head, right arm, below the elbow, right hand.

▸ Having filled each part, now imagine your body filled with the warm coloured light that you have breathed in and then directed to all parts of your body. All of you, head to toe, is filled with your favourite colour, warm and heavy.

▸ Relax and continue breathing gently, noticing what it is like to be where you are now.

▸ Open your eyes and come back when you are ready.

You can find a short video that highlights some points from this chapter at https://www.youtube.com/watch?v=GKe76Kby20Y or by scanning the QR code.

— Chapter 9 —

WHEN OUR THINKING BECOMES RIGID AND FIXED

Hijacking makes us hold on to our beliefs with a vice-like grip.

Due to the hijacking of the amygdala in trauma fear, we can latch on to our version of events with a life or death intensity.

How might we tell that our strongly held beliefs are springing from trauma? Trauma beliefs are all about survival. The limbic area of our brains is flooded and our frontal lobes temporarily disabled. From here, we latch on to beliefs from a place of desperation. These beliefs are rather like two-dimensional drawings, powerful but lacking nuance. Two-dimensional thinking does not allow for possibility and subtlety in the way that three-dimensional thinking does. Primitive fear can drive all our responses and actions such that we are simply not open to other perspectives. We become binary. Our beliefs can feel like imperatives that do not allow for flexibility, curiosity or fluidity. We may see evidence of this in our fast-changing political and cultural environment that increasingly appears to disrespect or even denigrate facts in favour of 'my fake news against yours'.[1] There is no middle way. Like a train travelling between only two stations, in trauma there can be no options other than success or failure, or safety or danger. This is the case in the following story.

---

1   Smethurst, P. (2022). 'Getting to the Essence': Working Towards Truth in Psychotherapy. In S. Wright (ed.) *The Change Process in Psychotherapy*. London: Routledge (quoting D'Ancona, M. (2017). *Post Truth*. London: Random, p.20).

TRAUMA STORY: Priti in the hospital[2]

In the aftermath of her car crash, Priti is utterly convinced she will survive. In the hospital, she develops a heart problem and is rushed into surgery. Then Priti becomes convinced she will die. No amount of reassurance makes any difference and she screams in protest, terrified of the surgery. Explaining and being rational does not begin to cut it; she is tenaciously certain of what she believes. In the end, Priti needs to be sedated. Later, she becomes convinced that one of the nurses is giving her the wrong medication and is not to be trusted. Normally a polite, restrained person, Priti becomes off-hand with the nurse, staring at her and complaining about her to others. If her truth is challenged and contradicted, however gently, she becomes angrier, feels more alienated and digs in further, in her conviction that she is right. The nurses seem oblivious and remain kind and calm, but Priti's dad Raj becomes embarrassed by her behaviour. Privately, the nurses reassure him. They tell him that Priti's intense convictions are a natural response to something catastrophic happening in the centre of her life and world. She is terrified.

Priti's concrete certainties are her attempt to make sense of an out-of-control world. Yet her trauma (fearful) conviction can mean that she develops skewed perspectives about what is going on. Logic will not work, and only makes her dig in to her certainties even more. She is not soothed until someone she trusts gently says how scary this must be for her. Sometimes things need to come to a crescendo and be fully expressed within us before we can let them go. Sometimes we just need someone to 'get it', at the right moment, and cut through to us. We might be aware of the extreme nature of our powerful trauma responses, yet at the same time be in thrall to them. We hold on to our beliefs with a desperate commitment until something breaks in. In the next two cases of developmental trauma, we will see how Julia is dramatically blinded to the needs of her kids and how Callan's trauma leads him to live by someone else's rules. Both have quite a journey

2 Priti is inspired and adapted from GB Paralympic athlete Martine Wright's story: *Unbroken* (2017) London: Penguin Random House. Used with her permission.

to move from a trauma position to a place of being able to give and receive care.

TRAUMA STORY: Julia moving from trauma to care

For Julia, the stress of being a single parent to children with special needs becomes overwhelming. As the pressures ramp up, the trauma of her past meets the trauma of her present. As Julia struggles with all the things she has to do, she feels utterly alone and she believes it is 'her against the world'. This repeats the situation long ago when she was scapegoated in her original family. Now, when she gets super stressed and her children play up, she responds to them as if they are attacking her. In her trauma-filled mind, they become the family who were cruel to her long ago. She feels trapped and imprisoned, yelling at her children, who of course become deeply distressed.

Julia's way out of this trap begins when she sees the wobbling lips of her children. She knows she needs help and reaches out for help to her support group at Complex Needs.[3] A person she trusts makes some truthful statements about her and she calms down. First truth: she is a traumatized person. Second truth: the ability to care for herself and her kids properly has been lost recently due to excessive stress. Julia writes down some true sentences and uses them to calm herself and think properly: I am not in a prison. They are my kids, not my cell mates. Recognizing her own emotional needs, she can now see those of her children. She acknowledges she has four kids to look after, not three. She has a kid inside her.

As Julia moves from a trauma position to a connected position, she becomes aware of the impact of what she says and does on her children. She can now begin to care for them. When she shifts perspective, Julia knows she has extended her mind. She sees that she needs to help her children with their feelings, giving them understanding and information about how to operate in the world. She has to help them connect up the building blocks in

---

3   Complex Needs is a therapeutic service for people with complex mental health difficulties provided by some local authorities.

their brains and she connects her own. She sees things differently now. She is not alone with her kids: they are all together.

Julia describes moving from a trauma position to a care position as being like clearing undergrowth in a forest. The more work she does on this, the easier and quicker the task becomes. Repeating what is true helps. We can be so sure of our fixed beliefs that we go through life not questioning them. Sometimes, as in the following case of Callan, it may take another trusted person's challenge to stop us in our tracks and make us reflect. Then we may be able to think properly and consider whether we are operating from rigid or all-or-nothing trauma thinking, and what we might need to shift or soften our perspectives to be able to consider other ones.

TRAUMA STORY: Callan and his family rules

The eldest of five children, Callan grows up in a highly controlling environment. His scary, domineering father, who had grown up in foster care in Scotland, survives in his adult life by ruling the roost. He can never risk being out of control, not again. Callan believes everything his dad tells him. His mum is a nervous person who never challenges his dad. On the receiving end of his dad's aggression and control, Callan is desperate to earn his love, so he diligently cares for his younger siblings and keeps them in line. This pattern continues into his thirties. In some parts of his life he becomes independent – he goes to college and gets married – but he continues to see his parents every day and defers to their expectations, particularly around the family. When his adult brother makes a career move that Callan doesn't approve of, Callan tells him to leave his job, in no uncertain terms! It isn't until Callan's wife tells him that stepping in like this might not be appropriate that he starts to examine his beliefs.

It is extraordinary for Callan to have his certainties challenged, but because he trusts his wife, he begins to question some of his own thinking. Callan signs up for a self-help residential therapeutic course that a friend recommends. He needs time to think, away from his environment and especially away from his parents who still live nearby. It is in the safety of this community that Callan begins to talk about how scared he felt as a child. Then he makes some painful discoveries about where these fear-bound beliefs come from. Callan had been convinced his parents did not love him. In fact, he was terrified they did not, and this terror fuelled his convictions about what was right and what he had to do to survive. Callan weeps, remembering how alone and scared he had been.

One of the tutors on the course explains a few things:

- How beliefs work after trauma: If we are not safe, we latch on to beliefs for dear life, as if they are gospel. Because no one tunes into us, we do not learn to properly trust others to help us with what we feel. Instead, we banish our vulnerability and develop a rigid code to live by. Callan recognizes that it was a survival imperative for him to be strong and a mini-parent. This code of behaviour came to dominate. Yet his frequent meltdowns tell another story, of a wobbly little boy there had never been space for. As an adult, Callan fervently believes these vulnerable feelings are bad.

- If we feel safe with and properly known by others, we develop a bird's-eye view in our minds: From an elevated position, we can see things from more than one point of view at the same time. In a healthy environment, a child learns that the dog next door is sometimes sleepy but can also be scary when he barks. And that Granny is also his mum's mum. This kind of flexibility is very important for us to learn in order to navigate all the complex possibilities of life. Developmental trauma can prevent this flexible thinking from developing properly in our brains. Callan is amazed and enlightened to know this, but not sure how he can change his rigid thinking.

Callan is then encouraged to find a language for 'little Callan' – his emotional self – to speak. This is hard at first, as he is ashamed and so used to banishing his emotional self. Yet gradually he develops more curiosity and space for the unloved vulnerable little Callan and starts a dialogue between him and his adult self. Initially, his adult part has no idea how to respond to his vulnerable self and easily gives up, but, with practice, he starts to use his imagination to connect with this aspect of himself. He notices that what his vulnerable part most needs and wants is to be heard. When his adult self understands this, he begins to be an advocate for the emotional needs of his neglected and banished inner child. Over time, this change of perspective starts to really make a difference.

Very gradually, and with much support, Callan is able to flourish as a more balanced person. As he gains skills in attuning to little Callan, he becomes more confident. He moves from parent to becoming an equal adult with his brothers. He learns to respect their choices, even if he feels they are 'bad' ones. He also learns to set boundaries with and keep an appropriate distance from his father.

Callan's deeply held beliefs have a logic of their own and are rooted in his trauma experience. Like uprooting a plant in his garden, he needed to employ much patient spadework before his rigid thinking can be loosened and freed.

Trauma responses do not just operate at the level of the individual or family. It may be a leap from where we are, but we could consider where our wider world operates in ways that spring from trauma. Could fear be at the root of the polarized nature of our national and international debates? For politicians, fear of not being elected or fear of the dominance of other powerful countries may sometimes drive their policies, which does not allow them to operate from a considered or more reflective place. Of course, many such fears are realistic and we need to respect fear's messages. However, when encountering polarized positions, it may be useful to hold information about the powerful workings of trauma in our minds. We might consider whether our responses spring from realistic fear or are, in fact, reactive and survival-based and not thoughtful and measured. Knowing how the legacy of fear operates on the psyche, how might we practise resisting labels and easy definitions and solutions? Can we take a deep breath and enable ourselves to open up a space to consider and reflect on possibilities, allowing for nuanced responses to complexities, rather than right/wrong, good/bad, them/us?

Much courage may be needed to face the eye of the fearful trauma storm and to become aware of and challenge the rigidity of thinking that can emerge from it. As someone I work with said, 'Grey is a harder sell than black and white!' Often, though not always, it is in the safety of a secure relationship or friendship, or reflecting on the vast interconnected complexity of nature, that we can find the strength or be helped to question ourselves, bear uncomfortable things and take the risk to drop our fixed positions. These are the words written for Julia:

2D to 3D
Fear
Clinging on
Jumping on my soap box
Sure about everything
Or am I?

Think!

Fear powers my beliefs
Drives so much
Now I'm sad for that fearful child
And the noise quietens
Tight grip releases
No need to be certain
I can see others' needs
Not just mine

BREAKING-FREE POINTERS FOR WORKING WITH TRAUMA FIXED BELIEFS

▸ When we observe fixed, binary, simplistic, all-or-nothing or rigid thinking, this might be a response to the overwhelm of trauma.
▸ We sometimes need someone to understand empathically or something or someone we trust to 'cut through' to enable us to release our fear-bound response and for the penny of wider understanding to drop.

▸ We are more likely to be able to adopt a bird's-eye perspective (and see other perspectives) when we feel safe, known and not so horribly cut off and alone.

▸ An atmosphere of calm and trust will help us soften and soothe our rigidity.

▸ Softening rigid thinking can take much patient spadework as we develop it to protect ourselves. It it can feel so convincing!

QUESTIONS FOR FURTHER REFLECTION

1. Do I notice when I dig into a rigidity in my own thinking? Might this emerge from trauma? Are there some aspects I would like to relax in myself? What helps me develop my bird's-eye perspective and more flexibility towards ideas and other people's different views?

2. Do I notice a rigidity in my own body when I am fixed in my thinking, or frightened? Might stiffness or tension give me a message about some fear or stress I am holding right now?

3. Do I have a sense when someone's certainty comes from fear rather than an integrated thoughtful position? What are the signs of this in your life, our world?

4. Can tenderness act as an antidote to rigidity? If so, how might we foster this as individuals and as a society?

JEWEL MEDITATION

Take time to consider a jewel with multiple sides. Choose the colour of the jewel. Then decide how many sides it has. Move in your mind from one facet to another. Imagine the light being different as it enters the jewel and refracts in different directions. Take time to enjoy the beauty of the jewel you have created.

Next consider a problem that you are concerned about. Take time to enumerate different ideas and perspectives that you or others have in response to this problem. Imagine you are moving around the jewel as you do this, taking space. As you consider them, imagine the jewel as the problem and the perspectives being the multiple sides exuding different coloured light. Take a slow breath with every side, taking space for the different perspective in your mind and body. Notice if any hierarchy emerges about the 'answers' or any judgements. These may emerge as bodily sensations, perhaps somewhere you tend to hold stress. If any emerge, notice them, then return your perspective to the jewel. Your responses are simply part of the jewel, just one facet of the whole. You can honour your responses and remember that the whole jewel is most beautiful when all sides are seen.

You can find a short video that highlights some points from this chapter at https://www.youtube.com/watch?v=QXWdDsZx-a8 or by scanning the QR code.

— Chapter 10 —

WHEN WE DISCONNECT

When we are overloaded, we switch off from what we cannot bear. We do this in order to survive.

Our minds have a circuit-breaker, like the protective mechanism that protects an unstable electricity supply. When we are overwhelmed by trauma, we can become spaced out or not quite present. This mechanism could be considered to be one of 'nature's small mercies'.[1] The disconnect protects us from feeling too much, from being too vulnerable. It also helps us carry on living when something is too frightening for us. Disconnect can happen in an instant if something triggers us, or as a response to something that feels too risky. It can also become a state we live in all the time.

TRAUMA STORY: Jade, the carer

Jade has become a carer for her mother who has dementia. As a single mother with a full-time job and her own teenagers to attend to, one of whom has special needs, she has a great deal on her plate. At first, when visiting her mother, Jade becomes weepy when her mother lashes out at her or becomes like a needy child. After a while, she feels nothing, hardly registering any emotional response at all. In the netherworld of her existence, Jade lives in a kind of psychological fog. It reminds her of the baby brain she felt after giving birth: she finds it hard to think clearly about anything or make decisions. She just ploughs on. Jade can't connect with things that were important to her before, they don't give her joy or

---

1   Herman, J. (1997). *Trauma and Recovery*. New York, NY: Basic Books, p.43.

meaning. Occasionally, she has a gnawing anxiety about money at night, but mostly she feels numb. She vaguely knows she is not the same woman she was before – all this caring for others has eroded her, but she doesn't spend time thinking about it. If she ponders it too much, she thinks she might break completely.

Disconnection as survival

For Jade and for so many around the world who face unbearable situations, disconnecting from emotional distress and pain is necessary for survival. When illness or disaster strikes, there is much more for us to be frightened about than before. How can we live with an awareness of how fearful we are? It is too much, so we disconnect. In war zones, the incessant sound of guns can become like background noise, and it may be hard to register it emotionally. It can feel that we stop caring. Blanking out our responses to the traumatic event allows us to function or simply survive what is in front of us every day.

So, how does this happen? Disconnect or *dissociation* occurs when the emotional (limbic) region of the brain becomes overwhelmed. This was the case for Jade under the sheer weight and ongoing demand of her daily experience.

Imaging tests show that the brains of individuals with dissociative symptoms are smaller in the hippocampus and amygdala regions that affect memory and emotional responsiveness: we do not remember, or feel.[2] This mechanism protects us from too much reality.

Studies on war veterans show lower levels of the stress hormone cortisol in their systems, so their bodies no longer physically register danger. They have become physiologically unresponsive to stress. At the more severe end of the dissociative continuum, we can be so cut off in our everyday life that we regularly lose whole chunks of time. A more moderate manifestation might be feeling emotionally unresponsive and seeing life as though through a pane of glass. However, as humans we are wired for connection, so, as with Benita and Caleb's story, our disconnect solution often comes at an emotional cost.

---

2   www.ncbi.nlm.nih.gov/books/NBK568768, accessed 09/01/24.

TRAUMA STORY: Blended family Benita and Caleb (1)

Benita, a young mother with a painful history, meets Caleb through an online group for sole parents. Caleb has a history of abusive relationships and knows much about surviving hardship. Caleb spent years struggling and reflecting on his past. Now he has met Benita he wants to give all of himself to her.

Benita is attracted to Caleb's ability to fight for their kids and is also deeply attracted to the depth of his personality. She has never met anyone like him. Caleb also adores Benita. He notices she hardly speaks of her childhood and wonders if she has truly grieved for all she has lost. When he comes to her for tenderness, she is either blank and non-responsive, or endlessly distracted and caught up with her responsibilities. Benita thinks Caleb is the most wonderful man she has ever met, but knows she is unable to connect with him in the way that he needs. This worries her. It seems that a part of her is dead, or clogged up, unable to fully experience joy and delight in Caleb.

What happened to Benita to make her so unresponsive? The process of disconnection is called 'dissociation', and it helps to understand what this term means. As we have seen, in order to survive a terrible event, our brains dis-associate; they do not associate with it. If we are disconnected, it does not mean we don't feel things. The opposite is true. We feel so much but we cannot access our emotions. As is so often the case with trauma, it may be useful to know Benita's back story.

TRAUMA STORY: Blended family Benita and Caleb (2)

When she is five, Benita's sister Adele slips down the bank of a river and is swept away by the current of a weir. Dad dives in but is unable to save Adele. After little Adele drowns, Dad crumbles, begins taking drugs and drinks to assuage his guilt and grief. Finally, the relationship between Benita's parents collapses and Benita hardly sees her dad again. When the subject of seeing her dad comes up, Benita is told that he is unable to cope. However, what this version of events misses out is how terrifying and painful it was for Benita to lose not only her beloved sister, but also the love and support of her dad. The horror of this double abandonment is powerfully held within Benita.

This is the underlying trauma that shows up in her numbed-out body and mind when Caleb comes close to her. When Caleb tells Benita how much he longs for more closeness with her, Benita is genuinely surprised as she feels as close to him as anyone in her life to date! What more does he want? Benita feels confused. Yet, Caleb seems to want something else. She asks herself: can I learn to trust Caleb more? Am I afraid? She doesn't feel afraid, she just goes blank and doesn't know what to do. Benita wonders whether she is somehow bracing herself for (another) disaster with Caleb, but he repeatedly shows her that he is not going anywhere.

Benita begins to understand that there is a discrepancy between past and present: the bracing and numbness are legacies of what has gone on before. Now the couple see that Benita's painful losses are coming into their present. Caleb tells Benita that he simply wants her to hang out and enjoy being with him without having to fix anything. This is uncharted territory for Benita but instinctively she knows that she wants to follow this path with Caleb. Benita and Caleb consult a couple's therapist and learn some tools. They learn to 'linger' and respond to each with small gestures of tenderness. When they do this, Benita is surprised when some feelings bubble up about her sister Adele, buried so long ago.

Benita and Caleb also go to a support group for newly blended families, to move beyond practical parenting and find space for their feelings too. Together they decide to adopt a more deliberate 'feelings first' principle. This has different strands. If one of the children comes in from school upset, they are not left alone. One of them immediately takes time to seek out the child in their bedroom and have a conversation. The family also spend time sharing over mealtimes using exercises they learned in the group.[3] They consciously decide that they no longer want things to be left unaddressed, as this caused suffering in the past. They both

---

3   One exercise the family learned was the 'Rose and Thorn', where a good and difficult thing is shared in turn by each family member.

have a powerful longing to be fully alive, and trust that this means opening up to feelings, however uncomfortable, scary and difficult that this sometimes is for all of them.

How dissociation works in more depth

After her sister's death and her father leaves, Benita continues on in life, not fully encountering the emotions associated with what has happened to her. There are good reasons for this, the primary one being Benita's need to focus on survival. Of course, she knows at a factual level what has happened to her and her family, but she has memory gaps and she has not *processed* the experience. A gulf emerges in her mind between her everyday life and the overwhelming experience. The emotional memory of what happened to Benita is stored in another place yet continually interferes with her ability to respond to life.

The power of disconnect

Caleb and Benita have to work hard to reconnect to feelings. Being cut off can so easily become a way of being. You may have had the experience of listening to someone telling their story, but they seem strangely disconnected from the meaning or heart of what they are saying. Or they seem to make light of something that seems weighty and serious. They may deny something's importance or even its existence. You may suppose they do not care about their story, or have any connection to it. But the truth is likely to be very different. There is a line in the film *American Beauty* (a 1999 film written by Alan Ball and directed by Sam Mendes) spoken by the character Ricky Fitts: 'Never underestimate the power of denial.' Our disconnected minds protect us from pain: the power of this mechanism should not be underestimated. Denial can be an endless merry-go-round. For some, directly facing what we are emotionally disconnected from may not be so possible, as is most striking in the following case of Max.

TRAUMA STORY: Max, the refugee

Max grows up in Germany in the 1930s in a climate of rising fear for Jewish communities. When he is ten, SS guards come to his house and take his parents away. They are eventually taken to Bergen-Belsen concentration camp. Max never sees them or any member of his family again. He becomes one of the unaccompanied children on the Kindertransport, arriving in England as a refugee and living in an orphanage.

Excelling academically, Max makes the most of the opportunities that are presented to him, working assiduously to build a future for himself and eventually becoming a highly successful businessman. Unsurprisingly, his response to terrifying experiences is to surround himself with order and control. He has huge capacity for detail which serves him well as a business leader. Max also has a great capacity for love and enjoys relationships with others, but always from a distance. He has a great love of beauty in all things: friendship, the arts, theatre, concerts and opera as well as popular culture, but he is not able to sustain an intimate relationship of trust in his life. Max's life has a wide canvas. He contributes much to the furtherance of young musicians, but he cannot allow himself to entrust his vulnerable self to another person. The wounded, traumatized part of himself is covered with a sheath of protection.

Is it possible to reconnect?

The degree of disconnection from experience and the possibility for reconnection varies in relation to the severity of the trauma, as can be seen with Jade, Benita and Max. As Steve Taylor writes in his book *DisConnected*: 'A small minority of (hyper-disconnected and traumatized) people are trapped inside their own mental worlds like prisoners in solitary confinement, alone with their own impulses and desires.' Steve goes on to outline how such hyper-disconnected people are frequently attracted to power.[4] There are many examples of hyper-disconnected leaders in our world who become dangerous

---

4   Taylor, S. (2023). *DisConnected*. Winchester: John Hunt Publishing, p.19.

because of their lack of empathy for other people. Such deeply disconnected people are unlikely to change. One of the consequences of being on the receiving end of a regime without empathy is that certain groups are dehumanized. One of the consequences of being dehumanized is that we erase or hide from this painful experience by dissociating from it, putting it in another place in our mind. Trauma begets trauma. The process can be overt or hidden, and cumulative. (See Chapter 19 for more on this.)

The inner workings of dissociation

Let's think about some inner workings of dissociation. If we are in an environment that dehumanizes our experience, we can then begin to cancel our own responses. Disconnection can happen without us being consciously aware of it. This phenomenon, as a kind of secondary seepage of dissociation, is just as important to understand. This is when we take in the treatment of erasure and then repeat it in our own minds. *We treat ourselves as we were treated.* It is part of dissociative trauma that when we have a feeling or response, then we cancel it.

A person who lives under a regime that does not allow freedom of speech learns to not speak their truth but also to not even think it. We may carry this erasure of ourselves in the form of lost self-esteem, or not knowing our own minds in our dealings with another person or life situation. Social media may make us more fearful to say what we think and feel, in case we are cancelled, attacked or misunderstood. We devalue our feelings because we were devalued; we neglect ourselves because we were neglected. In big and small ways, we cancel our inner reality.

Ways to work with disconnect

Though dissociation can cause problems and suffering, it does not have to be a life sentence. There are many ways for us to combat disconnection. We can learn to pay attention to and honour feelings, not forget or dismiss them. We can be subversively defiant in order to keep ourselves alive. We can learn to properly listen, actively using our imaginations to endeavour to understand and connect with what we hear. We can be determined to connect and reach out to others. Connection helps soothe us and feels good: we are naturally empathic and wired for connection. When we connect it can feel like coming home. A kind act helps us, the other person and any witness.

In a world that often favours and rewards disconnection, we can work on wiring up and connecting. We live in a climate that rewards competitiveness and tough choices that may bring us success but may make us feel less connected and more alone. We can ask ourselves: what are the experiences and who are the people who bring us joy and life? How can we replenish ourselves and soothe the parts of us that have become cut off and disconnected? Can we be thoughtful about what makes us feel disconnected? How can we practise owning our own truth and honouring it? What helps us come back fully to our own minds? In our last example – of the lost and unloved boy Jonah – it is the gift of an animal that makes all the difference.

TRAUMA STORY: Jonah and the dog

Until the age of six, Jonah lives in a care home without hugs and emotional warmth. Unsurprisingly, he is numb and unresponsive in his adoptive family. The family are consistent and loving, but Jonah has been so hurt, he finds it hard to trust them. One day, the dad comes home with a rescue dog called Bounce. Bounce is shaky at first, approaching Jonah tentatively. Bounce has also been hurt. The frightened, numbed-out boy instinctively senses and resonates with the tremulous acceptance in the dog and the two are instantly inseparable. Through touch comes a soothing and reciprocity that brings the disconnected, battered and fearful Jonah to life. Bounce senses safety too and, from the first moments together, never leaves Jonah's side. The duo that is formed is transformational: Jonah settles in his new family and he becomes much happier about going to school.

Though ways into reconnection can be found, being reluctant to change is instinctive – protective of more hurt. We may be anxious about looking too deeply under the surface of things. Maybe we are like a plant that is finding a way to grow, if not flourishing. After all, disconnect is a strategy that gives us a sense of safety and allows us to survive and avoid pain. Yet a deep part of us may wish to remember and take stock of our experiences, if only we have the space and safety to do so. Ultimately, it may be possible to bring into visibility what has become erased and bring ourselves more fully to life. If we have fallen into a black hole of trauma disconnect, we may need to remember a time before this happened. Over time, maybe we can then contact those parts of us that are resilient and find ways to connect with them again.

We are hardwired for connection: herein lies the potential for joy. These are the words I wrote for Benita:

Cancelling my reality
Keep forgetting what I feel
Can't keep track
Angry?
Allowed?
It'll end badly
Can't say
Don't trust
Don't follow
So cancel?
Reality cancelled
I cancel it
But I want to trust my body
Feel it's mine!

BREAKING-FREE POINTERS FOR WORKING WITH TRAUMA DISCONNECTION

▶ Disconnect or dissociation is our mind's safety device that protects us from pain or horror. However, it can be a device that lingers well after it is needed.
▶ Signs of disconnect are feeling in a fog or feeling numb in response to what is happening around us. We can be so disconnected that we are unresponsive to stress and danger.
▶ We can know the facts of what has happened to us but remain

emotionally cut off from an experience that remains *unprocessed* in our minds and bodies.

▶ Highly disconnected individuals are so trapped in their impulses and desires that they have little or no empathy for others.

▶ Paying attention to thoughts and feelings helps combat disconnect.

▶ We can be defiant in response to dehumanization in a world that can favour disconnection.

▶ From babyhood, we are wired for connection, survival and safety. Connection soothes us and is deeply consoling.

▶ If we have become disconnected, can we remember a time before the disconnect happened and connect again with what was important then?

QUESTIONS FOR FURTHER REFLECTION

1. Do I recognize a part of me or someone else that seems disconnected in a way that causes a problem? Might the disconnection be a clogged up or unprocessed trauma experience? What might my body and mind need to help me reclaim *me*, body and mind?

2. Do I ever deny or cancel my own or another's experience in a way that makes me or them less than fully human? What do I feel when I hear of others doing this?

3. Can I develop an open curiosity to parts of myself that I cut off from? Might journalling or some form of self-reflection or creative process be a way for me to move towards connecting rather than perpetuating the disconnect?

4. How might I actively foster my connecting up with others whom I trust and want to be close to? What might help me to do this?

EXERCISES TO AID RECONNECTION

▶ When you feel numb and disconnected, make a list of as many pleasant things, objects or events as possible. If you are with trusted others, enlist their support if you find that you cannot think of many.

▸ Draw an imaginary line round yourself in your mind, like a child's drawing (see the exercise at the end of Chapter 7). Imagine on the surface of your skin the numerous nerve endings. Stimulate these with a loofah while taking a bath, or gently brushing or stroking your arms and legs.

▸ Practise asking parts of your body what they might need to feel soothed or connected and more alive. Push your feet into the floor or your legs together. Notice whether you feel a little more 'you' or more 'here'. Or notice what it feels like to feel the support of a wall or chair behind you, or the bottom of the chair behind your legs. Notice if this feels good or just a little bit safer.

You can find a short video that highlights some points from this chapter at https:// www.youtube.com/watch?v=p6M2xtOxHmc or by scanning the QR code.

— Chapter 11 —

WHEN WE FRAGMENT

The power of trauma shatters experience into fragments.

Let us recap. When we suffer an intense experience, we might need to separate ourselves from it in our minds in order to manage daily life. In Chapter 10, we explored how an overwhelming event can create a 'gap,' or disconnect, in our minds, separating ourselves from a painful experience. As a result, we are protected from it. It is no longer accessible to us.

A further facet of trauma is our mind's way of fragmenting our experience. Let us consider how things normally work. We all have different ways of behaving in different situations – responses that we might see as different aspects of ourselves. For example, our professional self, where we are focused and restrained, may be a very different identity to the person we are with our children. We may be able to hold all these identities in our awareness, moving fluidly between them without even thinking about it.

In conversation, we talk about ourselves being 'in one piece' but trauma can rupture our sense of coherence. Then we might experience a *loss of balance* between our different selves, with some becoming overly dominant while others are hidden away for safe keeping. Under intense stress, our mind helps us by dividing up our feelings and responses, *sending them underground into compartments*. We do this in order to preserve a semblance of normality in an attempt to save us from knowing about our pain. This happens without our conscious awareness. These feelings, responses and memories are held there until a safe space for expression is provided. Sometimes, we are able to function well in normal life without any conscious awareness of the hidden pockets of trauma.

In the following example of Adam, his hidden fragment of fear is caused by a one-off experience as a toddler. When he is triggered again by hearing similar sounds years later, at first his emotional reaction seems incomprehensible and out of proportion.

TRAUMA STORY: Adam and the fireworks

Adam is petrified by hearing an exploding firework outside his room when he is three years old, an experience of which he has no conscious memory. When he goes to a party as a nine-year-old, the neighbour lets off a rocket. Triggered and terrified, Adam screams uncontrollably for several minutes, allowing no one to come near him. He does not understand why he responds like this and feels deeply ashamed. He hides behind the shed and his friend's dad comes to find him. They sit together in silence for several minutes until the man turns to him and gently says 'Afraid of fireworks, hey? Join the club. We all have things we are afraid of...' and puts his arm around him. Adam feels a wave of relief inside. Maybe he is not abnormal after all. Later, hearing about what happened, Adam's mum remembers the exploding firework incident on Bonfire Night when Adam was small. He had been alone in his room and she found him quietly sobbing and shaking. She and Adam are amazed that this memory and emotional response is hidden within him and they are glad and relieved to make the connection.

In Adam's story, the fearful memory triggered by the release of the firework is re-experienced as a powerful emotion that is released when it pops up years later. We might imagine that the sudden loud sounds make tiny Adam feel profoundly unsafe, and so his mind sends the fragment of fear underground for safe keeping. Connecting the original traumatic event with a springing up of fear that occurs years later is an 'Aha!' moment for Adam and his family. From then on, they understand his general sensitivity to unexpected noises and are careful not to retrigger him with fireworks if they can help it.

What are flashbacks?

As with Adam, fragments of trauma – or flashbacks – may bring with them intense emotions, or they may present as a sensation, image or memory – or a mixture. Depending on the severity of the trauma and the degree of overwhelm, the entire flow of our trauma experience can become fragmented, shattering like shards of glass. *Our minds hold on to these fragmented memories, body sensations, responses or images without context or narrative.* The fragments then operate as separate entities, leading to reactive behaviours and responses that seem disproportionate and not related to present reality.

Since the coining of the term shell shock,[1] now better understood as PTSD, scientists have observed that many war veterans suffer from fragmented highly charged flashbacks, startle reactions and night terrors, all part of a hyper-aroused fight/flight nervous system. Metaphorically, the psyche is in pieces. Some elements we might experience in bold type while other aspects are erased entirely.

Like our mountaineer Joe in Chapter 3, such fragmentation can, in severe cases of PTSD, become deeply disorientating and scary and, unless treated, can get worse over time. We can suddenly and involuntarily experience a body memory, sensation, thought, emotion or image. These are all fragments; kinds of flashbacks. They may be in response to an external trigger, or they can just happen. They may have no time stamp. It may or may not be possible to make sense of them or understand what they relate to. If they are not understood as flashbacks, such responses can appear ridiculously out of proportion, bizarrely inappropriate or exaggerated reactions to what is currently happening.

---

1   On 13 February 1915, the term 'shell shock' was used for the first time in the medical literature, in a paper in *The Lancet*. The paper is now seen as seminal in the literature on war neuroses. The author was Charles Samuel Myers, Director of the Cambridge Psychological Laboratory. Myers' view of shell shock was not universally accepted in the wartime literature. Myers, C.A. (1915). A contribution to the study of shell shock. *The Lancet*, 185(4772), 316–320.

How living with fragmented experience can affect us

If we experience this severely, living in fear of the intrusion of thoughts, memories and sensations can erode our confidence and ability to organize our thoughts, making daily life impossible. We can feel at the mercy of flashbacks. At a less extreme level, as in the following case of Zara, fragmentation may intrude in a more subtle way, for example affecting her child's ability to adapt to a new situation.

TRAUMA STORY: Zara from the orphanage

Zara lives the first years of her life in an orphanage, after being abandoned by her family of origin. At the age of seven, she experiences difficulties in adapting to her life with her adoptive family and feels sad and alone, particularly at school. She is often frightened and startles easily. During a brief spell with a play therapist, Zara is able to draw pictures of her early life, not whole pictures but fragments, including the hats that the nurses wore. These memories of her abandonment are indelibly encoded in her memory in the form of images.

At this point, it is as if Zara's mind is a like a garment full of holes. Drawing the hats helps her begin to weave the garment of her mind back together, stitching the threads of the images, the memories and the fearful emotions into a whole narrative. She divides her story into chapters with titles such as: Looked after by nurses, The smell of cabbage, Scratchy blankets, Scary cries of babies. In this way, she is able to integrate the fragments and assimilate the experience into a coherent narrative. Then, when she sees the images and remembers the sounds and smells in the orphanage, Zara can begin to make sense of what happened to her when she was separated from all she knew. This work transforms her trauma, increasing her ability to feel safe in her current life. She then gains confidence and starts to enjoy school, particularly after she receives affirmation from her teachers for the lovely story she has written. At the end of the year, she is awarded 'Pupil of the Year' in recognition of overcoming significant challenges in her life.

How flashbacks work at a deep level inside us

As we can see with Zara, flashback fragments are often visual. She feels emotions in response to the visual memories. Traumatic memories are stored in the lower or reptilian brain, the part of the brain that drives the primitive actions of the body. We call these memories 'implicit', as they are often lodged there without much narrative, deeply encoded in the body and mind.[2] As they did with Zara, the implicit memories can helpfully manifest themselves later in a safe, creative space, in her case through her drawing images of what she remembered – they were the 'way in' to her trauma transformation.

Flashbacks triggered by smell, sound and touch

Fragments can intrude in involuntary body and mind responses to smell, sound and touch. They can relate to a one-off or more prolonged trauma. The original traumatic event would have had a beginning, middle and end, but fragmentary flashbacks have no such sequence. In the following case of Billy, the trigger is smell.

TRAUMA STORY: Billy on the farm

Billy grows up on a farm. When he is young, one of the older farm hands exposes himself to Billy when they are alone together working in a barn. Shocked and then ashamed, Billy tells no one, burying the memory deep within himself. Many years later, he finds himself on another farm and smells the same mix of hay and tractor oil. It takes him right back to that overwhelming and shocking moment. In an instant, the fragment of memory erupts into his consciousness and he finds himself weeping and shaking uncontrollably. Disturbed by the power of these symptoms, Billy seeks advice and help from his GP, who recommends booking

---

2   Explicit memories are ones we have conscious awareness and maybe a narrative about. Implicit memories are held at a deeper level, unconsciously. They might include habits and knowing how to do things, such as riding a bike. In terms of trauma, implicit memories can be held in our bodies, in images, in emotions and sometimes an uncanny sense of just knowing or perceiving something.

a session of EMDR (Eye Movement Desensitization Reprocessing) Therapy.[3] After taking a history, the clinician asks Billy to repeatedly follow his eyes along a light bar, left and right, and as he does so, to notice and report on any responses, memories and sensations that come up for him. At first, he weeps and is a little distressed as he recalls the incident once more, but he quickly recovers when he finds words to make sense of the experience. After repeating the procedure a couple of times, Billy's arousal returns to usual levels. Later, when he visits the farm again, he remains perfectly calm.

Flashbacks can also be auditory, such as hearing voices. A person may be afraid when they hear voices that they may have a diagnosis of schizophrenia, so it can be informative and a relief to consider that such a symptom could be an auditory flashback – a trauma symptom – and not a mental illness.

In my work, I find that people are often relieved to discover that we all have multiple identities within ourselves. This is part of being a healthy human being and part of our human experience. For example, when we feel ambivalent about something, we say things like: 'A part of me would like to go to the party, but another part of me would prefer to stay at home.'

How fragments can spin off with a life of their own

The fragmentation in trauma is different. Like Zara's holey garment, the fragments are sometimes hardly held together at all and this can cause us difficulties. Our responses might feel very strange, they might unexpectedly spring up from within us and may not make sense to us or others. These fragments can spin off out of our

---

3 EMDR enables people to heal from the symptoms of PTSD and trauma. Using a combination of talk therapy and bilateral stimulation (left-right), it assists in reconnecting one side of the brain with the other. Repeated studies show that EMDR therapy can reduce the symptoms of trauma and is effective for single incident trauma and dispelling the charge of trauma more generally. EMDR can involve eye movements or a variety of bilateral stimulation, including sounds and tapping. EMDR would be a good treatment of choice for someone like Billy. For resources and further information see https://emdrassociation.org.uk.

control, so our confidence in ourselves is eroded, and this can be very disturbing. We might feel as though we are hanging on to our lives by a thread. Again like Zara, through understanding and informed support, there are ways to help our fragmented selves be sewn back together once more.

Without understanding we can easily judge fragmentary behaviour

Unfortunately, an understanding of how trauma fragmentation works is not always currently in evidence in our institutions and legal processes and we have some way to go before we become trauma informed across wider society. For example, when rape victims go through the court system, they frequently come across a number of difficulties. As Suzie Miller's one-woman play, *Prima Facie*, highlights, a person's recall of events in trauma is often patchy and their charged nervous systems reactive.[4] A female rape victim can be easily triggered by standing in the witness box in the male-dominated court room. A person can freeze under the repeated relentlessness tone of the interrogation, unable to remember the story in the clear linear manner that is required by the legal process. It is not always understood that, while the experience of the rape itself may be crystal clear, the peripheral details are not so vividly recalled. Recall can be patchy. The mind has fragmented. Through trauma, we can lose our usual ability to think.

A victim can be judged as being hysterical or exaggerating. This is short-sighted and sometimes cruel. I believe that there needs to be an appreciation of what is happening to them inside. A person's emotional responses are a natural part of the limbic brain's heightened arousal and their sketchy memory and lack of coherent narrative are part of trauma fragmentation. When we experience post-traumatic responses that take us over, we no longer have awareness of other parts of ourselves: we can only see the world through the lens of the dominating emotion or reactive response. The sad end result of our

---

4   *Prima Facie* by Suzie Miller is a one-woman play, premiered in 2019 and reworked into a novel in 2023. The play features Tessa, a criminal defence barrister who is sexually assaulted. The play won many awards and was performed by actor Jodie Comer.

societal and systemic limitation can be that someone can easily be retraumatized by a legal system (or other systems) that do not always understand their traumatized way of being. There are signs of hope, as trauma-informed protection and support during court processes are now becoming available for traumatized individuals and child defendants through registered intermediaries.[5]

Sometimes metaphors can help us understand. We might think of ourselves as having a symphony orchestra inside. Imagine the bass drum being dominant and unrestrained by the conductor. None of the other instruments would ever be heard, because the bass drum has an urgent priority that needs to be understood! Living with emotional parts that 'rule the roost' can feel frightening and disturbing, both for the person themselves and for the people around them. A part that has been dominated or drowned out can emerge in a raw 'unacceptable' way, eclipsing rational or logical thought.

We can involuntarily and suddenly change from being meek, uncertain and tearful, to spinning into an out-of-control rage, then zoning out and becoming unresponsive in an out-of-control switching of emotional states. When we are fragmented, we may say: 'A red mist came over me and I was lost to it.' Or we might report that we have done something that seems inexplicable and illogical: 'I don't know what came over me... I just found myself doing it.' Or we might lose chunks of time altogether.

Fragmented experience at one extreme

At the more severe end of the fragmented continuum, a person may be diagnosed as having dissociative identity disorder (DID) and need careful work with a specialist psychotherapist or psychologist to understand and reconcile themselves to the disparate facets of their

---

5   Registered intermediaries in the UK can be offered to support traumatized defendants through the court process, to work out through assessment the level of questioning that is appropriate for a defendant and to set ground rules with the questioning process. Whether an intermediary is offered is at the discretion of the judge. Judges often only permit intermediaries to support vulnerable defendants to give evidence, but not always to help them follow the full course of their trial, so the intermediary role, though important, could be more extensively embedded.

personality.[6] Each emotion has developed a set of priorities. In their particular and insistent ways, the imperative of each emotional part is to keep a person safe at all costs. Focused, slow-paced specialist work allows a person with DID to begin to understand these priorities, helping them to integrate what has been fragmented. As the person learns to stitch them together from a place of safety and acceptance, the different parts gradually become less distinct, pressing and powerful. Eventually, each part can be accepted and respected, with an equal voice around the kitchen table of the person's own mind.

Trauma-informed awareness helps with fragmentation

Working with DID illustrates a more general and important principle in working with fragmentation – namely the ability to develop an observing part of ourselves, using non-judgemental curiosity to be more aware of the workings of our minds. That way we can separate out inner tangled strands and understand them. This helps us to 'mentalize' or think about our separate 'split-off' feelings.[7]

The words of the poet Rumi encourage us to welcome all parts of us, through acceptance, which is part of mentalization:

This being human is a guest house.
Every morning a new arrival...
Be grateful for whoever comes[8]

---

6   Dissociative identity disorder (DID) was previously called multiple personality disorder and is a diagnosis used by clinicians drawn from the *Diagnostic and Statistical Manual of Mental Disorders, Fifth Edition* (2013, American Psychiatric Association). This condition can only be diagnosed by a mental health professional. In DID, two or more split off and distinct emotional parts have different priorities and identities. When one is dominant, a person may not be in control or aware of their actions. That is, one part of their personality may have no conscious awareness of another. In such extreme fragmentation, conscious awareness of the whole is not possible, while the split-off part might temporarily dominate a person like an eclipse of the sun. There are resources and information about DID at the end of the chapter.

7   In recent times, attachment theory has been expanded and further developed by Peter Fonagy and Anthony Bateman. These researchers coined the term 'mentalization', referring to the ability to reflect on and understand one's state of mind, to have insight into what one is feeling, and why.

8   Rumi, *The Guest House*, tr. C. Barks, www.scottishpoetrylibrary.org.uk/poetry/guest-house, accessed 09/01/24.

This really means being able to think about and understand our emotions and thoughts and those of others, and understand their priorities and concerns. This can be no mean feat: depending on the degree of traumatization, it may feel rather like the gradual process of learning how to tame a wayward horse, or perhaps a field of horses! The process of listening to, understanding, reclaiming and integrating the disparate parts can eventually mean that a person can transform from a grouping of unpredictable warring factions to, as someone once said to me, becoming like a scene from the TV sitcom *The Royle Family*, where all the parts co-exist peacefully together on the sofa, with no one part dominating the others but all living in harmony and working in balance as a team.

Such a person has moved from living a trauma-dominated fragmented life to enjoying a happy and peaceful internal co-existence. These words were written for those who struggle with disparate parts:

> *I am not one entity*
> *Parts went ape*
> *Other parts jumped in*
> *Meditate?*
> *Nothing touched them*
> *Too many frightened child parts*
> *But they're doing their best*
> *So I let them speak*
> *Welcome all parts*
> *You are all me*

BREAKING-FREE POINTERS FOR WHEN WE FRAGMENT IN TRAUMA

- Trauma's power can shatter our responses into fragments. We talk about feeling 'in one piece', but after trauma we can feel 'all over the place'.
- The fragments of trauma experience are like hidden pockets of memories, body sensations and images held without context or narrative.
- The fragments have no time stamp and can emerge within us

following a trigger or they can just happen. Sometimes, fragments can spin out of control and erode our confidence in life.

▸ A fragmented response to the world can be an exaggerated response to something or can mean that we simply erase something that happened altogether.

▸ Highlighted emotional responses are often part of trauma fragmentation.

▸ Our non-judgemental understanding of the parts of ourselves is our best chance of stitching ourselves together once more. Becoming educated about this facet of trauma matters in our world.

QUESTIONS FOR FURTHER REFLECTION

1. Are there parts of me that need safety and special attention so that I can reclaim all of me?
2. Am I ready to attend to aspects of myself that I tend to neglect or am afraid of? When a difficult memory or response emerges, can I meet it with a gentle embrace, rather than banishing it or running from it?
3. What kind of intimacies – with the natural world, with beauty, with friends or family, with sports activities – help me to feel safe and soothed by in order to attend to and reconnect with the more hidden aspects of me?

MEDITATIONS TO ASSIST INNER COHERENCE

Welcome all parts meditation

Imagine you have time to work on a jigsaw. All the pieces are on the table in a pile. As you sort and sift them, you start to place similar coloured ones together. Next you look at shapes that fit together, piecing them together until the shape starts to emerge before your eyes. As the pieces form patterns and contribute to the bigger picture, enjoy the inner satisfaction that building a whole brings you. Every part of the jigsaw, every part of you, is vital to your coherence and the uniqueness of you and each one of us.

Also refer to Jewel Meditation at the end of Chapter 9 and the body scan colour exercise at the end of Chapter 8.

SOME RESOURCES ON DISSOCIATIVE DISORDERS

- ▶ https://di.org.au – an international community network run by Sarah K. Reece promoting support and information.
- ▶ www.firstpersonplural.org.uk – a membership association open to dissociative survivors, their friends, family and professional allies.
- ▶ www.carolynspring.com – offers articles, blogs and trauma training.

You can find a short video that highlights some points from this chapter at https://www.youtube.com/watch?v=L6qObqwKQEo or by scanning the QR code.

Chapter 12

OUR BODIES HOLD IT

Trauma is enacted upon the body.

We may say that something is 'all in the mind', but our bodies and minds are more entwined than we might imagine. Our minds' responses to trauma, such as flashbacks, have been understood at least since veterans returned from the trenches after the First World War, but it is comparatively recently that the legacy of trauma on the body has been taken more seriously. Developments in neuroscience and brain research have helped with this.

Body memories

The term 'muscle memory' is frequently used when we are learning something new – a skill in doing something is installed as a 'programme' in our bodies. The same thing happens in trauma. Our minds may not remember (as we saw in Chapter 10) but our body 'holds' responses to our experience, which we might call a 'body memory'. Our bodies are receptacles of trauma: memories are imprinted, making trauma a hugely physical phenomenon. This happens in sexual abuse, Pat Ogden says: 'Those whose bodies have been violated continue to feel the battle ground of trauma physically: they relive it in their bodies.'[1]

After losing his son, singer songwriter Nick Cave wrote in his 2022 book, *Faith, Hope and Carnage*, about how the physical affliction of

---

[1] Pat Ogden is founder of Sensorimotor Psychotherapy and spoke these words on a trauma training for NICABM in October 2023. They are reproduced with her permission.

primal loss is not often talked about: 'There is an almost overwhelming physical feeling coursing through me...mental torment, of course, but also deeply physical...an interior screaming.'[2]

Nick also writes about 'the failure of language in the face of catastrophe'.[3] Yet language is what we have and it is peppered with indications of how embodied we are. We have gut feelings, broken hearts, butterflies in our stomach, heart ache, cold feet and stiff upper lips. When we are attentive to our body's signals, such as involuntarily putting our hand over our mouth, getting a lump in our throat or feeling a quiver in our belly, we find that our body is telling us its story. As in the case of Wilmer, below, if we pay attention, our bodies can powerfully protect us.

TRAUMA STORY: Wilmer's body message

Wilmer ends his long-standing relationship when he finds his partner's over-protection constraining and controlling. He has also felt dominated by his partner's sexual demands and wants to be free. He goes on online dating sites to meet someone new, for the first time for years. He finds the person very attractive, but is dismayed that they seem to quickly want sex rather than getting to know one another first. Wilmer's body freezes, he cannot feel aroused and bolts from the encounter. Afterwards, he wonders if his body was telling him it is too soon to move on, or maybe it is giving him a protective message – do not repeat the same submissive pattern?

Our bodies hold our experience

How do we treat our body? What is our relationship with it? Many of us might habitually ignore body signals and drive ourselves relentlessly forward in pursuit of our goals. We can put ourselves through stress with insufficient rest. There are often consequences to this: think about hard-working teachers who come to a half-term break only to go down with a cold. When we finally stop, our body often succumbs to infection or illness, making sure that we do take the time our body needs to rest and recuperate: 'The body keeps the score.'[4]

2   Cave, N. (2022). *Faith, Hope and Carnage*. Edinburgh: Canongate Books, p.42.
3   Cave, N. (2022). *Faith, Hope and Carnage*. Edinburgh: Canongate Books, p.45.
4   van der Kolk, B. (2014). *The Body Keeps the Score*. London: Penguin. This is a classic in-depth study of how trauma is held physically, based on research with Vietnam veterans.

Previous chapters have examined the deeply instinctive ways in which the body responds to the overwhelm of trauma. In Chapter 7, young Jon fainted at the bedside of his dying mother, a slump trauma reaction, his vagal nerve kicking in to 'save' him from pain. Other fight/flight trauma responses may manifest in the body as shallow breathing, jumpiness or the buzzing electricity of the city that we carry within. Our bodies hold so much of our experience in myriad subtle and sometimes mysterious ways. A young man told me that when he was living in an isolated state of self-restraint, he developed wounds on both index fingers. When he rediscovered his friends and fell in love, when life flowed through him again, they went away. Our bodies hold the legacy of life experience. In response to life's demands, we can become vigilant in posture, holding our shoulders in a chronic defensive brace. A person who has long been on the run from danger may or may not notice that their legs twitch the moment they feel threatened. Like Daniela in Chapter 6, our feet can be numb or habitually tense when maybe we have never quite felt safe enough to feel the ground beneath us.

Links between emotional distress and illness

When we are upset, we feel it physically. Sometimes, when an experience has been too much for us to process in our minds, its legacy can manifest in bodily illness. The British psychiatrist Henry Maudsley wrote in 1895, 'The sorrow that has no vent in tears may make other organs weep.'[5] Unresolved grief, as well as trauma, can be held at a cellular level, leading to chronic somatic symptoms and illness.

How does this happen? When tears of grief overtake us in an unexpected wave, we may, as a result of our trauma defences or conditioning, push them back down into a well deep inside us. This may or may not be conscious. Our body may give us an emotional signal, like an ache or a heaviness, but we may be scared to pay attention and dismiss it. We push through in our drive to survive. Understandable.

---

5   McDougall, J. (1989). *Theatres of the Body*. London: Free Association Books, p.139. The author quotes these words attributed to London's famous nineteenth century anatomist Henry Maudsley in a case study of a patient, Tim, whose uncompleted grieving she posits was linked to his cardio pathology.

Yet our tears are key to the expression of life and they deserve to be respected to enable us to find release.

Trauma in childhood often arises when the environment and circumstances provide no space for the expression of emotions, and this is termed as adverse childhood experiences, mentioned earlier.[6] Studies suggest that symptoms can emerge later in chronic health conditions.[7] Suzanne O'Sullivan has made an important study of psychosomatic illness in her 2015 book, exploring medically unexplained symptoms through a number of case examples.[8] We may develop chronic bodily conditions that are deeply woven into the fabric of our history and our experience. There is some research to show that persistent stress may be an antecedent to conditions such as heart disease, cancer or chronic autoimmune disorders like rheumatoid arthritis and fibromyalgia.[9] Traumatic body symptoms may include a speeding or irregular heartbeat, digestive problems, including irritable

---

6   Adverse childhood experiences have been defined as potentially traumatic events that occur in childhood (0–17 years), such as experiencing abuse, or neglect, witnessing violence in the home or community, and having a family member attempt or die by suicide. Also included are aspects of a child's environment that can undermine a sense of safety, stability and bonding, such as growing up in a household with substance use problems, mental health problems, instability due to parental separation or household members being in jail or prison. It has been shown that as the number and intensity of ACEs increases so does the risk for negative outcomes such as chronic disease, poor mental health, poor maternal health, infectious diseases, injury and risky behaviours during adulthood. Information from Centers for Disease Control and Prevention, US, checked 9 June 2023.

7   See www.ncbi.nlm.nih.gov/pmc/articles/PMC8462987 for Adverse Childhood Experiences and Chronic Disease Risk in the Southern Community Cohort Study (accessed 09/01/24).

8   Suzanne O'Sullivan is a consultant at the National Hospital of Neurology and Neurosurgery in London. Through case examples, her book *All in the Mind* (2015) explores 'medically unexplained symptoms' that occur in the same numbers in developed and undeveloped countries and account for 20 per cent of patients.

9   Agnese Mariotti, a science researcher in Lausanne, Switzerland, examines the effect of limbic stimulus to the sympathetic, adrenal, hypothalamic-pituitary-adrenal axis and complex responses, including hormonal regulation. If the stress is high and cannot be resolved and becomes chronic, the immune system will be compromised and it can have effects on organ health. Stress can also increase the levels of circulating cytokines and biomarkers of inflammation that can be a precursor to various illnesses, including cardiovascular disease. She also examines the effects of stress on the brain that may increase psychological vulnerability over time. Mariotti, A. (2015). The effects of chronic stress on health: New insights into the molecular mechanisms of brain-body communication. *Future Science OA*, 1(3). doi: 10.4155/fso.15.21.

bowel, or painful joints. We may look for the source of our difficulties in the right diagnosis or treatment, when actually our body is still reacting to *unprocessed experience – stress and trauma*. Although a medical operation may be necessary to heal us, having our bodies cut open in an operation may also be experienced as trauma, and touch previous unprocessed traumas.

Having respect for our bodies that hold so much

When we experience treatment we do not like, our bodies tell us. The difficulty can be that our environment may not have been safe enough at the time for us to tune into these messages. However, the body remembers something that we find traumatic, and *holds* the information.

If trauma is held in our bodies, it follows that working with our bodies is part of our recovery. Only when we start to notice our own trauma can we take steps to mitigate its effects and respect its messages and wisdom. We then become trauma informed.

Our bodies may need to release what they hold. The hiatus of trauma can stop our natural bodily flow. Remember the gazelle who is attacked by a lion? When the lion moves away, the gazelle will run for its life. This is because it has built-up energy that it needs to discharge. Humans also sometimes need to discharge energy following an overwhelming experience. This was discovered when Justin and Harriet had Relate sessions.

TRAUMA STORY: Justin finds his expression

Justin grows up in the shadow of his half-brother Franklin. Franklin is a troubled teenager and conveys his distress with outbursts of rage, often directed at Justin, whom he covertly bullies. Justin develops a strong distrust of others who become close to him, physically and emotionally. When triggered, he tends to withdraw from others. When he marries Harriet, the same tendency creeps in when the pair have a disagreement. When Harriet expresses her opinion strongly, Justin shies away and almost cowers from her.

Justin and Harriet book a couple of Relate sessions with a

sensorimotor practitioner.[10] Justin is encouraged to notice what he feels in his body before he cowers, and, with this encouragement, he courageously finds the words to express his fear to Harriet.

In recalling a cowering incident, and freeze framing the moment he feels fear, Julian is invited to let his body speak. He is surprised when his body involuntarily thrashes around. Though this seems bizarre, he is invited to respect and stay with this reaction without judgement. Waiting patiently for his body to give him the words, Justin is amazed to discover that his body is letting him know he is frightened and angry. It has been holding all the terrible things that have been inflicted on him by his brother – this is his 'bodily tantrum'.

His body pulled back from expressing the tantrum at the time in order to keep him safe. Instead, his body learned to cower and it is still doing the same protective thing in his marriage! Though it causes him uncomfortable anxiety at first, Justin begins to understand the legacy held in his body. When he notices the cowering defence, over time he trusts its signalling and allows his body to 'speak'. Justin feels liberated when he finds words for the fear that was trapped in his body. Then it is easier to tell Harriet what he feels about her strong opinions and he no longer needs to cower. They become more intimate. Justin's relationship with his body also changes.

Later, martial arts classes help him learn about his body's defensive structure. He explores Feldenkrais (a kind of movement therapy) and yoga to help him attend to its tensions, move differently and soften his posture. Justin slowly learns to 'love being in his own skin'.[11,12] Caring treatment starts to bring him moments of joy. Now, rather than cowering, he lengthens his back and holds his head high. He feels released as he properly inhabits his body for the first time.

---

10 Sensorimotor psychotherapy was developed by Dr Pat Ogden and is a method that enables an uncoupling of physical responses and trauma-based emotions. It enables individuals to work with physical sensation to move beyond their trauma (see https://sensorimotorpsychotherapy.org).

11 'Loving the Skin You're In' from the Merry Hell album, Head Full of Magic, Shoes Full of Rain.

12 Moshé Feldenkrais developed an exercise therapy in the mid-20th century that repaired connection between the motor cortex and the body. There are two ways to practise the Feldenkrais method, one a verbally guided way in groups and the other one through hands-on treatment called functional integration.

In the past, Justin's cowering was necessary to defend himself. His body developed an expression of permanent defensiveness. With a little help, he is able to uncouple his emotions and his bodily held defences, calming and transforming both.

Learning to listen to signals from our body

Our body does its best to signal its messages to us, but it is not always easy to slow down and take time to notice them. The first step may be to stop and check in with our bodies. Taking such steps does not need to be difficult. A little goes a long way. I have outlined some ideas or possible 'ways in' to connecting up with our bodies in the questions for reflection at the end of this chapter.

When our body is suffering, we can help it by consciously giving it repeated messages of safety. It may be that our environment is part of the problem and not so easy to change. When our environment is safe, we can train ourselves to notice elements of it that will nourish us. For instance, finding a favourite cafe, walking in the forest or taking time to notice the pleasure of the sun on our face can all feed and calm us and reclaim our equilibrium and balance. We can ask ourselves, what does my body need now to feel safe? Or what does my body need now to express itself? This present-day reality checking needs to be persistently repeated, as the pull-back to the internal bodily perception of fear can be strong. It can take time and the repeated determination of our minds for our bodies to 'believe' we are safe. Consciously linking ourselves to our five-senses perception (sight, hearing, taste, smell, touch) can bring us to a calmer state internally, and help our bodies regulate and relax.

Doing this can be easier in theory than practice. We saw in Chapter 3 how trauma can repeat. Body-mind habits become ingrained and are often unconscious. In addition, the way we treat our bodies can directly re-enact abuse and neglect, making us see our physical selves as hated objects and receptacles of harshness. Instead of listening to our body and paying attention to its instincts, needs and signals, we may drown out its signs or treat it as a rubbish bin. We may numb our pain in substance abuse or addictive behaviour that brings temporary relief but also a multitude of problems. We are trying to manage our distress, yet our bodies can suffer at our own hands, even in overdoing something that is good for us in an unproductive or damaging way.

Body neglect and burnout

Chronic or prolonged stress is a precursor to burnout. When we are burned out, we struggle to pay attention to the world around us and respond appropriately to daily interactions. We struggle to respond appropriately to our bodies. There are some mitigations for burnout at the end of this chapter.

If our bodies can be a place for us to heal our trauma, we may be at a loss about where to start. We can begin simply and quietly, being open to experimenting and seeing what happens. When we find ways to slow our bodies down and notice them, we may discover that we like the attention! The hormone dopamine gives us a pleasurable sensation when we treat our bodies with care. This may encourage us to repeat whatever feels good and to celebrate ourselves, tending to our bodies like a most loving parent with a baby.

The sense of instinctive safety we long to feel in our deepest selves is linked to the child that we once were. We have all seen a young child sleep, surrendering their weight on the front of their parent's body. It might strike us as a beautifully moving scene of deep trust. Such connectedness may produce a pang of longing somewhere in our own bodies, an echo of a need long ago to be held in the safety of another's body. Whatever our treatment in the past, when we begin to use our minds to pay attention to our bodies, we can change our relationship to them. The body is no longer a recipient of bad treatment, but a resource and ally to connect with, heal and celebrate.

Score keeper
Work for me
Hold my pain
Be my barometer
Tell me what next
Hold me up
Be my rubbish bin
Need anything?

BREAKING-FREE POINTERS TO ASSIST OUR TRAUMA-CARRYING BODIES

- Trauma is a physical phenomenon. How we treat our bodies may be a response to trauma. We can repeat bad treatment on ourselves, through a lack of awareness.
- Trauma can be held in our bodies in a myriad of ways, in our protective or defensive postures, in the way that we drive ourselves to survive, or hold emotional stress physically as a burden, contributing over time to the development of chronic dis-ease.
- The good news is that our bodies can become part of our recovery from trauma. Awareness of our bodies is an important part of becoming trauma informed.
- We can give our bodies repeated messages of safety that counter trauma and allow our spaces to release and soften. We can learn to treat our faithful bodies with the respect they deserve.
- Our bodies produce dopamine when we feel pleasure. Dopamine counters and rebalances us when we hold too much of the stress hormone cortisol.

QUESTIONS FOR FURTHER REFLECTION

1. What sensations do I enjoy? How do I know that I like these?
2. What is the bodily information that tells me about pleasure?
3. What inner information gives me the message that I am safe?
4. What inner information gives me the message that I am not safe?
5. Are there any illnesses or patterns of illness, or a part of my body, that frequently 'speak' to me? If so, might this have some psychological meaning or relate to an earlier trauma?
6. Is there any way of thinking, or action, that might help me respect my body messages more than I perhaps do, or learn to love myself at a cellular level?

IDEAS FOR MITIGATION OF BURNOUT

Stress makes it harder for us to maintain attention and make new memories. In burnout, we struggle to pay attention to the world around us and respond appropriately to everyday life.

- ▶ Evaluate stimuli realistically. Find a trusted friend or mentor who can help you talk through what you perceive as threatening and remind you that a stressful situation isn't necessarily something to be worried about. They may see things clearer than you.
- ▶ Evaluate your priorities. Decide what really matters. Are the things you are doing supporting your own and others' development? What can you cut back on in order to have more time and energy for the things that matter?
- ▶ Have a routine that brings you life. Routine helps you to show up to what is important when you would usually spiral and give up on things. Life-giving activities reduce stress and help you think clearer. Try taking exercise and making coffee dates to punctuate your days.
- ▶ Take a step back if you can. A change in plans is not a failure. Life is a marathon, not a sprint. Remember to pace yourself so you are a long-term whole and healthy person.
- ▶ Document your triggers and get to know your particular early-warning signs of burnout.
- ▶ Remember:
  - – Burnout is common. It is okay to struggle.
  - – Burnout has biological roots. You are not doing anything wrong. This perspective might help counter any self-imposed criticism which can lead to shame (see Chapter 15).
  - – Burnout is miserable but is a season that will end. Take care of yourself, rest and set up a less stressful environment if you can.

You can find a short video that highlights some points from this chapter at https://www.youtube.com/watch?v=gBJ26Vy2axI or by scanning the QR code.

Chapter 13

WHEN TRUST IN OTHERS IS BLOWN APART

Other people can traumatize us.

Hell is other people.[1] (Sartre)

People can wound each other. Paradoxically, the corollary can also be true: other people can be our salvation and help us heal. This chapter explores this dichotomy of the double-edged sword of relationships: hurts from others may be at the heart of our trauma, while just as often recovery depends on the quality of love and understanding of those around us. (The following chapter explores what happens more deeply when, after trauma, our cries for help are not heard.)

How do relationships, especially those formed early, traumatize us? Trauma has its own logic. Not just about an experience that hurts or derails us, *our trauma responses are related to our survival.* From infancy, we depend on the care of others. Sometimes this care goes awry. Our caregivers may come too close to us and invade our space, or neglect us when we need them. If power is transgressed in such ways in our early relationships, in response we might have an ongoing tendency to submit to others too easily, avoid, withdraw, not engage, resist or fight other people. We do these things because relationships *do not feel safe* to us. We still need others but *trust is broken*, creating an impossible circle.

---

1   A famous line from *No Exit* (1944), a philosophical play by the French existentialist Jean-Paul Sartre (1905–1980).

Psychologists think about our ability to relate to others as relating to our particular *attachment* style. Attachment theory was originally developed by John Bowlby who described attachment as a 'lasting psychological connection between human beings'.[2] Many of us (approximately two-thirds of infants) develop a *secure enough* attachment in infancy, where we feel safe with others and within ourselves when separate from others.[3] The other *insecure* attachment styles develop when we are not responded to sensitively or consistently. They are distinct styles of relating to others. The next three cases in this chapter illustrate avoidant, ambivalent and disorganized attachment styles.

Avoidant attachment and trauma – when trust is broken early

Our first case is about a child, Shona, who has an avoidant attachment style, which occurs when a child is not responded to at an emotional level.[4] Depending on the severity of our early experience, these attachment styles overlap and interweave with trauma. Shona has a history of neglect and is a little girl who on the surface seems friendly and responsive with everyone but inside is deeply traumatized.

---

2 Bowlby, J. (1969). *Attachment. Attachment and Loss: Vol. 1. Loss.* New York, NY: Basic Books, p.194. John Bowlby (1907–1990) was a British psychoanalyst, and the first attachment theorist. Attachment means an emotional bond with another person held over time. In a young baby, attachment is necessary for survival. John Bowlby made a study of the anxiety children feel when the bond is less than optimal and the ongoing effects of this that continue throughout life. In the 1970s, psychologist Mary Ainsworth expanded on Bowlby's original work. Her groundbreaking 'Strange Situation' study revealed the profound effects of attachment on behaviour. Researchers observed children between the ages of 12 and 18 months as they responded to a situation in which they were briefly left alone and then reunited with their mothers.

3 If we are securely attached as a child we would show clear signs of distress when our parent left, would greet them when they returned, then would soon return to our childhood tasks of play and exploration.

4 If we are avoidant attached as a child (approximately 20 per cent of the population), this is likely to be caused if a parent does not respond to our needs in a reliable and sensitive manner and ignores our distress. We may carry avoidant traits on into adulthood and may tend to avoid and disconnect from our own feelings.

TRAUMA STORY: Shona – a bouncing ball – avoidant attachment[5]

Shona's birth parents lead chaotic and wild lives. Neglected as children themselves, they remain emotionally adolescent and have not developed into mature adults. When bingeing on alcohol, they forget to look after their kids. Social services are involved and Shona is put into care and looked after by a series of foster parents. They report that Shona appears to trust everyone (superficially), responding to strangers in exactly the same way as she does to her foster parents. To protect herself, Shona does not form deep attachments – she never properly relaxes with anyone. She is like a ball, bouncing from person to person.

It is a human need to be known, to be found, to be properly seen and safe with another person. If we have this experience, our minds and bodies and nervous systems relax. It is a precious gift, a platform from which we can grow and flourish. Shona's trauma wound is her emotional and physical neglect by those whose job it was to provide this platform, a primary betrayal that shatters her capacity to deeply trust. Sharing feelings makes her vulnerable and doing so feels profoundly unsafe to Shona. Her protective solution is to avoid her feelings. Without the inner barometer of her feelings online, she is extremely vulnerable to further abuse. How? Because two things happen at once on different levels. Superficially, her attachment need for safety shows in her over-friendliness to everyone, at the same time as not properly trusting them. Her parents did not attune to her feelings, so she has learned to cut off from them for safety. From this position, little Shona cannot easily sense danger. Connecting to an avoidant person can be hard if they are not connected to themselves. Donald Winnicott called this 'game of hide and seek' a 'disaster' if there is no emotional 'finding' of a person who deeply needs it.[6]

5   Adapted from Sally Donovan's story of adopting her own children, *No Matter What: An Adoptive Family's Story of Hope, Love and Healing* (2013) London: Jessica Kingsley Publishers. Permission given directly from the publishers.
6   Donald Winnicott (p.187) wrote, 'It is a joy to be hidden and a disaster not to be found.' Winnicott, D. (1965). The International Psycho-Analytical Library, 64, 1–276. London: The Hogarth Press and the Institute of Psycho-Analysis.

How avoidant attachment with trauma may manifest later

How will Shona develop into adulthood? Her way of relating and trauma patterns, like tentacles that reach down into crevices, are deeply engrained and repeated. We might imagine that grown-up Shona might feel safest with quickly formed relationships, moving on and avoiding true connection to others, rather than risking putting down deeper roots of safety that will withstand challenges. Or she might find herself in a relationship with a person she loves and wants to be close to, but when that person offers her warmth or affection, she might run a mile. Of course, on a deeper level, she longs to be nurtured and loved, but feeling close to other people sets off her inner trauma alarms, feeling as intense to her as being trapped in a burning building.

Ambivalent attachment and trauma

We now consider our second flavour of attachment, which occurs as a result of *inconsistent parenting*, illustrated by the following story of Cassy.[7] The mixed messages we can receive being in relationship with someone with ambivalent attachment can be so contradictory, I tend to liken the 'push-pull' as being similar to the two ends of Dr Dolittle's mythical animal, the pushmi-pullyu, with the two ends of the animal directing operations in opposite ways![8] This seemingly perplexing shifting of behaviour can certainly be seen in Cassy.

TRAUMA STORY: Cassy – ambivalent attachment

Cassy feels so deeply inadequate that she constantly finds fault with her husband, fearing his rejection. After her dad was killed, her mother was erratic, sometimes needy and demanding and often emotionally rejecting and absent. Cassy spent most of her

---

7   If we are ambivalent (anxious) attached (approximately 10–15 per cent of the population), this is likely to be caused by parental inconsistency. Such a child may demonstrate needy and clingy behaviours and is not so easily soothed.

8   Pushmi-pullyu is the name of a fictional animal with two heads at opposing ends of its body, along with very sharp horns on each side of the head, in Hugh Lofting's *The Story of Doctor Dolittle*. I am using it as a metaphor for someone who acts in a contradictory or ambivalent manner, pulled in two directions at once.

childhood anxiously trying to second guess what might happen next. As an adult woman, Cassy is constantly afraid that her husband will reject or neglect her. So she goads and tests him, picking fights, imagining slights and then erupting angrily. At other times, she clings on to him, whining and desperate like a distressed child. Her husband Trent's tolerance is worn thin when Cassy seems intent on endlessly digging up the foundations of their relationship. It becomes a not-so-merry dance of cat and mouse.

After a particularly whirring sequence of pirouettes by Cassy, Trent, exasperated, says: 'The more you push me away, the more I think you need me! Just let yourself be loved, you grumpy little shit!' They both dissolve in hysterics and from then on these words are repeated between them as a kind of code when Cassy's desperate behaviour around love and need emerges. After the code words have been spoken, and humour dissolves the tension, Cassy is more able to see herself and her 'grumpy and needy child inside' from a slight distance. She begins to bear her feelings, find words for them, understand and forgive herself for the way she is. With repetition, this helps.

The next step is to be able to imagine and think about what Trent is thinking and feeling. Due to her early disturbances, Cassy has no inside template of a consistent other person acknowledging her with attention, affection and acceptance. Trent is a great guy, loves her, but when she is in her trauma place, Cassy simply cannot believe this. She jokes that she needs post-it notes with 'Trent is a good guy' around the house to remind her of this truth when fear fills her and she becomes a toddler all over again.

A hallmark of this kind of trauma and ambivalent attachment experience can be dramatic shifts in behaviour from neediness to coldness to outbursts of violent rage. Cassy has this kind of inconsistent template that plays out in her attachment dance with Trent.

Disorganized attachment and trauma

Now let's think about our third attachment style, 'disorganized attachment'.[9] Caused as a result of experiencing extreme fear in childhood, this impacts around 10 per cent of the population. This percentage is much higher for children of abusive or drug-addicted parents. Trauma is at the heart of this experience. It follows that if we are profoundly hurt by other humans, we become physiologically wired not to accept or expect good things in relationships from then on. We are not just avoidant or ambivalent about attachment and closeness, we are terrified of them. People feel profoundly scary to us. If we have disorganized attachment, we will be easily triggered into a state of hyper-arousal (overwhelmed with emotions – the red zone mentioned in Chapters 1, 4 and 5) or hypo-arousal (apathetic or unresponsive – the blue zone in Chapters 6 and 7).

In the following case, Chantal and Ben's adoptive children sadly had terrifying early experiences, which show in their unusual behaviour.

TRAUMA STORY: Chantal and Ben and their children – disorganized attachment[10]

Chantal and Ben adopt two siblings aged seven and four, who had violent and neglectful experiences in their birth family. Sometimes their lack of safety is painted in primary colours. When triggered, the seven-year-old sometimes goes ape, ransacks his room and yells to his family that he hates them. Other behaviours are more under the surface: the colours of distress more muted. Out of direct parental supervision, the children constantly gather objects from around the house and store them in random places. Understandably this is perplexing and infuriating for their parents. Ben says it is like living with gremlins!

---

9   Attachment theorists later came up with a further category termed disorganized. We will have disorganized attachment when our parent leaves us feeling terrified and does not attune to our needs. For such a child, when a parent returns, the infant looks terrified and withdraws, or clings and cries while simultaneously pulling away. Statistics on attachment styles from Siegel, D. (2011). *Mindsight*. London: Oneworld Publications, pp.168–9.
10 Adapted from Sally Donovan's story of adopting her own children, *No Matter What: An Adoptive Family's Story of Hope, Love and Healing* (2013) London: Jessica Kingsley Publishers. Permission given directly from the publishers.

After some years, Ben and Chantal attend a workshop on trauma and attachment. Later, the specialist they meet there becomes someone they consult about their children's behaviours. He says the aggression and object collecting are both signs of their lack of safety. He suggests Ben and Chantal try a new regime of 'maximum contact' at home, playing with their children more consistently and attentively. Rather than leaving the children to prepare meals, he says they can all eat baked beans for a period of time! The important thing for the moment is putting contact first and practicality second. He also recommends that the next time the four-year-old is rageful, the parents keep as close to him as possible, physically holding him from behind saying, 'I know you are angry, I understand that you feel afraid. I am here and am not going anywhere.' With the increase in empathic active attention, Ben and Chantal notice that, quite quickly, the children settle down a bit and play up less.

Incident trauma and societal trauma can also profoundly impact our ability to trust others

These three cases illustrate developmental trauma, but *incident or event trauma* can also disrupt our capacity to trust others. Many people will recognize that moments of extreme crisis or turbulence – like having one's first child, having a partner return from war or losing a job – can put more pressure on a relationship than it can sustain and a house of cards can easily come tumbling down. At such times, relationship cracks that might exist untroubled in times of calm can easily become chasms. This is explored in the film *The Best Years of Our Lives* (1946), through the portrayal of the relationship between veteran Homer, with his fiancée Wilma.[11] Homer returns from war traumatized, with both hands missing. The trauma shatters Homer's capacity to trust in and accept Wilma's love and he dramatically tries to push Wilma away.

Everyday family tensions can have lighter fuel poured over them

---

11   William Wyler (director) (1946). *The Best Years of Our Lives*. RKO Pictures.

in a crisis such as a global pandemic, which was experienced traumatically for many. Think of the huge numbers of children who no longer trust in going to school. It is easy to get frustrated with a person who digs their heels in, becomes secretive, is not open with us, is prickly, defensive, or endlessly looking for faults, but it is important to understand why they might behave like this and to see the bigger picture. *Trauma may be the undercurrent that we underestimate or miss altogether: their trust in others may be damaged.* We can ask the question: what happened to this person that led them not to feel safe?

When trust is broken what can be done?

When we are angry or frightened, overwhelmed and upset, we need another person to provide an acknowledgement of how we feel. That makes us feel safe and that we belong in our tribe and in our world. Having emotional acknowledgement is like being on the right frequency with a musician's tuning fork: feeling someone else match our resonance calms us profoundly. It sounds simple, but it is not so easy to give or receive if this 'tuning in' was not done for us. We can continue to feel unsafe inside and with other people, even if others around us are safe and attentive. *Trust takes time to build, and patience and repetition.* Dealing with their traumatized children requires Ben and Chantal to actively find the right emotional frequency to match and resonate with their children and repeat it. Trent finds a way to contact traumatized Cassy through humour. Of course, this is enormously demanding work for someone who lives with a traumatized person. With practice, however, you can discover, like sound waves, the particular frequency and resonant quality of affection, attention and acceptance that reaches them and makes a difference. When Ben and Chantal found ways to tune in, their kids felt safe. Things do get better for that family. *The quality of the relationships we can offer our traumatized loved ones will be the greatest succour and help for the healing of their traumatized selves.*

Safety and relationships are bound up together

Humans are wired for two systems: relationship and safety. Optimally they co-exist happily. But if a relationship is compromised by trauma damage, our safety system is blown out of the water. Of course, as was the case for Homer, the opposite is also true and the two systems can get *entangled*. Reparation can sometimes involve a slow repair, a re-interweaving of the two systems to form a new braid, as our humanity is healed and transformed and we find a way to become at ease with ourselves and others again.

How we begin to build trust after trauma

I recently reread *An Evil Cradling*, the 1992 account by Brian Keenan of his incarceration as a hostage during the Iraq/Iran war.[12] For the first few months, Brian is incarcerated alone and suffers much dehumanizing treatment. After some months, the journalist John McCarthy joins him in his cell and they are held together for the remainder of Brian's four-and-a-half years of incarceration. Having John there with him ultimately enables Brian to survive the terrifying experience with his humanity intact. The following extract outlines the challenges of coming back to relationship from a place of extreme isolation and fear. Though most of us will thankfully never experience the horrors of incarceration, Brian's words, written after extreme hardship, shed light on the workings of trauma and his route back to life and joy.

> Fear of self and fear of the other re-emerged as the constant undercurrent of our first days together... But the breaking down of these fears, of these insecurities [...] was not an immediate thing. It takes a long time to come back to yourself. It needs a commitment to the courage of another person in order to approach them, be honest with them and know that you will not be shunned or rejected by them. (p.96)

Trauma can teach us that we should be afraid of our vulnerability and our trust in it can be shattered to smithereens. Yet in post-trauma growth, we may find a new appreciation of our own fragility and come to see our worth within it. Ultimately this learning can be transformational. Brian Keenan discovers his vulnerability in courageously sharing it over time with John McCarthy. This changes everything for him.

---

12   Keenan, B. (1993). *An Evil Cradling*. London: Arrow.

Even when we take steps towards making different choices and start to feel a little safer in our foundations, we may still not be able to resist the temptation sometimes to try to sabotage ourselves or what we have. Post-trauma work is not a straight line. When triggered, we can easily dig up our own foundations. Recovery is usually a bumpy road. It takes time to build a trellis of support where we can flower. Like Cassy, that fearful, protective part of ourselves may surface and repeatedly derail us and our loved ones. When this happens, can we remember our trellis and learn to trust in weaving our threads back together again?

These are words written to Cassy:

I've been drowning
For so long
Not trusting
You or anyone
To be my lifeboat
Yet so wanting
You to know my experience
My thrashing about – not knowing what to do – is scary
Maybe help me?
Such a relief
And hopeful

BREAKING-FREE POINTERS WHEN TRUST IS BROKEN AFTER TRAUMA

▸ A facet of trauma is broken trust in other people. If this happens when we are young, this can be impossible because we still need them to survive.
▸ If rooted in childhood, trauma can be caused by others coming too close or not close enough, and that means emotionally neglecting us.
▸ Some legacies of trauma may appear in us avoiding our feelings in relationship to others, or displaying changeable behaviour with others, or just being deeply afraid of any closeness.
▸ Trauma may be the undercurrent that we miss or easily underestimate when we struggle in relationships.

- Safety and relationship are two fundamental human systems, both of which can be damaged by trauma.
- Quality time and attention and acknowledgement of emotion can help heal trauma wounds.
- From being afraid of our vulnerability (a message that trauma gives us) we can find a new appreciation of our fragility and vulnerability with the right people around us. When this happens, lives are changed. We are helped and enabled to truly be ourselves, and freed from trauma's legacy and power.

QUESTIONS FOR FURTHER REFLECTION

1. Do I generally feel safe with others or by myself?
2. Can I practise checking in with my 'inner weather'? How am I feeling? Am I warm and flowing or cold and fearful? (See the end of Chapter 14 for an exercise on this.)
3. Do I (or someone I know) ever operate in ways that sabotage flow, openness, intimacy and closeness? Might that behaviour be based in fear?
4. Long ago, did I have someone to acknowledge my feelings so I learned to accept, attend and be affectionate towards who I am and what I feel? Does this experience sustain me? Do I do this for others?
5. Has an important relationship changed in my life? Do I want to find ways to allow that relationship in more deeply? If the relationship was not helpful to me, can I try to understand, forgive myself and them and let it go?
6. Do I have a relationship with an animal, a passion or love of nature that sustains me in a way that humans do not quite reach?

MEDITATION – WHEEL OF AWARENESS

Dan Siegel (Professor of Psychiatry at the UCLA School of Medicine and founding Co-Director of the Mindful Awareness Research Center at UCLA) has developed a practice following research with 10,000 people.

The idea is to begin to differentiate *being aware* from *the things we are aware of*. He uses the metaphor of a wheel to illuminate the hub of knowing, the rim to show what we engage with in the world, and the spokes of the wheel are our attention on those things.

The hub of a wheel is a place where we can develop attentiveness in our minds. Regularly dwelling in this place may be strengthened with practice, may help us become more reflective and less reactive, giving us choices about how we respond. From the hub, we are able to notice the sights, sounds, smells, sensations, thoughts, other people, anything that comes into our consciousness. The wheel may be a useful tool to develop curiosity about our own mind and our relationships with others. This is easily accessible through Siegel's website, https:// drdansiegel.com, where you will find wheel of awareness meditations to try (click on 'wheel of awareness').

MEDITATION ON BEING FOUND

Imagine being on a solo expedition and the weather turns nasty. You are alone in a wood and the night is drawing in. All the trees look the same and you begin tripping on roots. There are some rustlings and animal noises you do not understand and these make you feel increasingly alone and isolated. Suddenly, you arrive at a light-filled clearing. An idyllic cottage with smoke circling from a chimney is there before you. It looks strangely familiar. As you approach, the door opens and a person who loves you opens the door and smiles in delight. You are home. Your body drops in relief. You go inside and kick off your boots.

You can find a short video that highlights some points from this chapter at https:// www.youtube.com/watch?v=684dmZ42Ljg or by scanning the QR code.

— Chapter 14 —

WHEN WE CRY OUT IN DISTRESS

To survive trauma, we may silence our cries, sending them underground.

When in peril or subject to a wrong, we cry out in distress. When trauma is involved, our cries are likely to have the intensity of a wail. This chapter will focus on what happens when our cries of distress are not met. The focus here is on what John Bowlby called an *anxious attachment style* and how trauma interweaves with this way that we may have developed in our relationships with others long ago.[1]

Attachment revisited – how needs are sometimes not met long ago

Let us recapitulate on the essence of attachment theory in a little more depth. From the first moments of our lives as human beings, our relationships and *attachments* to others are essential for our survival. Our brains are undeveloped at birth. We need the attention and care of others for our brains to develop. We need and are wired for connections with others. If our physical and emotional needs are not met we may survive but we cannot thrive. In Chapter 13, Cassy needed to trust in the benign and responsive mirror of Trent's face to see her own feelings reflected and accepted. This interaction had not happened long ago, so she feared it now. Trauma got in the way of her attachment to him.

---

1   We may become anxiously attached (or preoccupied) when our parents or caregivers are inconsistently attentive. This anxious part of us may lead us to become overly dependent on others, unable to tolerate being alone, fearing abandonment and having difficulties setting boundaries.

Our need for acknowledgement, containment and validation

Emotional reflection from another is a physiological necessity for the regulation of our nervous systems: it is a primary reason why we fall in love and form close relationships in adulthood. This mirroring or reflection is a kind of *acknowledgement*. Another word is *validation*. This means that the other person is able to hold our experience in their mind's eye and heart without rejecting or judging it. Deep down, it goes something like this: 'If you see me and know I feel like this and do not reject me for it, I can accept that I have this feeling and be okay.' How these attachment needs are met determines how safe we feel and how we relate to others for the whole of our lives. If they are met, we know and trust that what we feel is *contained*. This word conveys the deep safety we experience in being able to express what we feel inside when someone does not reject us or our feelings but 'holds' us and them. If contained when we are little with our big feelings, we learn to trust that the other person is strong enough and wise enough to accept whatever we feel, no matter how terrible. The experience of acceptance and containment makes all the difference to our ongoing sense of peace and equilibrium in the world.

The 'value added' of trauma

Now we put trauma into the mix: imagine what would happen if our need to be mirrored, validated and contained by others was absolutely not met. How would it feel if the very people we seek out, our caregivers, were in fact 'scare-givers' – unpredictable, frightening or frightened? We would employ defensive strategies such as fight, flight, freeze or faint/flop (as discussed in Chapters 4, 5, 6 and 7). Yet the more afraid we are, the more we need other people. In such a predicament, we might then adopt other defensive strategies, running like Shona or Cassy do (see Chapter 13). Another solution or primary response to our fear might be becoming clingy and dependent, like a child in distress who anxiously holds on in desperation to the other person, refusing to let them go.

The anxious attachment of deep distress

One sign of awry attachment is a deep cry that springs from a void of need inside. It may not be overt, but may simmer under the surface, having its origins in experiences of being ignored, displaced or rejected, either long ago or more recently. You may have had the experience of being around a person who seems subtly needy to you. You may have developed that way of being yourself, as a desperate attempt to have a crumb of attention: maybe leaning forward in an intense way, demanding attention from others, locking onto them with your eyes, or sometimes becoming 'unreasonable'. If you are on the receiving end of this kind of neediness, you may feel an immediate, visceral response to move away, shut the other person down, judge them or rescue them in some way. They might feel just too much for you.

Why? Because you may sense a deeper distress, rather like that of an animal who is trying to alert others to their plight. You feel another person's desperate survival cry underneath their presentation – a plea for help – and its intensity may be scary. The ability to convey distress is a child's most primal survival response. To ask for help is a sign of hope for the future. *Yet if the child grows up in an unsafe or abusive atmosphere, that cry itself can be dangerous and make things much worse.* Instead of crying overtly, the child learns to disguise their distress and bury it. When this child becomes an adult, their cry of distress might emerge occasionally, but mostly it rumbles deep down in the lift shaft, so they exude a subtle atmosphere or aura of fear or demand, not fully known to even themselves. As is seen in Maya's story, the pleas and desperation may emerge in relationships.

TRAUMA STORY: Maya and her son

Maya becomes estranged from her adult son after they have a big row. She cannot tolerate what she sees as his unreasonable lashing out. When she joins a support group and shares her story, Maya has space to reflect on her part in the dynamic with her son. She cannot understand why he seems to be always angry with her.

In her early life, Maya was very frightened of her unpredictable father who erupted violently, particularly when drunk.

Her mother was helpless and frightened, appeasing and collusive of her husband's drinking. Little Maya was terrified but kept quiet.

Maya has a child when still a teenager. Quite quickly, she marries a man whose personal power makes her feel safe, and with whom she is in thrall. She tolerates his mood swings but finds them extremely frightening. Maya whines and pleads with him but at the same time is subtly supportive of her husband's extremes of behaviour, going along with his whims. She never challenges him when he shouts at both her and her son.

Now, in the support group, Maya is challenged about the estrangement with her son. Someone asks: what is your part in it? Why is he angry? Defensive at first, Maya comes to see that despite her pleadings and wailings, she has been subservient and passive, tiptoeing around her husband rather than being a protector of her son. Her cries fell on her husband's deaf ears, partly because she believed they would: her distress was imbued with fear. Maya begins to realize the ways in which she has failed her son and has dismissed his cries for help, as well as not being attentive enough to her own. This is a breakthrough in her understanding, though very painful to admit. Maya finds a therapist who helps hear and contain the painful cries she carries inside. Then she begins to reach out to her son in much calmer and more conciliatory ways. She begins to hear his cries and understand them. As she does this, the atmosphere softens like gentle rain between them.

Our capacity to turn away from distressed cries

Maya's whining and cajoling with her husband was a veiled cry for help: a trauma defence born of desperation. There is nothing meek and mild about such a request. It has the life and death quality of a terrified baby's cry, making demands on others to act and save them. However, the more Maya whines, the more it enrages her cruel husband, who ignores her, which only makes her whine more. This part needs to be met in order to be healed, not in an appeasing manner, but in a way that fearlessly understands. It does not need caretaking or rescuing, but must be engaged with directly. Yet how human it is to avert our gaze when we find something too shocking or painful, or if it does not fit with our ideas of how things should be. We can just not see things or people we do not want to see, so we dismiss them. We may reflect on the ways in which this gaze aversion is perpetuated in our society and our world when we encounter someone or something that is out of sync with our experience and makes us feel uncomfortable and inclined to dismiss or judge. This can happen at an individual and organizational level.[2]

TRAUMA STORY: Ezra and volunteer Jane

Ezra arrives in the UK as a refugee from a war-torn country, having travelled thousands of miles in danger in the back of many lorries, seeing many terrible things, including shootings and people dying from their injuries. Arriving in a safe country he applies for asylum but the process is long and confusing. He feels he is being treated with suspicion and hostility. For many years, his case is not attended to, so his status is in limbo.

For Ezra, travelling to the safe country was a destination of hope, but life on the streets is a struggle. Travelling around the city, he notices that people look uncomfortable when they see his unkempt appearance after he has slept rough, or they ignore him altogether. He feels like an outcast. It undermines all the strength that has got him here, and leaves him feeling isolated and alone. In his home country, Ezra was outgoing and confident, but here he finds himself shrivelling away. If someone offers him kindness, he tends to latch on to them intensely because he is so unused to emotional contact and needs it so desperately.

One day, Ezra hears about an International Group that meets in the centre of the city, offering welcome, food and a chance to wash clothes. On arrival, he is met with a no-nonsense warmth. There are rules and clear boundaries. Ezra feels safe when there

---

2   Woodcock, J. (2022). *Families and Individuals Living with Trauma.* London: Palgrave Macmillan. Woodcock (p.52) states: 'Gaze aversion is the term Louis Blom-Cooper used to describe the host of helping agencies that failed to notice that four-year-old Jasmine Beckford was being systematically starved and beaten to death by her stepfather and neglected by her mother. It is a good term that sums up what happens when we fail to see something clearly because it is too shocking and painful and doesn't fit with our preconceived beliefs.'

are steps to follow. There is a regular timetable and jobs are fairly allocated. More than anything, Ezra notices the atmosphere of acceptance in the group. The volunteers look him in the eye, learn his name and treat him with a demeanour of calm consistency. Someone always comes to sit with him over dinner and he is able to talk if he wants to. The other guests seem relaxed and talk with one another, play games, make jokes and share their experiences. Ezra feels as though he is properly seen for who he is in the group, even if sometimes he feels down and doesn't want to engage. It feels like a sort of family. They don't judge him, are not afraid of his appearance, do not pry or ask questions but allow him to be. It is the first time he has felt safe since arriving in the country.

One day, one of the volunteers inadvertently riles Ezra while serving him lunch. Jane tells him he cannot have a second helping of dinner. Ezra erupts, all the bad treatment and the terrible things he has witnessed bubble up to the surface of his mind and he lets out a wail of desperation. Jane is shocked by Ezra's powerful reaction, but holds on to herself inside, continuing to look at him kindly, saying nothing and not moving her body. Her heart is beating and she is frightened she has done the wrong thing, but she remembers the trauma-informed training the volunteers did. The facilitator told them that an antidote to trauma can be to allow a person to 'complete their circle'. She remembers the description of the smell of orange zest coming into the air, then naturally falling when the skin of the fruit is broken. This was a metaphor used by Pierre Janet.[3] She remembers that every experience needs a precursor, action and completion. She needs to let Ezra complete his circle. He is upset, but it isn't really about what she has done. When Jane gives Ezra space, he is able to express and contain his emotion within the safety of the group. He soon calms right down.

---

3   Pierre Janet (1859–1947) was a pioneering French psychologist, physician, philosopher and psychotherapist in the field of dissociation and traumatic memory. He used the metaphor of a person breaking an orange, and the zest being released into air, emitting odour, then falling to the ground to describe the beginning, middle and end of each experience that we have. Experiences need to be seen in their entirety. Trauma cuts across these natural circles of expression, so it is therapeutic to allow ourselves the idea of re-instating a completion of our experience.

Safe spaces

This atmosphere of safety in the International Group soothes Ezra's inner cries of distress and relaxes his tense body that is primed for rejection and hardship. The group has developed 'concentric circles of safety' with repeated and consistent rituals, procedures and steps that are soothing and containing. They do not reject his cries, they do not judge him. This experience of being in the group goes some way to healing his hurt over being discriminated against for being homeless and people averting their gaze from him.

Unflinching non-reactive responses

We might think of one powerful force needing to be met by another equal to it. Perhaps we do not imagine that loving acceptance is a powerful force but it is a precious commodity. The plea of the child or vulnerable person may be subtle and veiled, or overt and stridently insistent, or even hostile. Ezra's powerfully expressed distress is met with calm understanding and the gift of space by Jane, who 'contains' his pain without judgement. His cry quickly dissipates and Ezra naturally completes his 'circle' of experience. We can practise open listening, not flinching, reacting or becoming repulsed by the powerful whine of a distressed person. When doing this, we are not focusing *on* but reaching *through* the signs of trauma (while understanding them) *to hear the subtext of pain underneath*. From this place, we are more likely to be able to offer a person unconditional warmth and acceptance. Of course, this is not always easy to achieve in practice, for a number of reasons, explained below.

Setting boundaries kindly

Sometimes a person can be so desperate to be heard that they can be overbearing or attempt to manipulate us or not know when to stop. You may find yourself becoming overwhelmed and traumatized (for more on how trauma is catching see Chapter 19). For your and their protection, it can be very important to kindly set limits and be firm. You do not have to acquiesce to all a person's demands or pander to every whim. If you do, a person is likely to feel less secure in the environment. Like sheep sheltering against a wall in bad weather, boundaries make us feel safe. They are important trauma mitigations.

It is healthy to challenge and say when something is not acceptable. The International Group had clear guidelines about what the boundaries were and they trusted in them. This helped Ezra feel safe. It is not always easy to hold boundaries at the same time as allowing someone to complete their circle – it takes practice to develop careful skill and judgement.

Dual awareness of our own responses

We can develop the skill of 'dual awareness' when in a challenging situation with another person.[4] It takes practice, but while listening and focusing on another person, you can, at the same time, move your attention inside and notice how you feel. I have sometimes called this our 'vertical axis'.[5] The horizontal axis is our focus on the external world. With inward attention, you can learn to ground yourself inside when you feel that you are being squashed or demands are being made of you that you cannot meet. If you notice stress impacting you physically and halting your flow, you can regularly check in with your body for your 'inner weather' (see end of chapter) for information and focus on keeping breathing and feeling your feet grounding you on the floor.

Keeping proximate with others

Irrespective of their style and how they manifest, a person's distressed cries need to be met with robust *strength* and *proximity*. Sometimes we think we need to come up with solutions when actually we may

---

4   Trauma specialist Babette Rothschild speaks about developing dual awareness at https://youtu.be/HlM8XV7vIFs, first as the capacity to distinguish in our minds between feeling upset and what is happening in the here and now. And second, to distinguish between our internal sensations, which may be giving us the message we are frightened, and our external environment through our five senses, which may be giving us information that we are actually safe. The video was accessed 09/01/24.

5   Smethurst, P. (2017). Borders and boundaries. *Therapy Today*, 28(5), 28–32. This article explores training offered to volunteers working with refugees and asylum seekers in London.

simply need to be there with kindness. When a desperate cry for help is responded to with contact and proximity, it can be quickly transformative. If we are *proximate* with someone and carefully watch their face, we will observe details. Those details will give us thoughts and ideas about how we should respond to them. It takes courage to trust this instinctive skill in ourselves, but if we have benign intention towards another person, we can trust that this is likely to be communicated to them.

Compassion

As humans, we know when we are properly received and understood by another person. Unflinching compassion can be conveyed in small ways: in looks, a smile, a soft tone of voice, a small gesture, a comment or an act of kindness. A person cries for help when they have been treated with a lack of empathy or ignored when in need. Wounds are created when we are disregarded, dismissed or attacked or when our safety systems have been threatened. As also discussed in Chapter 13, the origin of the trauma may have emerged in the arena of other people, so our whole nervous system is stressed and we feel beleaguered and desperate. The corollary is also true: the *right* treatment can also heal. Our own capacity to contain and create safety for a traumatized person is vital. Just a sprinkle of our relational empathy or contact goes a long way. In fact, too much could leave a person feeling swamped and confused.

Understanding the push-pull solutions of distress

Being distressed brings dilemmas and 'solutions'. We might reflect on the choices we make or have made ourselves, when we have been in pain or frightened. A child who suffers abuse will sometimes plead for it to stop, but continue doing what makes their abuse worse. They can repress their own cries of distress. A child may tolerate what hurts them in order to remain close to the abuser. Fear tells them to do this. Being close to others is imperative for us as humans. As a result, *we can sacrifice safety, and we silence our cries of distress or protest, for the sake of safety and closeness*. The sacrifice may make this seem an easy solution, but the reality is likely to be a tug of war and an excruciatingly difficult choice to make. This kind of trade-off often occurs in situations of domestic abuse. We may decide we need to keep close to important others at all costs, because there is always a possibility that our emotional needs may be met one day. What a dilemma to face.

We hold on, or we cry out.

These words were written for Maya:

You don't hear me
You sit over there
You don't help me
You won't help me
No one can really help
But there's a cry
From somewhere
I hope I'll be brave enough

BREAKING-FREE POINTERS TO HELP US HEAR TRAUMA CRIES

▶ The burying of our distress can be a result of trauma that is rooted in the anxiety we have felt long ago around others and can lead to feelings of deep desperation.

▶ To have the full repertoire of our feelings (not just profound fear) accessible to us as humans, we need to have our feelings reflected in another's face, acknowledged and validated. We need to trust that they have space for what is in our heart and mind, without dismissing or rejecting our experience or our feelings.

▶ If this has not happened sufficiently for us, our distress, like a deep cry, may remain unheard inside, not heard or properly known, even to ourselves.

▶ As a result, we may exude an aura of fear and demand that may cause others to shy away from us and avert their gaze.

▶ An antidote to this trauma is imagining with compassion an unheard or sometimes strongly heard cry, and allowing ourselves and others to 'complete the circle' when distressed.

▶ Safe spaces, consistent boundaries, developing dual awareness, unflinching non-reactive responses, remaining proximate, no non-sense calm, warmth and loving acceptance can all help to contain distress and mitigate this aspect of trauma.

QUESTIONS FOR FURTHER REFLECTION

1. Can I practise checking in with my 'inner weather'? (See following exercise.)

2. Do I recognize fear showing up in a relationship characterized by appeasing and placating or rejecting? If so, are there some changes I would like to make to change the dynamic? Might I need some help and support to consider how to do this?

3. Have I had the experience of being around someone who feels as though they have a chasm of unmet need inside? What is my response to such a person? Am I drawn to them or repelled by them? Maybe both?

4. Can I trust the idea of being calm and *proximate* with someone in distress as a powerful emotional commodity?

5. How welcoming am I of others who may be different? How do I respond to those who do not hold my values or someone whose views I think are 'wrong'? When might I avert my gaze in the face of an overwhelming need or demand? Would I like to expand my capacity to be welcoming?

6. Can I practise listening with benign acceptance or 'unconditional positive regard'?[6] This involves becoming aware of our bias and knowing how that could influence our responses. Developing such awareness allows us to bracket our judgements and biases, should we wish to, while consciously focusing on understanding and accepting the other person.

7. Can I practise being emotionally containing and developing active

---

6   The term 'unconditional positive regard' was coined by Carl Rogers in 1956 and is the basic acceptance and support of a person regardless of what the person says or does, especially in the context of the therapy that he researched and developed as client-centred therapy. The main factor in unconditional positive regard is the ability to isolate behaviours from the person who displays them. It is a powerful concept.

listening skills? Or consider inviting someone to be my emotionally attuned mentor or confidant, and be theirs too?[7]

EXERCISE IN CHECKING INNER WEATHER

Take some time for yourself, in an environment where you feel comfortable and safe. For a few seconds, check in with yourself, and do a weather check. Is your mood fair and tranquil, with a hint of a storm cloud on the horizon? Does your breath come easily and evenly, or is there some inner turbulence? Are you warm and flowing or cold and fearful? If there is some disquiet in your system, what are its signs? Is there something you can do to attend to your needs right now to create a more balanced weather picture?

Use nature to assist you. Think of your mind as a sky, blue and clear. When a thought comes, maybe it is a cloud that you can watch as it moves along and fades into the distance. Maybe, if you feel a part of you in distress, you can imagine that your legs are trunks of a tree, holding your weight, but also rooting themselves into the ground, where goodness and riches can be found and drawn up to feed and nurture you.

EXERCISE TO HELP REACH THE MARGINS

Imagine kneading bread. The bread has been proving and growing in consistency and now you scoop it up into your hands and begin working with it.

Pull the consistency, stretch it and bring it back into itself, taking care with edges. Imagine that these edges are like the parts of you that can be overlooked, the broken parts, the parts that are not quite smooth, but they are part of you nevertheless. They are the wounded bits of you that you want to attend to, so that you are not tempted to despise these broken parts in someone else.

---

7   There are resources to support us developing active listening online: see https://mindtools.com or www.samaritans.org.

You can find a short video that highlights some points from this chapter at https:// www.youtube.com/watch?v=kpkh1EPR2rE or by scanning the QR code.

Chapter 15

THE LEGACY OF SHAME

Shame can have a magnetic quality, drawing us to the conclusion that we are culpable, sometimes when we have committed no crime at all.

When I look back upon my life, it's always with a sense of shame, I always think I'm to blame.[1] (Pet Shop Boys)

We all need a little shame, it can correct our behaviour and help us reflect. In a traumatic experience, shame can have a particular purpose. If we are in a dangerous situation, shame protects us. It makes sure we are not seen and heard and, as Janina Fisher writes, 'puts the brakes on behaviour that would be punished'.[2] Trauma is the danger and shame is the conclusion we then often reach – that we are wrong and bad, often when we have not done anything wrong at all. The difficulty is that shame's message – that we have done something wrong and that there is something wrong about us – can linger long after the event. *Shame becomes about us, not what we have done.*

Like Finella, our lawyer in Chapter 4, the unbearable feeling of culpability in shame can permeate us and keep putting us in the dock. This is because shame's roots are often deep and powerfully held. As in the following example of Jase, shame can frequently spring from an experience of being marginalized for being different in some way.

---

1   Pet Shop Boys (1987). 'It's a Sin' from the album *Actually*.
2   Janina Fisher is an international trauma specialist. This is a quote from her seminar Undoing the Damage: Healing from Trauma-Related Shame, in 2023, and is quoted with her permission.

TRAUMA STORY: Jasmine to Jase

Jasmine has never felt good about herself since she was a small child. Mum is kind, but even she seems to do little to protect her from the other members of the family picking on her relentlessly.

Jasmine also has a secret that she guards fiercely: she does not feel comfortable in her own body. She sometimes wishes she was a boy. She is deeply fearful that if this is known, she will be rejected. In her teens, Jasmine often thinks that one or other of her friends is off-hand or critical of her, which sends her into a downwards spiral. She has many 'friends' on Instagram and always compares her own image negatively to them. She cannot imagine they will accept her if they know the secret about her gender orientation. The fear of rejection gets into all her interactions and sometimes paralyses her. She constantly fears not matching up in some way, but is scared to talk openly to her friends about her fears, in case they reject her completely. It is a real bind. When she is alone she ruminates endlessly, feeling anxious about the things she says and posts on social media. She feels wretched and isolated, trapped by fears about making more mistakes, and exhausted by her feelings of fear and shame.

Things ease for Jasmine when she finds an online support group for non-binary people and others who wish to be more fluid about their gender identity. For the first time, she speaks about her fears and longings with others who have similar feelings. She finds herself relaxing a little inside and grows in confidence. She takes the risk of confiding in her mum and is surprised and pleased when she agrees to call her Jase and refer to her as 'them', not 'her'. Mum even says she will tell Dad to do the same, and not goad Jase about it. This relieves something inside: having Mum's support makes all the difference.

Jasmine is now Jase and 'them', and things feel much better. Mum reminds Jase they have always loved art and encourages them to start attending an extra-curricular art class where, with the support of an encouraging and understanding teacher, they feel connected to others in a climate that accepts all contributions and people openly and without criticism. Finding one or two others who do not identify as solely 'male' or 'female' and pursuing art helps Jase to begin to be self-accepting and less critical. Jase has found 'their people', a non-pressurizing environment without judgements. As shame eases, creativity flows. When doing art, Jase feels a special freedom emerging inside and is quietly proud of the results. Maybe they are worth something as they are?

What causes shame?

Jase's fear and shame loosens when it is spoken and understood. As with Jase, shame often starts with bad treatment or the absence of good treatment, which has a heavy toll on our ability to develop healthy self-esteem. Sometimes, shame is created unintentionally when we remain silent rather than step in to support someone. It is then that fear and trauma can take a hold. Jase fears that, as a non-binary person, they are not acceptable or loveable in this world. Shame can be very painful and wrapped up with fear. Jase's *fear of judgement turbo charges their shame*. This is a frequent and painful spiral.

How shame operates inside us

The insidious part about shame is that bad treatment gets replayed inside, depriving us even more of self-worth. Like a hidden operator and often not consciously aware of it, Jase replays the fearful self-deprecating messages of 'not good' inside. Someone who feels they have made a mistake long ago can become highly anxious, compelled by an inner imperative never to make a mistake ever again – a situation that can become tortuous, often developing into a destructive cycle (there is more exploration of this in Chapter 18).

I think of shame as having a sticky quality, rather like Velcro binding us to a thought pattern that hurts us, but often under the surface and out of our awareness. Where one thought goes, another can follow, until we are surrounded and overwhelmed by shameful and fearful thoughts. In this state, we can often feel as though we are drenched in shame, soaked to the skin. Like driving rain or hail, shame can really hurt us, having a whipping, relentless quality. It is so pervasive it eclipses the possibility of light or good things breaking in. When this happens, our self-esteem and confidence are eroded as we are under attack from a plethora of shameful and self-deprecating thoughts. A client describes this as being driven by a voracious dog whose hunger can never be satisfied. Being in such a situation can be utterly exhausting. Shame leads to *strain*, as we become worn down by its barrage of demands telling us that we should be different from who we are.

Society can reinforce shame but its roots are often in childhood

Jase's distress about their orientation is fed by social media, where their vulnerability is highlighted, reinforced and distorted by anxious comparisons. This significantly fuels their shame messages and, as we will see in the next story of David, technology that can disconnect us from each other becomes a potentially dangerous platform for shame. Unlike guilt, which stems from a specific act, shame is usually created in relationships and often, like Jase, has its roots in childhood.

How shame grows and can be protective of more hurt

Imagine a child being in a frightening and out-of-control situation. Perhaps someone does not respond to the child, so they do not feel safe. Believing that they themselves are wrong and bad at the core, when everything is terrifying and painful, gives the child a modicum of control in a dangerous situation. Children can and often do grow up feeling lousy about themselves, and believing they are in the wrong becomes a kind of damage limitation position – *I will get me before they do*. This shame default can become an out-of-proportion part of us and can dominate and define us as adults too. The following story about David has some of the same features and further illustrates the under-the-surface spreading feature of shame.

TRAUMA STORY: David and the WhatsApp message

A naturally sensitive person, David is born with severe cystic fibrosis. Constantly wheezing, and smaller than his classmates, he does not fit in with the 'norm' and is hurt by frequent bullying for being small and unable to do sports at school. Looked after by his parents into adulthood, David is relentlessly cheerful around them, on some level hoping that if he is chirpy he will be more acceptable. Maybe his humour will somehow compensate for his disability and all their sacrifices and make them happy. Underneath all this, he feels as though who he is and what he does will never be enough.

His parents take care of him diligently when he has numerous lung infections. Yet their stoicism also makes them tense and they endlessly bicker with each other. Eventually, they become too elderly to care for David, who is then moved into supported housing, where one or two devoted friends visit him regularly. On the outside, he is cheerful but brittle. He sometimes has a sharp tongue. He jokes, but never expresses appreciation. Inside, he is full of self-loathing.

David's friends have a lively WhatsApp group, where they communicate with each other about visits and grocery shopping. One day, David reads something on the group chat that he finds critical and offensive. In an angry impulse, he responds to this criticism by messaging his closest friend in the group, calling the person a 'miserable tosser'. Unfortunately, instead of sending the message just to his friend, David mistakenly sends it to the whole WhatsApp group. David immediately feels a terrible wave of shame and anxiety flood over him, with the old messages of culpability and unworthiness.

We can develop 'defences' against shame

David's story is a good illustration of typical defences against shame. It is so painful to know that we feel inadequate, or that we have been hurt or our emotional needs have not been met. It is also painful to make a mistake, to feel *in disgrace*. So, we guard these truths like a vault inside us, becoming skilled at rationalizing and defending ourselves from such acknowledgements. Other shame defences are being prickly, justifying ourselves, latching on to explanations, being critical of others and lashing out. When we do these things, we often sadly reinforce our inner shame messages.

There is a famous scene in the film *Good Will Hunting*,[3] when, in a seminal moment, a professor (played by Robin Williams) empathically

---

3   Gus Van Sant (director) (1997). *Good Will Hunting*. Miramax.

repeats to his student (played by Matt Damon): 'It was not your fault. It was not your fault.' The student eventually breaks down in tears as he begins to realize the full weight of the shame he has been carrying for so long. Hating or blaming ourselves feels extremely painful. So is being let down by others who we depended on. The words of permission, 'It was not your fault', or in another context, 'You are allowed to make a mistake', can be powerful if they penetrate us at a very deep level. It helps us forgive ourselves and begin to let shame go.

Ways to mitigate the power of shame

The WhatsApp incident acts as a catalyst for David. He tells his closest friend how miserable he feels about lashing out. Rather than being offended, the wise friend suggests he joins a support group for other cystic fibrosis sufferers. When David begins to see, through getting to know the others like him, that he is not culpable for his predicament, he understands how attacking himself has damaged him. Like the student in the film, with his trusted friend he acknowledges his pain and his truthful story as his tears flow. He then turns towards himself in compassion and begins to reclaim the good in himself. However, as David discovers, *building shame resilience* frequently takes longer than is suggested in the film.

Why changing shame can be challenging

Shame can be a tricky customer and can often take some excavating. This can be particularly hard because of shame's tentacular nature; its causes can be deeply buried. We have seen with Jase how bad treatment led to fears about not matching up and being rejected. In classical portrayals in art of the Seven Deadly Sins, Shame's eyes are often cast downwards and his head is covered. When we are in a state of shame, our instinct is to withdraw from others and hide our shameful state from them. Our bodies are very much part of shame. We flush, feel sick, wish to curl up into a ball. We tell ourselves it is just better not to admit how bad we feel. A childhood belief can tell us that there will surely be bad consequences if we do: *shame is so often bound up with fear.*

What can we do about shame? We are not born with shame. We can ask ourselves: have we ever seen a tiny baby who is bad? Shame is constructed from experience and there are ways to mitigate and counter its power.

Becoming aware and conscious of our shame messages

One antidote to shame is to develop curiosity about the shameful messages we have inside. Shame tells us that nothing is enough, that we are not enough. Over time and with practice, we can develop mindful awareness to first notice our shame messages and acknowledge the pain that our shame protects. Imagine when we have done something shameful, taking time simply to acknowledge 'this hurts'. *It is so excruciating to feel separate from others and unloveable, but acknowledging pain helps.*

When we cross our own moral code

Shame can occur when we have actually done something wrong, when we transgress our own moral code – David feels bad about being rude to someone else. These 'transgressions' can vary in severity. Army veterans and health workers who witness or make 'mistakes' in the line of their duty and service can hold deep and lasting shame and a kind of emotional injury when they transgress their own moral code. Such a person can feel contemptible, cannot forgive themselves and often has a long road to travel to recover and find ease with themselves once more. (Zach in Chapter 16 has such a journey to make to reappraise the story he has deeply held about himself.)

Acknowledging our inner shame messages

It can help to see shame messages as *one story*, not the *whole truth* about ourselves. From this position, their power over us can begin to decrease and forgiving and loving messages can begin to emerge. This can take patient inner work. When triggered by shame, David thinks of the power of its negative messages being like a wave, sometimes as a sensation in his body. Noticing the messages without judgement helps him. Instead of becoming submerged by the power of the negative messages (the wave), he learns to imagine herself as a surfer riding over it. In that more powerful place, he notices and voices the pain and remorse about his action and consciously brings to mind good things about himself, stepping up his self-care. He starts to treat his body with more gentleness too. With this inner work, he is learning to self-soothe to counter his shame.

A determination to operate from a place of self-worth

David becomes an impassioned fundraiser for cystic fibrosis research. This generosity outweighs the negative pull of shame: he feels rightly proud of this work. Shame grows in a world where disability or difference is judged as 'less than'. *This second mitigation comes from determinedly operating from a place of worth, not shame.*

We can learn to accept difference and become wary of accepting narrow judgements. We can also practise treating ourselves as if we matter. When David finds a sense of worth and self-esteem and speaks out about it, his confidence grows and this dispels his shame. Understanding his shame helps nudge him towards other possible ways of thinking: he sheds shame, like a skin. For example, he realizes his parents maybe do not need his defensive humour as much as his loving appreciation. Shame does not like to be spoken about or brought into the light. Recognizing and speaking about shame deprives it of its hidden oxygen. As Brené Brown[4] writes: 'Shame hates having words wrapped around it. If we speak shame, it begins to wither.'

Building bridges to others

A third mitigation can be finding a bridge back to other people. Part of David's healing involves being honest about how mortified he is about hurting someone else. Their forgiveness is healing. To reconnect with others, he needs to tolerate being vulnerable. We may repeatedly get tripped up by shame: typically it does not just neatly and magically vanish. It can be slippery and shape-shiftingly elusive, tending to

---

4   Brown, B. (2012). *Daring Greatly*. London: Penguin, p.58. Brené Brown has conducted much research on the way that shame is held individually and within organizations and her books, podcasts and Netflix talks on the subject are recommended.

reinvent itself in order to evade loving and accepting messages. It takes David much conscious work to untangle its power and have confidence in using his shame mitigations. When shame tells him to cover and hide, he urges himself to speak out and reach out. This takes courage!

Shame perpetuates fear and protects us from pain. By practising risking and owning his fragility, David can allow himself to make a mistake and not descend underneath dark waters.

These are his words, giving voice to the truth of his shame:

Shame came around
I must hide away and
Be alone
This shoal
Of shame
Gets in
Everywhere
When all I
Need is
Compassion
And touch

BREAKING-FREE POINTERS FOR COUNTERING TRAUMA-FUELLED SHAME

▸ We are not born with shame, it is constructed from our experience.
▸ When in trauma, shame can be a conclusion that we reach. It can be protective, putting the brakes on behaviour that we fear would be punished.
▸ Shame, believing that we are bad, traps us in our trauma, and fear of judgement turbo-charges shame.
▸ Shame can bind us to hateful or judgemental thought patterns that hurt us.
▸ Shame leads to strain, it eclipses light, goodness and joy.
▸ We can defend against shame by being prickly and defensive, justifying ourselves, latching on to explanations that keep us in the 'right', becoming easily critical of others and lashing out.

▶ Building shame resilience takes time. One way to become curious about our shameful messages is to 'hold them to the light' and speak about them. That way we might begin to see that they are not the whole truth about ourselves. Shame withers when held up to the light.

▶ When we free ourselves from negative blame/shame messages, we may begin to believe in our own inherent worth.

▶ When we do this, we can become more determined to operate from self-worth – it feels better!

▶ Shame may tell us to duck, dive and hide. The corollary is to deprive shame of its oxygen by being vulnerable and open, building bridges with others whom we have hurt or who have hurt us. In time, we may notice this brings a greater sense of freedom.

QUESTIONS FOR FURTHER REFLECTION

1. Do I recognize my own tendency to put myself in the dock, to first imagine my own culpability in life situations? Do I think I am bad?

2. Is it possible to speak my shame or acknowledge its painful message?

3. If shame is a very old story, how did it help me survive?

4. Is it possible to have a dialogue with shame and boot it out when it relates to an old message rather than a present-day actuality?

5. Can I allow myself to make mistakes and learn to tolerate them with compassion, rather than heap coals on myself for my failings?

6. Can I locate how shame is held in my body and let the messages go with softness and tender care?

7. How can I develop shame resilience or operate in ways that do not give my shame more oxygen? Does it help to develop ways to acknowledge my own fragility and vulnerability without judgement? Do I need to be vigilant about perpetuating my own and others' shame, recognizing its power and tentacular nature?

8. What helps organizations and institutions to avoid developing shame cultures? If shame leads us to cover up mistakes and hide faults, what practices can we employ to counter this?

DIALOGUING WITH SHAME

▶ Imagine that within your outer shell there is a shadow version of you that you want to hide from the world. What resides there are all the things that you despise about yourself. It is also a repository for all the negative messages others have given you about yourself.

▶ That part of you needs your attention right now. Ask it what it feels about you and what you have done today. Let it have a voice and try not to judge it. Write down what it says and ponder the words.

▶ As you notice what your shadow part says, be curious and see how you want to respond. Does what your shadow part says surprise you or shock you? Can you be thoughtful about this shadow side? How has it helped you survive?

▶ Imagine from a benign place you talk to your shadow non-judgementally and maybe let it know that you hear its feelings and understand them. You may be able to give the part a different, more realistic or kind message.

You can find a short video that highlights some points from this chapter at https://www.youtube.com/watch?v=oNZsrPUGkG8 or by scanning the QR code.

— Chapter 16 —

OUR PAINFUL HEARTS

Trauma breaks our hearts.

In 1890, Vincent van Gogh painted an old man sitting in a chair with his head in his hands. He called this painting *At Eternity's Gate*, and said he found it 'unutterably moving'. It is a powerful depiction of human vulnerability.[1] Those of us who have been heartbroken may have a memory of the physicality of the experience. Grief and pain can come on us suddenly like a squall of rain, sometimes bringing relief and even clarity in their wake. As Malcolm Guite writes: 'It is hard to see through tears but sometimes it is the only way to see.'[2] We only mourn because we love.

Overwhelm and grief overlap and interweave

Those who have suffered trauma in the midst of being heartbroken may have a painful predicament at the centre of their experience. The traumatic aspect – an overwhelm *story* – can overlay a *pain story*. Trauma gives us *too much experience to digest.* If we have suffered previous losses, there can be a domino effect, where one loss reverberates with a previous one, and one before that. As we get older, inevitably more friends and family members die and the effects can be cumulative. It can also create guilt, if we realize that the latest death has had little effect on us compared with other deaths.

---

1   *At Eternity's Gate* was a lithograph and oil painting by Vincent van Gogh completed in Saint-Rémy de Provence.
2   Guite, M. (2014). *Word in the Wilderness*. Norwich: Canterbury Press, p.155.

How trauma responses protect us from pain

Trauma responses are there to protect us from too much painful over-whelm. Yet our responses can block us and lock us in, so it is hard to move on. They can lead us to contract protectively or defensively from our unbearable pain or a grief that we cannot resolve. For example, a person who has suffered the loss of a beloved may be so overcome by intrusive, tormenting and troubling traumatic memories connected to the shocking process of their death that their grief is blocked and unable to be expressed. Locked in to the trauma memories, they may be unable to remember the goodness and beauty in the relationship that might bring some healing. This is the case for Kay, whom we first met with her son Jon in Chapters 7 and 8.

TRAUMA STORY: Kay's traumatic memories

When her husband of over 20 years dies of cancer, Kay feels as if she has exploded and her insides are full of debris. Graham's last months are turbulent and deeply disturbing. He is frequently in pain, which the NHS medics struggle to manage, partly because of staff shortages. By his bedside the whole time, Kay finds his agony unbearable because of her position of utter powerlessness. A fiercely private person, Graham is unwilling to tell many people about his diagnosis, and their younger children are not told that his condition is terminal.

After Graham's death, Kay pushes her feelings down and soldiers on for months. She suffers particularly with traumatic memories. In her dreams and waking reveries, she keeps seeing Graham horribly struggling for breath. Haunted by his pres-ence at home and the pervading smell of his cigarettes, she is convinced that she needs to rescue him from beneath the ground where he lies buried. In whirling guilt, she berates herself and the medics for decisions they made about Graham's treatment. Kay is consumed by angst. She feels as if she is going mad and hardly sleeps for weeks. In addition to being in intense sorrow, her mind is in a kind of backwards anticipation. Memories feel important and urgent. Her mind fixates on the isolated agony of the bedside, taking her down guilty and tortuous rabbit holes. She has no control. Separated from normal life, Kay hardly relates to others. She feels as if she is in her own glass coffin, alienated from her family, who appear to not understand. She shies away from people's platitudes, however well meaning. She has no peace.

A good and wise friend tells Kay that grief can be a kind of madness. She suggests that Kay might choose an object, a talisman that reminds her of Graham, and keep it under her pillow to reach for in the night. Graham loved collecting semi-precious stones, so Kay chooses a smooth piece of hematite that he had found. When her stomach twists in the painful reality of Graham's death, the stone reminds her of the solidity of his love and grounds her. In these brief moments, she feels Graham's love for her as well as the heartbreaking reality of his absence. She grieves deeply and then she sleeps.

At other times, the trauma returns with power. It feels then as though the terrible manner of Graham's passing is pressing down on Kay like a freight train. How can she begin to accept the way he went? Does she even want to accept it? At dawn, she finds herself visiting a quiet meditation garden situated very close to her house. When she is overcome by the intense emotions, it somehow helps to sit on a bench and feel connected to the wild flowers and colourful roses that remain simple and beautiful.

Kay struggles on with life's demands for a long time. After eight years, she attends the funeral of one of her friends, exactly her age, who has died of pancreatic cancer. She had been part of her life with Graham. Although long after Graham's death, Kay cannot stop crying as soon as she enters the church. She is embarrassed as she is not really crying for her friend, but for Graham. It is as though her feelings have been building up inside her for years and are suddenly released. She has not cried like this for a long time.

How we navigate fear in the midst of grief

As for Kay, grief in the end tends to find its own route out. There can be much physiology to navigate first – often the physiology of fear. The first line of C.S. Lewis's memoir after the death of his wife of four years reads: 'No one told me that grief felt so like fear.'[3] I believe that this happens when trauma and grief become entwined. Trauma responses can weave their tendrils around our grief experience, as they did for Kay, constricting grief's natural flow. Trauma's fine filigree can be hard to spot and hard to untangle because we can be so convinced of its messages, sometimes so turbo-charged and urgent. Some of its messages may be our mind's way of protecting us from the pain and the heartbreaking reality of our experience.

Ways to release fear's hold and ways we avoid pain

It may be important to release fear's hold and untangle it from our grief. Becoming aware of the language we use may help. Edith Eger tells us that fear's favourite words are: 'I can't! You can't! I told you so!' (I would add: *They are wrong! I have to do this!*)[4] When we say such things, our protective fear response may be appearing 'in disguise' as a determined unwillingness to accept some difficult reality. For example, we may be determined to forget someone who has hurt us; or we may scapegoat someone else. We may be determined to not accept a loss, holding on to a person like a ghost. Imagine a parent of two boys. One of them is missing, so the dad obsesses over finding him on the internet, while in the process he ignores the son he has. Trying to forget, obsessing over something else or digging our heels in is not necessarily wrong, but is our mind's way of trying to keep us away from our pain. Society can reinforce this: well-meaning friends and relatives can say, 'You should be over this by now.' Even if they don't, we can fear that they think it.

The paradox of pain

It is a paradox: we can become freer by attending to and releasing our pain. It is human to feel afraid to do this. Yet, maybe with help and encouragement, we can begin to locate our fear and practise attuning to it with curiosity in order to discover what its roots and

---

3   Lewis, C.S. (2015). *A Grief Observed (Readers' Edition)*. London: Faber and Faber, p.3. (Original work published 1961).
4   Eger, E. (2020). *The Gift*. London: Random House, p.156.

story are. (At the end of the chapter is an exercise to help find fear at a bodily level.) As Tamsin Calidas writes in her memoir after a night of terrifying storms: 'Sometimes facing the thing you fear the most can be empowering and incredibly beautiful.'[5] Caught in a whirlwind of fear, escalation might feel far from beautiful, yet if we do not address our trauma and face our fears, we may need to employ ever more desperate ways to escape from the pain bound up with them. Fears can lead us on a merry dance. As we saw in Chapter 5, an ever-pressing need to avoid, numb and run from our painful heart is frequently at the heart of addiction.

In other situations, the healing of pain can be blocked by beliefs that reinforce protective fears. We may justify our decisions endlessly, for example telling ourselves to continue to guard a secret. Pain and truth can be feared like a bomb, as can be seen in the following story of Zach, when a terrible secret ripples out over a whole family system.

TRAUMA STORY: Zach's toxic secret

At the age of nine, Zach walks in on his 'uncle' in the act of sexually abusing his younger brother. His dad left months before, and since then a close family friend who Zach loves and they call 'Uncle' is always in the house helping his mum. In a horrified daze, he walks out of the house and down the street. Later, the brutish uncle threatens him with violence if Zach utters a word about what he saw. Dare he tell his mum? Surely this will only make things worse for her. Terrified, Zach buries powerful rage and pain in his heart. Only his nightmares show him how scared he is.

After a few years, his uncle dies and Zach tells himself that the problem is over. Yet his inner horror remains unspoken as Zach guards the bitter betrayal and toxic hate for his uncle in his heart. This hate is part of his trauma response, it helps him keep the secret and protect the family. On the other hand, he feels wretched and guilty about his brother, so keeps distant from him, not allowing himself to contemplate the meaning of that terrible

5   Calidas, T. (2020). *I Am An Island*. London: Random House, p.58.

betrayal or the impact it has had on his life.[6] To appease his guilt, he often sends his brother and his family generous gifts. Tying himself in knots, Zach preserves the painful emotions in aspic at the centre of his heart, while on an everyday level banishing them.

When Zach marries and has his own children, he is often guarded and combustible with his new family. He finds it hard to hug his kids. Things become rocky at home. In desperation, Zach goes to his GP who listens carefully and then refers him to a trauma specialist who helps him make sense of what has happened without judgement. The trauma specialist says that his hateful thoughts and images are manifestations of trauma that are still alive in his heart and mind; his trauma and his brother's trauma are not his fault. Validation is a primary need of us all and Zach weeps with relief; the trauma specialist's words make sense and help him feel immediately less fearful. But he wonders what he can do about this pain, shame and guilt. The trauma specialist asks if he can imagine himself as very small and suffering deeply. Can he see an image of the child that he was in his mind's eye? Can he imagine caring for his suffering and embracing that child? Can he even find a way to love him?

This new curiosity about himself is a game changer for Zach. He has never considered himself as small and vulnerable, just a miserable, failing brother. Feeling horribly compromised having witnessed a terrible event has eclipsed his sense of his own suffering. He can see how scary and confusing the betrayal was for a little lad. Beginning to feel some compassion towards himself makes him feel softer inside. Maybe softness is not the same as weakness? It certainly feels like a relief to Zach.

Zach begins to understand the roots of his suffering and how scared he was long ago. When he was small, his uncle was a scare-giver, not a care-giver, and was monstrous to his brother who he knows carries the emotional scars to this day. Yet the crime was not his or his brother's. To survive, Zach learned to be a 'strong

---

6   Zach suffers from 'moral injury', a term used of someone who has broken or *has witnessed someone close to them* breaking their own moral code. Such a person is compromised at a value level and the experience typically affects their identity and their ability to trust others. Moral injury can be a result of warfare. Blaming ourselves in shame is frequently a part of moral injury, often covering deep pain entangled with trauma fear.

man' but he begins to see that this is not true strength. The more heartbreaking truth is how vulnerable they both were. He is still not able to talk to his brother about what happened but he is able to hug him (and his kids) more tightly these days, which feels good. He imagines his brother and he may be able to talk once their now elderly mother has died.

Consequences if we do not acknowledge pain

With specialist help, Zach is able to face, understand and release his powerful protective fear and the pain it guarded. Speaking the language of the heart can take great courage. Even though we may not be in a complex situation like Zach, we humans naturally fear and are on our guard to avoid pain. Guarding and holding in pain can create huge internal pressure that is so often only released in red mist rage, as we saw in Chapter 4. Our pain can fill us to the brim so we cannot see another's. It can take a long time to allow ourselves to face our pain and sometimes our minds 'forget' it (see Chapter 10). Situations can get complex, layered and tangled, as they did for Zach. Sometimes, things need to get worse before they get better.

Speaking or finding ways to express our pain

It is often when we take the courageous step of admitting our vulnerability and pain at a place of rock bottom that change can begin to happen. Something can shift if we consciously find ways to express pain in ways that feel right and authentic for us. Philip Robinson, survivor of the *Marchioness* pleasure-boat disaster on the Thames in London in 1989 that killed 51 people, including some of his close friends, suffered a great deal in the aftermath and later trained as a professional singer. He said: 'Singing is a way that my soul can talk to tragedy.'[7]

Unlocking the secrets of our hearts requires slow steps and careful thought. There may be a long road to travel, with many bumps, and we might not know what we will find at the end of it. To face the truth is a journey of faith and hope.

7　Sherman, C. (2019, 14 October). *The Quest to Cure PTSD*. Psychology Today. Philip Robinson is Chief Executive of the Yellow Heart Trust founded in 2002 that awards grants for those suffering from PTSD and/or issues related to addiction.

Competitions of pain

We might reflect on how many individuals and groups are locked in cycles of hate and violence. At the centre of such a cycle may be a wounded heart that, due to fearful messages, cannot be acknowledged, healed or relinquished. Woundedness may not even be known about consciously. Hearts can be defended and hardened and accrued with layers of justification, sometimes leading to us entering into a competition of pain with others, intractable cycles at family, societal and inter-country levels. (Cycles of destructive behaviour that originate from trauma are considered in Chapter 18.) When full of pain, it is so human for us to push our pain out rather than find its locus within us. To be healed, pain first requires acknowledgement.

The pull of continuing on in survival mode

As there was for Zach, there can be a balm in meeting pain truthfully, but for a long time it may feel much easier to keep going in survival mode. Our minds might be trotting along the same paths, but underneath we may suspect that we are living in ways that do not bring out our best selves. Maybe we skate over our painful experiences like a frozen lake, unable to stop for fear of what happens when we fall.

What we most need when in pain

Yet perhaps what we long for is being caught and held. When surrounded by our tears of loss and pain, we may long for another person to just be there with us, unflinching and strong. Maybe we might reflect on whether we have received this from someone else at some point in our lives? Or, we may recall what it has felt like to witness another's tears – maybe we felt moved and privileged like van Gogh. Do we feel humbled when a friend, child or partner takes the risk of sharing their vulnerable heart with us? That person is no longer skating or falling but has landed with us on a ledge of painful recognition. It is an act of courage to be honoured.

Witnessing another's pain

I believe that witnessing another's tears is a profound privilege. Time stands still. Tears let us know we are alive and may bring important messages, if only we can give space to listen. The release of tears also brings physiological benefits.[8] Edith Eger writes: 'Love is a four-letter word spelled "TIME".'[9] Can we respond to the expression of another's painful heart with love, offering a priceless quality of *unlimited time* that gently holds and heals, gluing us together in our shared humanity?

Pain's long road

The pain that we hold in our heart's centre may not be known and it may take time for us to uncover and understand. We can be like the princess in the fairytale 'The Princess and the Pea', who cannot locate the source of her painful discomfort. On a societal level, commitment to finding nuanced, layered and complex truths can be anathema in our current climate, which on one level prizes emotional sharing, but on another is frequently reactive and pain-averse. In summary: we can so easily live with a painful story buried inside us.

Yet, thoughtfully facing the painful truth of our experience can release us from its power and help us to grow. Fear may protect us from a pain that feels too much for us to bear. This is a paradox of pain and the purpose of fear.

These are the words written to Zach:

Pennies dropping
My revelation:
It's okay to be vulnerable
To state a feeling
And let the pennies slowly drop in relief

I validate me

---

8   Crying has physiological benefits: releasing endorphins (painkillers), dissolving stress hormones (cortisol) and releasing the connecting warmth hormone (oxytocin).

9   Eger, E. (2022). *The Gift*. London: Penguin Random House, p.72.

BREAKING-FREE POINTERS FOR HEARTBREAKING TRAUMA

▶ Trauma gives us too much experience to digest. The 'too much' of an unbearable situation can linger and trauma memories and responses get tangled with our ability to properly grieve.

▶ We can contract in fear from pain about a horrible reality we have experienced.

▶ Fear tells us we cannot bear pain. The paradox is that if we can face our pain (even a little), it may bring us freedom.

▶ It can be arduous to untangle fear's defensive messages that snag up our painful hearts: *I told you so! They are wrong! I have to do this! I don't want to talk about it.*

▶ Our painful heart can be so full up to the brim that we cannot see another's.

▶ We can get into a competition of pain, thinking ours is greater than another's.

▶ Unlocking the painful secrets of our hearts can take time. Pain can be elusive and hard to locate but it can be worth the effort of seeking it out – our pain is our truth and knowing it can help us grow and be more open to others.

▶ We long to be caught and held when in pain.

▶ When someone shares their vulnerability with us it is a privilege to be witness to it.

QUESTIONS FOR FURTHER REFLECTION

1. What is my relationship to fear? Are my fears realistic or unrealistic? Are they perhaps protecting a painful heart and old messages about myself? What is the pea under my mattress?

2. Do I have a curiosity to side-step fearful inner messages by practising intentional statements that begin: *I can, I want, I am willing, I choose*?

3. Like Zach, we are born to love – but we can learn to hate. Will what I do and reach for today stem from a loving or fearful or hateful place within me? How might I open my heart and validate my own or another's experience?

4. What is my relationship with my or another's tears and painful feelings? When I bear witness to someone's tears or my own, can I honour them and be thoughtful about their message?

RIVER MEDITATION ON PAIN

Imagine a river flowing. When you have a painful memory, thought or body sensation, try to acknowledge it, pay attention to it on an in-breath and then imagine sending it down a river in your mind on an out-breath, letting it go and relinquishing it. Take time to watch the current carry it off downstream. (This way you can find a route through your sorrow, fear and pain.) If the painful memory, thought or body sensation returns, simply return to the practice, treating yourself with the gift of spacious time for just a few precious moments. This can become a simple practice to repeat and deepen.

MEDITATION ON OPENING UP THE HEART

Sit comfortably in a chair and relax as much as possible. Lower your shoulders, loosen your jaw, feel your feet firmly on the floor and take a few deep breaths. Notice the breath going into your body and coming out again. Imagine that your breath, as you breathe in, is the loving kindness that you wish for and need. When you breathe out, you send this loving kindness out to the world. Do this several times, and feel your chest begin to soften. Maybe move your shoulders back a bit to allow more space for the breath to reach your heart. Can you feel a sense of bodily spaciousness in the giving and receiving of loving kindness? Enjoy connecting up with the things that matter, and sending loving kindness there. Honour any connection of care, compassion or sadness that this opens up in you, and thank your heart for having the intention to open up to goodness in this exercise.

You can find a short video that highlights some points from this chapter at https://www.youtube.com/watch?v=Hk8uXTeJiWA or by scanning the QR code.

Chapter 17

THE LEGACY OF LONELINESS

Trauma can leave us feeling cut off and alone.

Loneliness is an important aspect of modern life: referred to as a pandemic in the 1990s, and by *The Economist* in 2018 as 'The Leprosy of the 21st Century' and by *The Lancet* as 'A public health problem'.[1] Olivia Sagan cites the impact of contemporary societal factors on loneliness: 'War, economic desperation and impacts of global warming have pushed millions towards a particular kind of loneliness.'[2] She refers to the fact that the number of people who are displaced for the first time in recorded history is now topping 89 million and she reflects on the global impact of uprootedness and our sense of dislocation and disconnection to others. Kataryna is an example of such a person, who, in addition to loneliness, has an ongoing fear about the safety of her loved ones far away.

TRAUMA STORY: Kataryna displaced from her home

Kataryna and her young daughter Anastasia left their homeland after bombs began to fall, leaving her husband and 18-year-old son to fight the war. They are hosted with a family in a safe country, and her daughter goes to school. Kataryna is grateful for the safe place. She gets on well with her host family, who are nothing but kind, driving them around and attending to their needs. But her particular inner hell of anxiety, loneliness and profound longing

---

1 Cacioppo, J.T. and Cacioppo, S. (2018). Loneliness in the Modern age: An evolutionary theory of loneliness (ETL). *Advances in Experimental Social Psychology*, 58, 127–197.

2 Sagan, O. (2022). The loneliness epidemic. *Therapy Today*, December, p.37.

for home tugs at her from the pit of her stomach, keeping her awake at night. At Christmas time, it gives her deep solace to meet up with other Ukrainians and celebrate with their particular traditions, food and music. In this way, she feels solidarity with the others on the front line in her mind and heart. It soothes her gnawing loneliness.

Loneliness can begin early

Of course, there is truth to the existential truth that we are all essentially alone in life. To mitigate this, it is human to connect to others and this brings many joys. Yet there is much that disrupts our sense of being bonded and belonging to one another. So often, our experience of loneliness threads its way back to our earlier lives. As explored in Chapters 13 and 14, as humans we are wired for connection, and our primary sense of safety and the development of our brains are fundamentally bound up with important others. If our connections to other people were shaky, disturbed, unpredictable, compromised or non-existent when we were infants or children, or if trust has been broken through abuse, neglect or abandonment, our trauma will penetrate deeply and give us *a sense of ongoing absence of solid others.*

Having our trauma not seen or understood is profoundly lonely and triggering

We have explored how other people can traumatize us. There can be a secondary traumatization, because if what is at the heart of our trauma is hidden and not understood, we are likely to feel profoundly alone. *Lack of understanding of our trauma adds to our woundedness and perpetuates our loneliness.* Loneliness might be a hallmark of our trauma and a lack of empathy can be a trigger. As is so often the case, as our lives unfold, our wounds can be touched repeatedly, flooring us until we properly comprehend them (see Chapter 3).

The link between loneliness and shame

This link is important, as many of us who feel alone blame ourselves for feeling alone, thinking it is our fault. The truth may be much more complex. There are a multitude of socio-economic and adverse life factors that can pile up, leading to a person feeling alone and up against the world. In an individualist society, there can be an idea that we can solve our own loneliness by our own effort, but if the experience begins early in our lives or as a result of a life-changing trauma, there may not be such an easy fix.

TRAUMA STORY: Reclusive Steve

For Steve, nothing is the same after his wife of 50 years dies in a car crash. A quiet and insecure man, he has relied heavily on Jean as a bridge to negotiate the world. He grew up isolated and sometimes frightened by the unpredictable mental ill-health of his mother. Having Jean's solidity changed him – he has been deeply dependent on her.

In the immediate aftermath of the tragedy, Steve is swept along by the kindness of others. As time goes on, his friends and neighbours no longer know what to say and they tend to reach out less, and Steve does the same. He feels awkward around them. They stop mentioning Jean, which feels hurtful and leaves him feeling more alone as, at first, she is the only thing he wants to talk about. When he feels as if they don't want to know, his withdrawal is gradual but profound. After a while, when friends and neighbours engage with him, Steve starts responding blankly, which they find hard to deal with. People start to talk about him as 'odd' and he gains a reputation for being crotchety and awkward in his community.

Gradually, Steve's position in society becomes further eroded as the community centre he frequents closes its doors due to cuts. He starts hoarding milk bottles, not opening his post or answering the door. Steve becomes reclusive and increasingly obsessive. Money worries start to set in as his benefits do not keep up with inflation. On the outside, he cuts himself off from others and makes himself unreachable. He keeps his wife's coat on the hook in the hallway and won't invite anyone inside his home. In his emotional world, his life-changing loss remains unprocessed. Emotionally, he is unable to let his dead wife go. He guards the pain that remains inside him like an untouchable inner vault. It is easier for Steve to hold on to his private agony than to reach out and risk further loss and pain.

One day, Steve's nephew rings and tells him that his daughter Lisa is sick. Steve is upset about the child and remembers he used to like writing children's stories. The next day, he writes a story for Lisa and sends it to his nephew. That phone call is a lifeline and changes everything for Steve. His nephew is so impressed and moved by the quirky story that he shares it with a friend who is a children's book illustrator. One thing leads to another, and Steve is encouraged to write more stories that are illustrated and eventually published. Steve loves going to his hut in the garden and thinking up stories that might connect with a hurting child. He feels less stress when he revels in his imagination. When creativity flows from his lonely vault, he feels better.

Finding ways to connect mitigates loneliness

If you are trying to relate to a person in the throes of traumatic loneliness you may need to be prepared to go the extra mile for them, if you can. It is unfortunate that Steve's friends stop talking about Jean, as what he most needs is for his pain to be *acknowledged*. This may not be so easy to achieve in practice. A trauma sufferer may be so caught up and trapped in their symptoms that, even if you reach out to them, they may be unable to connect with you and therefore push you away. It is easy to give up, not make the effort, or judge them, not understanding the bind they are in. Many human tragedies happen not from deliberate unkindness or unwillingness to connect, but by a failure of imagination and ability to connect.

The prison of loneliness

The truth is that once we have been hurt by life, like Steve, we can harden ourselves or retreat into a defensive response so easily in order just to survive. We may know we do not feel right and may have a sense of when this change happened, but do not know how to feel better. The loneliness of developmental trauma can feel like being locked in without a key.

Unconditional love and links with loneliness

Many have suffered emotional neglect in childhood or received messages that are conditional. In order to be comfortable about being ourselves at a deep level and safe in the world, we need to have received enough consistent loving acceptance and affection when we were at our most vulnerable. Only then can we develop a sense of inner security that allows us to trust that a relationship is stable and intact and can weather setbacks, conflicts and differences of opinion or disagreements.

If, as a young child, we are soothed and our relationships are restored enough of the time, between the ages of two and three we will develop a deep-down sense that safe and important people continue to exist in our minds even when we cannot see or hear them. Psychologists called this object permanence.[3] If this developmental process has been compromised, we may struggle to feel this security in our later intimate relationships. Instead, we may feel fearful of abandonment and easily go to a fearful, painful, locked-in, scared and lonely place or tend to be continually hurt by real or imagined slights or offences.

The spiral of loneliness

If we have experienced deep and isolated loneliness as a result of the trauma, we can then learn to expect it. We can keep on doing the same

---

3   Many of us can tolerate some degree of relational ambiguity. This means having a capacity to not be completely consumed by worrying about another person's rejection of us. When we argue with our loved ones, we can later bounce back. Even if they are not physically with us, we can trust that we are held in a loving way in their mind. All these involve object constancy – the ability to maintain an emotional bond with others despite difficulties and distance. This idea was developed by Jean Piaget. Object permanence is a cognitive skill we acquire at around 2 to 3 years old. Explanation from Psychology Today, August 2018: www.psychologytoday.com/us/blog/living-emotional-intensity/201808/are-your-loved-ones-out-sight-out-mind (accessed 09/01/24).

things, even though they do not fill the void: sometimes it feels safer to stay with what we know rather than risk doing something new. Steve's fruitless litany of anxious rituals are a manifestation of, and not a solution to, his fearful loneliness.

Loneliness impacts our bodies

There is a physiological aspect to this. 'A lonely body is a stressed body,' writes Noreena Hertz.[4] She goes on to explain that our bodies become exhausted and overly inflamed in chronic loneliness. The stress is ongoing and so our bodies do not easily relax. Loneliness is often associated with depression and other mental health difficulties and may also be linked with illnesses such as cancer, heart disease and high blood pressure. In his stressed state, Steve's trauma-fuelled rituals perpetuate his suffering and overall ill-health until he becomes open to something different after his nephew offers him a lifeline. Steve goes on to learn that, as literature and philosophy have pointed to for centuries, being lonely can be transformed by creativity.

It may not be easy to soothe deeply lonely people

Steve is able to take a journey of growth with his loneliness, but some of us continue to feel like Robinson Crusoe, marooned on a desert island, distant from everyone in our inability to trust others. We may have relationships but find difficulty in being open and honest with others, so the relationships do not satisfy us and rather perpetuate the loneliness. It is ironic. What ought to be a source of nourishment may in fact just feel like everlasting hard work. Relationships do not reach the spot. If we feel deeply alone we may be very dismissive of any kind of care – if it has never been there for us and we defend against needing it. We may become attached to a single friend, only to scurry, crab-like, back into our habitual loneliness the rest of the time. Ironically and sometimes tragically, we can be left to continue and perpetuate this failure to connect.

4   Hertz, N. (2020). *The Lonely Century*. London: Sceptre, p.24.

The impact of long isolation

Someone with a deep sense of being alone may fear others, so an enforced isolation such as a pandemic lockdown might suit them well on one level. They may find socializing and being with others a strain, so the break is a relief. On another level, such a person may long to be loved and cared for, but they may fear it even more deeply. Chronic and reinforced loneliness may be one of the legacies of a long pandemic: when we are barricaded in, we may miss out on the most important things. Someone who struggled with a tendency towards loneliness prior to the pandemic may be too fearful to emerge after so much isolation. Fearful separation becomes reinforced and, for some, remaining apart can feel safer than connecting with others. Loneliness is easily reinforced. Yet we are built for connection and without it there can be consequences. Covid-19 was experienced by us all very differently: enforced isolation also made many of us more aware of the vital necessity of contact and touch, how much closeness we missed and how much the lack of it affected us. There were some wonderful community-led responses that offered support, particularly to those who live alone. I wonder how much such initiatives have been sustained, now that the pandemic is over. What is the legacy of prolonged separation on us as a global society?

Ways of mitigating loneliness at a community level

How can we respond to pervading yet maybe hidden loneliness in our community? Even the most prickly, isolated person is likely to welcome the question 'What is going on for you?' if they believe it is sincerely and openly asked. We can ask ourselves, what do they need me to understand? If we are honest with ourselves, we may sometimes be a little afraid of not knowing what to do when we hear the answer. It is not always easy to know how to speak to a neighbour who appears awkward, alone and isolated, but a two-minute exchange may be more meaningful than we will ever know. To look someone in the eye and give them space and time to respond to a question can feel risky, yet compassion is a two-way street, linking us creatively with others, relieving our own loneliness. There are health benefits to care. Caring for another slows us down and soothes our vagus nerve, increasing the health of our immune system and heart.

Sometimes it can help to have an inner 'word with ourselves', take a breath and soothe the part of ourselves that is scared to take risks with strangers, and not be disheartened if it doesn't work out smoothly or our offer is rejected. To take the risk of connection: *something good may happen.* A person living alone may find it easier to talk when strolling side by side with someone, rather than feeling the pressure of eye contact face to face. If we feel alone, what is spoken about is way less important than the engagement or a connecting gesture of kindness. A little goes a long way. These are words that I wrote for Steve:

> *I long to be got*
> *I long for deep*
> *For someone to*
> *Reach what I feel*
> *And need*
> *Hurts*
> *Lows*
> *Everything*

BREAKING-FREE POINTERS WHEN REACHING LONELY PLACES AFTER TRAUMA

- ▶ This aspect of trauma may be exacerbated by the increase of global dislocations, disconnection and the dereliction of individuals and communities.
- ▶ Socio-economic and adverse life conditions can foster isolation and loneliness.
- ▶ If we feel profoundly unseen by others early in life, we can find difficulty believing that others hold us in mind if they are not physically present, leading to insecurity and loneliness. This primary trauma can be reinforced as adverse life stresses pile up.
- ▶ If we find difficulty in deeply trusting others, relationships can feel like everlasting hard work. If care has never been there, we defend against needing it. Hence loneliness is not an easy fix.

- Our bodies can become chronically inflamed by loneliness.
- Loneliness can become transformed, as it was for Steve, by self-discovery and creativity.
- Acknowledgement of pain and simple acts of kindness can mitigate loneliness as we are wired for connection. Care of others does us good too.

QUESTIONS FOR FURTHER REFLECTION

1. Do I feel the hell of loneliness at times? Do I feel powerless to change this? What soothes this pain? What helps me feel alive and connected?
2. Do I recognize part of me that feels empty or alone? If so, can I learn to check in with my inner self and develop a relationship with the parts of me that I may have been afraid to know about?
3. Do I know others who live alone and are difficult to connect with in my community? How might I reach out to them, and/or let go of any judgements in order to imagine their loneliness or their loss?

A MEDITATION ON COMPASSION

Imagine resting back into hands that 'listen' and hold you, that want to accept the depths of you, that connect with you effortlessly, easily.

Imagine that the hands that listen, hold and support you are saying, *'I want to tell you that I am listening, that I hear you, I hold you, we hold each other. The weight is shared, we are together, understood. The power is shared, we are grounded together. We can change things together from this place of understanding, from this place of us. You are met with compassion. It makes all the difference.'*

From here, imagine someone else who is suffering and invite them into where you are right now.

Use your imagination to think about the nature of their suffering and what it might feel like to be them. Send them your loving compassion and hope for their recovery and healing.

You can find a short video that highlights some points from this chapter at https://www.youtube.com/watch?v=FKhivEeH8xY or by scanning the QR code.

— Chapter 18 —

THE POWER OF DESTRUCTIVE CYCLES

Trauma can make us go round in escalating circles, fuelled by fear and pain.

A destructive cycle can develop as a complex attempt to both express our pain and avoid it. Yet like a truck that has lost control, destructive patterns have the potential to inflict untold hurt.

What are destructive cycles?

These cycles can involve addictive behaviours such as alcoholism or drug taking (as was explored in Chapter 5), or they may manifest in subtler ways. Note these two truths about destructive cycles: first, if we are in one, it can be hard to see what is really happening, as we may be too fearful and trapped to see; second, the momentum of a cycle often becomes so compelling that escaping can be extremely difficult.

Destructive processes arise as a solution to the problem of emotional pain, so changing our behaviour takes personal courage – to face the pain and deal with it another way and find the right kind of help and support. A third truth: destructiveness can often be hidden amidst good things. In the following case of Sanjay, this discovery comes as a big surprise.

TRAUMA STORY: Sanjay – this is hurting you

Sanjay is a nurse who does long shift work. He loves his job and is good at it, almost to the extent that it dominates his life and his identity. Nursing reminds him of being the eldest back at home, caring for his five younger siblings. When their ducks were all in order, his mother was civil to him.

In his adult life, Sanjay feels safe when there is a mountain of responsibility on his shoulders. It is reassuringly familiar to feel that he can create order through sheer hard graft. On a deeper level, this behaviour is fuelled by a vicious inner critical voice that constantly presses him on to further heights – a voice that he took in from his mother long ago.

Sanjay leaves home for work early before his family are awake and is frequently not home until after bedtime. His kids start acting out: one of them is in trouble at school. His wife tells him he is working too much and becomes resentful of the burdens on her, but Sanjay finds his work so compelling that the stress at home makes him take on more shifts.

Sanjay finds meaning and purpose in attending to others in extremis – the more cases the better! Spreading himself thin is as natural to him as breathing. He expends huge amounts of energy reassuring his patients with a smile or joke when they are frightened and uncertain. Sanjay is like an actor who loves being on his stage. As resources are stretched ever thinner, Sanjay's shifts become extended and more frenetic, with fewer practitioners and more patients to triage. Yet Sanjay seems to have endless capacity. Everyone relies on dependable Sanjay to step in when there is a crisis on the ward. When his buzzer goes, Sanjay flies down the ward to respond.

Gradually, the cracks begin to show as Sanjay's sleep becomes disturbed. He starts having panic attacks. A cardiac colleague checks things out and his heart is healthy. He is referred to the hospital counsellor who tells him he needs to stop work and reset his mind and body. Sanjay is appalled: who will run the ward then? The counsellor is unequivocal: 'Your first priority is to you and your family, Sanjay. Yes, the need is great but what is happening is serious: your job is hurting you.' Sanjay stops in his tracks. He is flabbergasted. How can this be true? Yet, deep down he knows he has become caught up in his own Catherine Wheel and he fears he might spin out of control. Reluctantly, but with relief, he takes time off and has a big think.

Challenges of helping someone in a destructive cycle

Watching someone close to us who is in a destructive cycle of behaviour can be hard to bear, and can also be frustrating. You can be led on a merry dance when the person you love is caught up in the throes of a destructive loop. Though you may see what is going on, they may not. They may be afraid or unwilling to acknowledge the forces they are caught up in. The science of fear is complex, and being in an arousal state can even be exciting, compelling and addictive: think of the enjoyment of funfairs or ghost rides.

Looking through the presentation to the underlying fear

Though there may be an addictive element, when we are trapped in a destructive cycle we are likely to be frightened at a deep level. *Fear held in the nervous system often tells us to hold on and resist doing anything different as the vortex speeds up.* The power of this fear can be immense, and sometimes have a life/death intensity. Those who try to help or offer solutions are likely to be frustrated by this. They may be told something like: 'You say I need to get into the sea, but I am holding on to a raft for dear life!'

Respect for how a cycle has been a survival strategy

To help someone in a destructive cycle, it is important to begin with respect. The power of the destructive cycle and its baseline of fear needs to be acknowledged. After all, the cycle has helped us survive so far, and has become essential to us, is maybe bound up with our personality, and likely to be deeply engraved in habits of body and mind. Yet, the power of the destructive force can feel like desperately walking in quicksand – really hard to escape, even if we want to. On the other side, watching someone you love hurting themselves is a particular agony: all you want is for them to stop.

Illusiveness of cycles make them hard to grasp

Destructive cycles can be obvious to the observer, but when we are living them, they can be illusive and, like a nettle, hard to grasp. With conviction, we may justify what we are doing, while inside we are full of fears: fear of judgement, fear of losing what we know, fear of admitting that we are lost and hanging on by our fingertips, if the truth is told. One thing leads to another in destructive cycles, and pain often gets missed. We may go to great lengths to hide our terrified vulnerability (or project it on to others like Sanjay): hiding is a trauma symptom. Destructiveness can be hidden within good things. It is a paradox that the forces of creation and destruction flow closely together: the two currents may not be easy to distinguish or pull apart.

Asking difficult questions of ourselves

Our survival solution becomes the air that we breathe and our default position. The solution may not be all bad, in fact it may spring from good motivations and therefore feel imperative and easy to justify. Sometimes to change the destructiveness, we may need to be prepared to let go of something good. We can ask ourselves a penetrating question: is this behaviour *really* good for me and others? Am I balanced or is something skewed? Sometimes, like Sanjay, we may have a laudable vocation to challenge injustice or make a difference in the world, but we can still be hurting others or ourselves in the process. If we feel we have no choice about our actions and behaviour, the turbo charge of trauma may be what is hidden and keeping us trapped.

How we can lose our moral compass

As is often the case with destructive cycles that grow in momentum, we can so easily lose our moral compass, which can become part of the debris caught up in a trauma wheel. Imagine a young woman who experiences terror at the hand of an abusive and controlling father. She may escape his clutches, but remains on the edge of society – a highly vulnerable young person. We could imagine that she might cross a rubicon from trauma terror and rage to developing an inner compulsion to right wrongs. She then gets caught up in an underworld that brings criminals to their knees. After a while, her unconscious desire for revenge on her father leads her to become a vigilante, using violence to bring perpetrators to 'justice'. This young woman's destructive cycle emerges like a slowly turning vice as an attempt to help manage her pain and unresolved trauma.

The power of emotional charge is legion

With destructive cycles, there is so often a crescendo in the force of an emotional charge that we cannot relinquish because of the relief and distraction the behaviours bring us. It is so powerful and we feel so lost that our natural sense of right and wrong can be eclipsed. For our young abused girl, becoming a vigilante *makes sense from a trauma perspective*. She had been in real danger and her body and mind are now trying to keep her safe by punishing men. *To understand our trauma cycles, we need to be humble in understanding what they are protecting or are a 'solution' for.*

Examples of destructive cycles

Destructive cycles may reveal themselves in behaviour such as habitually shouting at the kids, overeating, overworking or automatically taking an overly defensive stance towards the world. A person may over-analyse everything, shop obsessively, over-exercise, break laws, use porn, endlessly perfect the domestic environment, fret about everything that isn't perfect, endlessly change location, go on multiple holidays or find a myriad of other ways to survive. We keep doing these things because they temporarily satisfy something, while we ignore the costs to ourselves and others. We tell ourselves: I just need to do this. But we might ask ourselves: what will I feel if I stop?

How can we stop the force of the revolving wheel? It is very difficult to change when our patterns take over our lives. Rather than choosing to wear the coat, the coat starts to wear us. In the case of the next family, the consequences of this can sometimes end in tragedy.

TRAUMA STORY: A cycle and its consequences

Bess and George have three children. Their youngest, John, is sensitive and withdrawn and is picked on at school due to his stammer. As a teenager, John spends a lot of time gaming with online friends. Bess and George try to restrict this, but back off when John lashes out at them. Secretly, they long for him to be like their older children, who are sociable and cheerful, not bringing them any real problems or worries. John senses their anxiety and frustration and perceives it as judgement and rejection of him. He withdraws more and starts to truant from school. Eventually, John leaves home and appears to be managing okay but secretly he is gambling, taking more risks and getting into severe debt and is threatened by loan sharks. He doesn't ring his parents, but they tell themselves he needs his space. They busy themselves with their other responsibilities.

One day, when John is 22, the doorbell rings and Bess and George open the door to the police. John has taken his own life: they have found him in a pool of blood in his bath. In horror, they discover John has been in debt to multiple loan companies, pursuing him to extract their dues. They didn't see this coming. The terrible truth is that in a paroxysm of shame and despair, John chooses to end his life rather than face the crippling shame of what he has done and bear the imagined disapproval of the world.

In their terrible loss, Bess and George are filled with their own shame, guilt and remorse. Had they driven John away? Could they have done more to help their son? Bess's mental health, in particular, declines dramatically. She is consumed with grief, and relentlessly berates herself. She cannot forgive herself for her failings as a parent. She cannot eat or sleep, and her quality of life diminishes massively.

George urges Bess to seek psychological help. They both realize they need to access support. They join a group of parents who have experienced the death of a child by suicide and begin to find profound solace in knowing they are not alone. They become campaigners for changes in the law regarding advertising around gambling and regularly speak in the media about John's story. They are determined to help raise awareness about suicide to prevent others becoming trapped like him.

Bess needs a great deal of help to soothe the consuming whirlwind of guilt and self-attack that propels her obsessively and relentlessly. It takes a lot of humility for her to admit that she was not able to control or determine the choices John made. She and George are also honest about their regrets. It is so painful to face them. It is so difficult to think about how their love did not somehow always reach their son. Bess finds it difficult to accept her pain and powerlessness. In time, she learns to befriend the powerful undercurrent of fear that has always been with her. Maybe, on some level, she had been somehow afraid in her parenting of John?

Being prepared to dig deep

Great courage is needed for us to take a long hard look at what is not working and reach for something different from our old patterns. Courage because this necessitates us facing our failures, our fragilities and our fears. Like a complex musical fugue with many interweaving parts, it may take some time and hard work for something painful and fearful to be worked through honestly and without flinching until some resolution is reached, slowly, step by step. To do this is an act of faith and hope. Sometimes, despite our best wishes, things go wrong and it is too late. It is a tragedy when the wheels spin out of control, and, as was tragically the case with John, the body and mind cannot take any more pain.

When we face our own or another's destructive cycle, maybe there is a point when we are faced with a choice: *do we choose life or death?* If I choose life, what difficult choice about *now* might I be faced with? What is the next thing I can do to follow life?

Reaching for something new after trauma feels like a risk but it is essential for us to grow. On the edge of what we know might something new be beckoning us, like a distant clarion? We might still be afraid and the drumbeat of fear may still be compelling, but at the same time can we still, tentatively, dare to reach for the something new?

The following words are written for Sanjay, the nurse. They might also fit for any of those caught up in destructive cycles.

I'm scared
I thrash about
This is how I live
Same old wheel
Round and round
Faster and faster
How can I stop

This endless repeat
Just trust

BREAKING-FREE POINTERS FOR DESTRUCTIVE CYCLES

▶ Destructive cycles are a complex mix – both an expression of and an attempt to avoid our pain.

▶ Destructive cycles are difficult for us to escape. Fear tells us to hold on and resist doing anything different as the vortex speeds up.

▶ If we are close to someone in a destructive cycle, the starting place can be to respect it. The cycle is a solution and has helped them survive so far. It may also be engraved in their personality, body and mind and it may be a herculean task for them to change – it's as natural as breathing.

▶ A destructive cycle is usually easier to see in someone else.

▶ We can be busy (in destructive cycles) hiding our vulnerabilities or projecting them on to others (like Sanjay).

▶ Destructiveness can be hidden within good things.

▶ It can take great courage to look at what is not working and reach out to do something different. A person will need a support framework that attends to all aspects of the cycle as a whole and be encouraged to take small steps of hope. Life can bring good things on the other side.

QUESTIONS FOR FURTHER REFLECTION

1. What do I do to excess? Do I get into repetitious cycles that I do not seem to be able to change or have control over? Might this be a pattern that saves me from knowing about something else? Might fear be at the centre of my cycle?

2. Am I 'revolving or evolving'?[1] Is the way that I am living bringing out my best self? Are things in balance? Am I prepared to make changes to further my own growth? Might this mean getting very

---

1 Eger, E. (2021). *The Gift*. London: Random House, p.152.

honest and uncomfortable with how I am and why? What might help me to begin to do this?

3. What gets my attention every day? (It is a truth that what gets our attention grows.) Might I develop an interest in learning about my own patterns of behaviour and studying them?

4. Do I choose life or death? If life, what helps me to pursue creation, not destruction?

MEDITATION ON FEAR AND CALM

Take time to go inside to focus on your inner life. Start with the head, then pay attention to sensations in the chest, torso and abdomen, focus on your backbone, arms, pelvis, thighs, knees, calves and feet. Pay exquisite attention to muscles, noticing any tension. Are there any parts where fear may be held?

Using your imagination, and staying attuned to the body, be aware of any part that feels as though it holds too much. Take time to notice any feelings that may come up in response to this feeling of 'too much'. Imagine moving from a place of momentum and 'too much' to entering a clearing on the savannah, where you can lie down and rest. There is nothing to do right now but to enjoy this time out. Notice what it is that has felt like 'too much'. Are you drawn to it? Notice what it feels like now not to be *in* the 'too much' zone but in a place of awareness, noticing and resting, letting the 'too much' go. Just for now, choose to be in a different place of restful reflection and restoration.

You can find a short video that highlights some points from this chapter at https://www.youtube.com/watch?v=f83XgjiQuow or by scanning the QR code.

— Chapter 19 —

YOUR TRAUMA, MY TRAUMA

Trauma wounds are catching.

No man is an island, entire of itself; every man is a piece
of the continent, a part of the main.[1] (Donne)

Trauma transmits between individuals, within families and organizations and at a societal level. The truth of this statement is powerfully revealed in the following story of Chantal at a conference.

TRAUMA STORY: Chantal, the adoptive mother

Chantal (from Chapter 13, who, with her husband Ben, has adopted two traumatized children) attends a social services conference for adoptive parents. She feels a buzzing exhaustion after being on the receiving end of her child's emotional outbursts (e.g. 'Go crap yourself, loser') for several years now. She has learned not to shout back, and any attempt to set up sanctions only succeeds in setting up a control war, which she always loses. After the conference introductions, the trauma-informed social worker begins to speak…

> 'One of the first things I have to remind myself when I meet a foster carer or an adopter in need of support is that I am not seeing the person they once were. Traumatized children can traumatize their carers.' Chantal feels as though a big finger stabs

---

1   Donne, J. (1923). Meditations XVII. In *Devotions Upon Emergent Occasions*. Cambridge: The University Press.

> at the middle of her forehead. Bullseye. I am no longer me, the person I once was. She is lost and what remains is wreckage and distant memories.[2]

Chantal feels the bullseye of empathy because her truth has been stated: her son's trauma has become hers. *Trauma touches trauma.* If we line up dominoes and touch one of them, they will cascade down. *We are impacted by another person's unprocessed experience.* Our responses to someone else's trauma can be profound or subtle. Such responses can take us by surprise when the trauma is not our direct experience.

The myth of the individual self

In the Western world, we tend to think mistakenly that the individual is paramount, autonomous and self-sufficient. As Richard Coles powerfully reflects following the death of his partner: 'We are a library of other people', pointing to the truth that we are all connected to each other, more deeply and profoundly than we may realize.[3] It follows that the *too much* of trauma is also picked up between us, yet trauma's inside nature can make this a hidden truth. Trauma can be absorbed from another person or from a trauma-laden environment. We can hold secondary trauma without knowing, its effects can remain trapped and unacknowledged. This can add another burden: when things are not seen or understood, we can feel guilt, confusion and shame *because we think we should not be feeling like this.* Being around her son's trauma leaves Chantal feeling like 'wreckage', with a strange buzzing tiredness. Let us think about why.

The transmission of trauma charge

Trauma – the charged stress response, frozen in time, often not known about or spoken – is like unprocessed data blocking our pipes. Chantal describes a 'buzzing exhaustion' and the word 'buzzing' is

---

2   Adapted and quoted directly, with permission through the publisher, from Donovan, S. (2013). *No Matter What: An Adoptive Family's Story of Hope, Love and Healing.* London: Jessica Kingsley Publishers, p.305.

3   Coles, R. (2021). *The Madness of Grief.* London: W&N, p.130.

worth examining with regards to secondary trauma and physiology.[4] Her son's primary terror (carried under the surface) has made its way into her too. Chantal's buzzing is caused by trauma cascading into her brain and body. We can look at the biology of this. Emotional charge affects the functioning of the limbic area of the brain. The buzzing is due to an increased charge of cortisol, caused by the reduced capacity of our brain's hypothalamic-pituitary-adrenal axis, the place where we regulate stress.[5] Chantal loves her son, and their emotional connection and her responsibility for him mean his stress buzz becomes hers. As we saw in Chapter 12, the buzz of trauma may contribute to a wide variety of bodily symptoms.

Trauma's buzz makes us constrict rather than flow

If we pursue our pipe metaphor, it can be seen how trauma might impede the free flow of our emotions because it simply clogs up our bodies and minds. How? Trauma's buzz tends to make our bodies and minds constrict *reactively*, holding on to our responses for the sake of survival, rather than acknowledging them and letting them go. Trauma tells us to contract and carry on rather than open up, trust and let go. This diminishes our capacity to respond fully to life in the present.

How we are impacted by others in trauma

The *same processes* occur whether we are traumatized ourselves or whether we respond to someone else who is traumatized. In the story of Ezra (Chapter 14), the volunteer Jane was immediately physiologically impacted by his powerful outburst. Her heart beats and she is full of emotional charge. On the *outside*, she 'contains' him and does not respond in kind. Neither does adoptive mother Chantal (above) scream back at her child, 'No, you go crap *yourself*.' However, just because we might not respond *externally* does not mean that we

---

4   Chantal's exhaustion is rather like the flop/submit response that was examined in Chapter 7. Living with her angry son has left her with a sense of painful defeat; she is resigned and robotic.

5   www.ncbi.nlm.nih.gov/pmc/articles/PMC3182008, accessed 09/01/24.

are not internally impacted by the 'too much' of trauma. Both Chantal and Jane carry the charge of trauma *inside* them. Sally Donovan describes the transmission of trauma in a graphic way: 'Trauma is like a big balloon; apply pressure at one end by squeezing it and it expands at the other end. The amount of trauma is the same, it just moves.'[6]

Emotional acknowledgement helps mitigate trauma responses

Thankfully, both Jane and Chantal are helped. If the pressure of trauma's charge causes us to *contract*, it follows that to counteract this, we need *places of emotional expansion*. The 'bullseye' of empathy is a necessary acknowledgement of the trauma that Chantal has sustained over a long period, and offers her huge *relief and release*, and some practical help follows. In the International Group in Chapter 14, trauma-informed checks and balances are set up to assist the team working alongside traumatized guests. Volunteer Jane attends a 'debrief' after the session and is able to share with a leader how scared she was with Ezra. *Acknowledgement helps trauma resolution.* When given space to do so, Jane releases the charge and lets it go. Next time she sees Ezra, she is fine.

What is covered up may emerge in other ways

Chantal's traumatization occurs through the overt aggression of her son, and the source of its activation seems clear. However, it is also possible that her son's trauma could activate an underlying trauma in Chantal. Trauma touches trauma in under-the-surface ways, when the original trauma is not known about, not acknowledged or simply covered up. Rather like putting a lid on a pressure cooker, hiding something and carrying on can add to trauma's charge and power.

---

6   Donovan, S. (2019). *The Unofficial Guide to Therapeutic Parenting: The Teen Years.* London: Jessica Kingsley Publishers, p.137.

Intergenerational trauma transmission

Trauma's effects can be quite subtle, like fine filigree reaching into the crevices of life. They can sometimes surprise us. We might reflect that our ancestors, only a few generations ago, resolved disputes by fighting duels. The legacy of violence in our cultural history may show itself in our contemporary appetite for the murder mystery genre, the emotional charge remaining and emerging in another way.

Organizations can become traumatized

It is easy to dismiss such ideas, but let's think about organizations that cover things up. Imagine a person working in a firm uncovers inconsistencies in pay levels. She decides to investigate past records and then discovers paperwork relating to a serious malpractice that was covered up. So, when she challenges the board, they become defensive and warn her off aggressively. Whistleblowers who threaten a culture of covering up truth are frequently scapegoated and blamed for being 'the problem'. Within such a scenario there may be an element of trauma fear infiltrating the organization's capacity to respond: *its culture has become no longer open and supportive, but rather defensive and constricted.* Gabor Maté writes that the things that 'appear to us now as normal need the greatest scrutiny...like crustacea placed in cold water, we haven't noticed the heat being turned up to boiling point'.[7]

Imagine that a person from a violent background is the founder of a business. He then goes on to treat his staff in rigid and threatening ways. Such an organization might then carry this entrepreneur's 'charge', tending to operate in 'red-zone' survival mode, where everything has high priority but attention to detail and the completion of tasks is low. In this way, *personal trauma has become scaled up into the collective*: the system has become traumatized. Too much 'red zone' can lead organizations to then become numb in the 'blue zone' and collectively 'miss' obvious wrongs and injustices or just glibly cover them up. This can be because individuals become frightened

---

7   Bramley, E.V. (2023). The trauma doctor: Gabor Maté on happiness, and how to heal our deepest wounds. *The Guardian* (Health and wellbeing), 12 April 2023, accessed 26/12/23. In this interview, Maté was speaking about his recent book, Maté, G. and Maté, D. (2022). *The Myth of Normal*. London: Ebury.

of red-zone conflict and hide in blue-zone unresponsiveness. The 'shadow' side of an organization is likely to emerge when rules are not enforced, poor performance is not held to account, and conflict and bad practice are not dealt with effectively and thoroughly. The heat is turned up but no one has noticed: the organization has become toxic.

Trauma transmission in families

We can think that our personal history does not connect to others. Yet the tentacles of trauma can emit confusion or perplexity in ways that are not clear cut. This can happen in families. As we reflect on our own personal histories, we might find that the behaviour of those closest to us might not always quite make sense, and this can sometimes get in the way of the flow of our relationship with them, leaving us subtly feeling not quite comfortable or safe. We might notice that when certain things are mentioned, a family member becomes uncomfortable, non-responsive or dismissive and brittle; or that they have an inexplicably strong determination to live a certain way, at the expense of other ways. *What is not allowed to be expressed and processed at the time can profoundly affect us later.* This can sometimes emerge later, as in the following story of Lin and his family.

TRAUMA STORY: Lin's displaced family

Lin's parents are traumatized by being uprooted and displaced, and witnessing the horrors of violence and civil war in their early lives. Reaching a safe country, they settle and fervently devote themselves to finding work. After marrying, Lin's parents quickly become pillars of their poor community. His father and mother become charity workers and are endlessly sacrificial. Then they go on to have their only child: Lin.

When he is upset as a young boy, Lin frequently receives a message from his parents that his feelings are not important compared to the needs of others around him. His parents also sometimes become suddenly very angry with each other, which scares him. To survive this, Lin dismisses his vulnerable feelings, blaming himself for his 'weakness'. He desperately loves his parents, but does not feel close to them and is wary of them. He makes his own way in life, throwing himself obsessively into his academic studies, where he has early success.

Some years later, after a number of setbacks, Lin collapses emotionally and is unable to function for some years. With some psychological help, he slowly pieces things together from his history. He understands that his parents' benign determination to help others sprang from their own traumatic early losses, having been displaced from their war-torn homeland. They are not bad people: they 'project' their own adversity onto the needs of vulnerable people. They had been determined to make things better for others but they had no space inside to grieve for all they had lost. This made them brittle and driven.[8] Their unprocessed loss and trauma emerged in their inability to deal with their own child when he was distressed, cruelly dismissing his feelings and telling him to be strong. Their strong belief system gave no space for Lin to be vulnerable, hence his emotional collapse later.

As he recovers, Lin feels a great sense of sorrow, for himself and his parents. He feels a sorrow weightier than his own: he expresses what they could not. Ultimately, his open exploration and the courageous sharing of his feelings becomes healing for him and his parents. They open up and find ways to talk about these matters. Lin is enormously relieved to uncover his trauma story and understand why he was afraid of his parents and of his feelings. His hidden trauma is transformed by the jigsaw pieces of acknowledgement and understanding.

Unprocessed trauma needs space

Lin's parents' trauma solution was to attempt to save others, but the charge of their unprocessed trauma emerged in their erratic and neglectful parenting. They were well-meaning people but at some level they could not bear the vulnerability of their own child. If we are not able to process big life events, we devise survival strategies to avoid

---

8   Psychological projection is a defence mechanism we unconsciously employ in order to cope with difficult feelings or emotions. Psychological projection involves projecting undesirable feelings or emotions onto someone else, rather than admitting to or dealing with the unwanted feelings.

our painful memories and feelings. These strategies can impact families in complex ways. It can often be that individuals in families pick up and carry the unprocessed feelings of other members. Unprocessed trauma may lead us to judge or blame others without understanding them, limit our capacity to feel peaceful or free in the present, or we may be over-fearful in our approach to life, unable to take risks or see life as a gift. We may feel an uncanny pull to explore or tell the story of a member of our family who has gone before and not quite understand why. For instance, a grandchild of a displaced individual may have a powerful wish to connect with place and locality, putting roots down in a way that was impossible for their grandparent. Trauma can show up in a tendency towards perfectionism or a wish to *put something right*, to somehow make up for what has gone before. In such ways, the scars of trauma can go through generations. However, trauma stories from past generations can be transformed. With awareness, we can make sense of what has gone before in a way that is honouring and creative. For example, in response to a parent's wartime experience as a displaced refugee, a person may find meaning and creativity in working to relieve the suffering of migrants.

We can become an 'overflow' for other people's traumas

Sometimes, as in the case of Lin, the legacies of family, intergenerational or institutional trauma become clear later when light is shone and difficulties are seen and understood. Sometimes trauma is revealed in uncanny ways: the grandchild of a war victim who suffered starvation might develop an eating disorder. This could be an example of trauma being passed down the generations. In other cases, like Chantal and her son, trauma can travel upwards, as Chantal becomes her son's overflow. Unravelling complex stories with openness and honesty is part of becoming sensitive to trauma. This can be a courageous thing to do, but can bring hope of changing old patterns that are stuck.

Becoming trauma informed and sensitive

To mitigate the effects of trauma in a family or organization we need to *step back and reflect in order to best scrutinize*. This way, we can become more alert to behaviour that does not make sense. We might observe in ourselves a puzzling lack of responsiveness to injustice, or perhaps a feeling that seems out of proportion to the incident that has triggered it. These might be signs of our own trauma, or responses to a trauma embedded in the system. Noticing the signs is part of becoming *trauma sensitive*. Often, *tell-tale signs of trauma are feeling 'too much' or 'too little' in response to something.* As we hold our ingrained behaviours up to the light, we have the power to change discriminatory, inflexible or stuck patterns of behaviour around us.

Triggers so easily lead us repeatedly down the same paths (as we saw in Chapter 3). However, becoming *trauma informed* and educated about the subtle yet effective power of trauma processes can begin to unfreeze and free up things that feel blocked. Becoming trauma informed may require us to have the confidence to *trust our intuition or 'felt sense'* when something feels wrong. In families, we can ask whether it may be worth having open and honest conversations about things that feel stuck or suboptimal. Are relationships strong and loving enough to withstand the challenge of this? Sometimes, even the possibility of having an open and honest conversation can soften us. Having the confidence to say no to something that does not feel right can take courage. Within an organization, it might take a resignation or sacking followed by an honest analysis of findings in the culture, and a resetting of intention, for a culture to be reformed. From this position, an institution might be able to think in careful and detailed ways about how it might respond more openly when challenged, and protect itself with robust checks and balances to provide a clear and open ethos. New information, rather like updates on a computer program, can allow for movement and growth. It can relieve a stuck system.

The legacy of societal trauma – how do we teach history?

When a trauma is historic and societal, in order to grapple with the hold it has over us, we may need to understand the nuances and complexities of the original event. One response to trauma is to simplify or whitewash complex truth. I recently visited Scotland, and learned for the first time about the Lowland Clearances between 1760 and

1830, when the landowner or laird removed tenant farmers from their smallholdings, forcing them to move elsewhere in the country or even abroad. The Wikipedia entry suggests this was voluntary migration, but the truth is more sinister. Many families were forcibly removed, often at gunpoint, and their properties burned. This is an example of the trauma response of 'too little'. It is human to rewrite complex and uncomfortable history in an attempt to simplify and neutralize it, put a gloss on the reality of trauma, or avert our gaze individually and collectively (see Chapter 14). Unless the truth is faced, it is likely that injustices and domination of one group over another are perpetuated.

Whether family, organizational or societal trauma, *we carry forward what we do not process*. This is what is meant by intergenerational transmission of trauma. We need space, time and attention to allow what has happened to us to be known about and given words and meaning. Doing so gives us more options and freedom. Of course, it is hard to speak up and step in when we perceive injustice, or try to change a system that is broken or not as safe or open as we would like. It is courageous to explore and give voice to something that has remained hidden. The process is likely to cause us discomfort, yet the rewards come in the experience of something new emerging.

These words were written for Lin:

When there is pain
What happens next?
Is it mine or yours?
If yours then
What do I do with it?

Can I give space to
My pain separating it
From yours
Honouring both
Broken threads woven
The cloth smoothed

BREAKING-FREE POINTERS WHEN WE PICK UP TRAUMA FROM OTHERS

▸ We touch each other's traumas in profound or subtle ways. The scars of trauma can go through generations: we carry forward what we do not process.

▸ We can become traumatized from being in a trauma-laden environment such as an organization.

▸ We are more connected than we know. The stress charge of trauma is catchy.

▸ We need a bullseye of empathy and space to step back and be thoughtful about trauma's legacy in a family, community or organization.

▸ Openness counteracts what is hidden in trauma.

▸ We can mitigate and become freer of trauma by having the confidence to ask questions, challenge behaviour that seems wrong and say 'no' when something feels wrong.

▸ New information can free up a stuck system and 'pipes' can flow more freely.

QUESTIONS FOR FURTHER REFLECTION

1. Do I know any institutions or relationships that seem to be unduly activated by stress or stress responses when dealing with life events? Might these spring from another place and time?

2. What might help me 'unblock the pipes' of my own ways of relating? Do I notice traces of trauma fear or a feeling of numbness in the presence of someone, or when I think about something I find challenging?

3. How do I, my family or my organization deal with life events? Openly and flexibly, or in a stressed or rigid way? Are there uncomfortable blocks and signals that my body is aware of? Can I step back and become thoughtful about my habitual responses, and trust my body to give me the information and signals if something is 'not right'? Can I free myself to question, do something different, or allow myself to begin to think differently to unblock the system?

4. Do I notice that I react markedly differently with certain friends/

family or in other situations, and could those differences be connected to trauma or triggering? Can I be thoughtful about any
trauma fear in me or another?

It may be helpful to revisit the meditation on fear and calm at the end
of Chapter 19 here.

You can find a short video that highlights some points from this chapter at https://www.youtube.com/watch?v=DFvS_HPqfaY or by scanning the QR code.

Chapter 20

TRAUMA BRINGS RESILIENCE: TEN STEPS TOWARDS POST-TRAUMATIC GROWTH

Don't waste a good crisis.[1] (Churchill)

It's never too late to be what you might have been.[2]

Beyond breaking free

Breaking free from trauma's power has been the focus in the previous 19 chapters. This final chapter partly acts as a summary of some primary ways to do this. However, breaking free is only part of our challenge. Building resilience and moving forwards after trauma is hard work. Building resilience means maintaining our course and learning how to continue to live in freedom. This chapter focuses on how, after we shed the trauma chrysalis that has encased, protected and restricted us, we might then go on to fly. I present ten 'resilience steps' that can bring both challenge and also new wonders. The word 'steps' implies that we should follow them in order, but how they work for us will be completely individual.

---

1   Winston Churchill, when working to form the United Nations after the Second World War, famously said this. Quoted 21 March 2019 by Guillaume Gruère of the Organisation for Economic Co-operation and Development (OECD).
2   This quote is attributed to the novelist and poet George Eliot (1819–1880) but others may have said it before: www.falmouthpubliclibrary.org/blog/the-curious-case-of-misquotation.

Resilience step 1: Stop and go inside

So often we speak about *moving on* after a tough experience, but throughout this book has been a call to first move *inside to identify trauma*. This can be one of the hardest and one of the most powerful trauma mitigations – taking the space to notice what is happening inside enables us to begin to reflect and think. We need to put on our own brakes. As someone said: 'Don't just do something, just stop and stand there!'

Changing gear

This can be a real challenge. Stopping to think can be hard because our trauma responses convince us to carry on doing what we are doing – trying to survive the best way we can. As Silvia Vasquez-Lavado writes, in response to the weight of trauma, we can endlessly 'pretty it up or hurry it up or drink it down or work it away'.[3]

Trauma responses play powerful tunes within, telling us what is happening or has happened and what we should do. Trauma often pushes the accelerator urging us to keep the status quo. In order to change, to mitigate trauma, we learn to pay attention to it. Bessel van der Kolk helped us to understand that our noticing brain is directly connected to our amygdala (alarm centre). Using our noticing brain as 'witness' to our feelings calms the body and restores safety.[4]

Stepping back to have a good look

The slower we go, the more we see. Sometimes it helps to imagine that we are looking at something from a distance, then we see more and we have more choices. We can ask ourselves: *are we thriving? Are we living our best lives?* Maybe we might feel too much or too little in response to life? Do we (or someone close to us) feel easily *overwhelmed, ramped up, disconnected*, or locked in to repetitive behaviours or looping patterns? As we have seen throughout these chapters, these may be signs of trauma.

---

3   Vasquez-Lavado, S. (2022). *In the Shadow of the Mountain*. London: Monoray, p.191. Vasquez-Lavado describes an extraordinary experience of leading a group of young female abuse survivors to the base camp of Everest and witnessing them being honest with themselves and each other.

4   van der Kolk, B. (2009) *The Body Keeps the Score*. London: Penguin, p.301.

It is counter-cultural to slow down

If we do have some trauma symptoms, *our current societal upheaval may be compounding them.* We live in an accelerated global culture and, as we explored in Chapter 19, trauma touches trauma – the domino effect. Speed matters and we need time to think and catch up with ourselves for anything to change. None of us can be immune to the global events that bombard us every day and the often-polarized narrative. All this can add to our sense of overwhelm, leaving us feeling helpless to know what we can do to help. Nationally and internationally, things feel more precarious and uncertain. An environment gasping for breath, wars and economic and political upheaval can feel as if the global tectonic plates of security are shifting beneath us. The changes and challenges of our world affect us all, taking us – individually and as families, communities and nations – on such a whitewater ride that we may increasingly be experiencing more trauma rather than processing and integrating our experiences.

Slowing down is a current pressing need

Learning how to regularly apply our brakes is an imperative in such a world. Someone I spoke with said, 'I just need to make my feathers go down.' This person knows she needs to access the green zone of safety mentioned in Chapter 1. How do we begin to do this? When we are living in the midst of current trauma, it may help to come at this sideways. The writer and poet Kerri ni Dochartaigh grew up in Northern Ireland at the height of the troubles. She writes: 'If you ever find yourself in a situation where you need to protect a child from bloodshed, find books about wild creatures for them, find a microscope; a magnifying glass, anything at all that helps the unknown make sense.'[5]

The idea of the Window of Tolerance is a tool

A bit of theory that might help. You will now be familiar with the 'too much or hyper' and 'too little or hypo' aspects of trauma (too much = overwhelm, which we have called the red zone; and too little = underwhelm, which we have called the blue zone in Chapter 1).

---

5   ni Dochartaigh, K. (2022). *Thin Places*. Edinburgh: Canongate Books, p.18.

As I said, the optimal regulated place to return to is the green zone, where we feel safe and calm. How do we foster our green zone? A trauma resource that many find helpful is the idea of the Window of Tolerance, first developed by psychiatrist Dan Siegel. When we have too much activation (red zone), or have zoned out and have too little (blue zone), *we have less toleration of our feelings*. We can be so aroused (or hyper, as we explored in Chapters 1, 4 and 5), or so shut off (or hypo, as we explored in Chapters 1 and 7), that our availability to be aware of what is happening to us in the present – our *'window'* – is limited. We might observe ourselves or someone else who is so unaware of their present reality that they appear to have a window of awareness which is as narrow as a tooth pick! The diagram below is a visual representation of the too much and too little polarities, above and below our Window of Tolerance.[6]

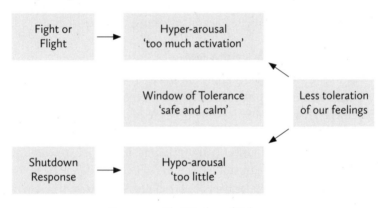

Figure 20.1: The Window of Tolerance

What we focus on grows – the discipline of staying in the present

One of our tasks, in post-trauma growth, is therefore to develop our attention to what is happening in the *present moment within us and develop an open curiosity and awareness about it.* That means awareness of both *our inner and outer world.* Over time, this tolerating of our own experience in the green zone, like a sash window gradually opening up

6   Adapted from Ogden, P. and Fisher, J. (2015). *Sensorimotor Psychotherapy*. New York, NY: Norton, p.69, and Siegel, D. (1999). *The Developing Mind*. New York, NY: Guilford Press.

to let in more air, will increase. We can then focus calmly for longer. In the green zone, we can begin to trust our feelings as a barometer for our lives. When we practise this, we expand our Window of Tolerance more and, as a consequence, the dominance of our too-much-hyper and too-little-hypo states decreases. What we focus on grows. What also helps increase our Window of Tolerance is developing an attitude of *kind attention* towards ourselves. We explore more on how we do this in step 2.

Resilience step 2: Awareness of trauma

Developing an awareness of our trauma responses is the clarion call of this book. A progression from stopping and identifying trauma, awareness is an *attitudinal stance*. It means learning to pay attention to what is inside *with a benign absence of judgement*. It means learning to accept ourselves, even the tricky bits.

Beliefs that block trauma awareness

We may have all kinds of beliefs that stop us being trauma aware – beliefs that tell us to minimize, judge or hide from our trauma rather than pay attention. I recently heard former President of Ireland Mary McAleese speaking on a podcast about her father, Paddy Leneghan, whose life was changed after witnessing a car bomb explosion on the Falls Road in Belfast, Northern Ireland, in 1972.[7] After the bomb, he went out to help a young woman, who died in his arms, and Paddy became traumatized as a result. Overnight, he changed from being outgoing and gregarious to a profoundly depressed person who sighed, but did not speak for several years. Many years later, Mary spoke with her father and asked him what he remembered about his experience. Astonishingly, he said that she was the first person to ask him what had happened on that day – the day that all their lives changed. When she asked if he had thought about getting help for his catatonic depression, he said, 'Who was I to say there was anything wrong with me?' Mary makes the powerful point that, in a climate

---

7   Professor Mary McAleese, President of Ireland (1997–2011), was interviewed by Alastair Campbell on *The Rest is Politics* podcast on 5 June 2023 about her father's story. She gave permission for me to mention it here.

of death and destruction, where so many suffer physical injury, psychological distress and pain are often judged to be way down in the hierarchy of pain. She speaks about a culture of stoicism, which is still prevalent in Northern Ireland today – that something troubling inside us is less important. This attitude is reinforced by a kind of pride that says you don't want to be looking for sympathy.

Challenging and loosening the power of our beliefs

Beliefs are not truths. If we hold on to them too tightly they can limit us. For example, we may believe we need to be strong but the truth is that it may harm us to banish softness. Loosening a fixed belief can enable us to drop some of our defences and claim our soft centre. If we cannot be soft or vulnerable, we perpetuate distress.

How? Because believing in a hierarchy of pain keeps trauma alive. In the aftermath of the Northern Ireland troubles, suicide, attempted suicide and mental distress are still endemic. As it did for Mary McAleese's father, hidden trauma can so often become another kind of (unacknowledged) explosion, causing untold suffering, going forward through the generations. Awareness of trauma really matters because if we are not aware, trauma can and does wreck lives.

Where might we see evidence of trauma?

We can look for narratives of *fear and anger*. These are common trauma responses that can dominate our individual, societal and political life. Of course, some traumas are caused by accidents and natural disasters. But many other traumas are caused by the way we treat one another. Myira Khan, psychotherapist and founder of the Muslim Counselling and Psychotherapy Network, writes about trauma: 'We are often treating the wound not the weapon.'[8] Part of becoming trauma aware is developing awareness of how we can cause trauma, human to human. Trauma can be caused by an unwillingness or inability to listen to other points of view, by power systems that disregard the vulnerable, by systems that skate over the surface by going for quick solutions or answers, by inflexible and polarized

---

8   Khan, M. (2022). Building resilience: Climate change anxiety and trauma. *New Psychotherapist*, 81, Autumn.

positions or by a hard unwillingness to feel or imagine others' feelings. We may also notice trauma when a situation becomes unbalanced, for example when there is a skewed championing of the individual to the detriment of the community. In response to any of the above, we might observe some of the symptoms outlined in these chapters.

How can we become trauma aware?

We can notice where power is and whether it is used for good – misuse of power creates trauma. We may need to pay attention when we notice that a part of ourselves or another person's pain is being dismissed, attacked, denigrated, ignored, not taken seriously or demonized. It is all too easy to ignore or gloss over painful experience. As we saw in Chapter 19 (on group responses to trauma), we can habitually disconnect, become inured to injustice and then it is easy to ignore it. To protect ourselves from discomfort, we can become anaesthetized to what misuse of power creates. Bad treatment of all kinds damages people, whether it is sexual violence, seeing difference as less than, being inured to the injustice of inequality or the exploitation of or disregard for the natural world. To mitigate this tendency, we can consciously develop a sensitivity to trauma. We can ask in a particular situation: is someone's experience or our own being squashed or overlooked? If so, we can choose to do the opposite – to see and honour it, notice it, name and challenge it, be compassionate and decide to operate from another non-traumatizing place entirely.

Development of curiosity about truth

For many of the individuals in this book, trauma is eventually dissipated. We can be transformed when painful truths are acknowledged – the fizz is released from the bottle. This takes curiosity about the charge of trauma that we might be holding. It is so easy to hide from the truth. We often go for simple sound-bite truths to try to avoid complexity. We blame others, and distort or avoid things that feel uncomfortable. Truth is often complex and it can be painful to face our own. We need to develop relentless curiosity to investigate what is true. When individuals and organizations become curious and open to understand complex things, we are likely to become less afraid to make mistakes. We then become less defensive, developing an open and thoughtful stance in relation to what is going on. At an organizational level, we can expand the bandwidth of our discussions. Curiosity opens up space, and space is an antidote to trauma.

Changing cultures as we respond to pain

On the one hand, we do not have to respond reactively towards wrong things. On the other, we do not have to go for easy solutions to make the discomfort go away. Either extreme is likely to perpetuate trauma and polarization. Reacting is an understandable human impulse, but in our trauma-fuelled reactivity often nothing much changes. We are on a merry-go-round. Part of post-trauma work is learning to acknowledge the charge of our feelings and then remain thoughtful about our discomfort, weighing our responses and actions carefully. Creating collective spaces where open and respectful conversations happen and where we can respond to each other's woundings can create change. Deep listening helps us attend to the painful under-current in our own or another person's trauma response. Looking at what may lie beneath the behaviour softens our reactivity and desire to judge and may also 'buy us time' to be thoughtful. By being aware of, empathic and thoughtful about trauma reactivity but not joining in with it, we will mitigate trauma's power. The impact of this could be huge, in our individual lives and within our families and workplaces.

Learn to trust, name and manage feelings

I have already mentioned learning to trust feelings, as our inner barometer. Part of this is developing the practice of naming our feelings. If we *name* our feelings, we learn to trust them to guide our choices and actions. Esther Perel says that post trauma it can feel as if a cast has been taken off our leg after it has been broken.[9] We need time to patiently learn how to use this part of us again. Of course, when we find our feelings and name them, we have to learn to tolerate them. When you are not sure what you feel, try

---

9 *Esther Perel: Where Should We Begin?* is an Audible Podcast that features anonymous couples who come for couple therapy. Esther makes this point in chapter 5, couple 4.

consulting a feelings wheel.[10] Feelings are fluid, we can help them move by writing them down. We may need to be patient learning to manage our feelings, whether they are too many or hard to find. This does not have to be all hard work, but we might notice that we prefer some feelings to others and they might not always appear in an orderly fashion!

Moving to the outer world – setting boundaries because we matter

As we learn to trust our feelings, we also begin to gain confidence in setting boundaries. Setting limits protects us from life's overwhelm, so that we begin to feel safe and calm in our own skin and like 'us' again. We stitch ourselves together through working out what we are able to manage and what we cannot. Part of this skill is in learning to trust what resonates with our needs from the inside out. (There is a needs audit in Appendix 1.) Asking ourselves what we or someone else might need is a good question to repeat. This was part of war reporter Raphael's journey in Chapter 1 – some of dealing with his trauma was working out that going to war zones was perpetuating his trauma, so he needed to limit his exposure. Post-trauma work is learning to become robust and consistent in attending to our own best interests. Learning to attend to our needs after trauma can be a big job, like turning round a big ship – it takes patience, determination and time.

Traumatized people need understanding

We traumatized ones often need special care. We may not be always able to give accounts of ourselves. We may not be coping with all we hold on a daily basis. We are likely to not always be able to think properly or be coherent. We may have an ongoing difficulty in trusting our own feelings or those of other people. This is not our fault, our difficulties are an expression of our desperation caused by our trauma wounds. Some of the individuals in the stories of the book may appear to have recovered easily from their trauma. The reality is often a longer and slower struggle, with bends and setbacks along roads to recovery. Sometimes, only a long journey

---

10   https://feelingswheel.com, accessed 27/01/24.

enables us to see how far we have travelled. Let us have a sense of awe about the things we are still able to manage while carrying a heavy load. Let us be astonished about how far we have come. We may not easily overcome or succeed. Many who have suffered trauma in their early lives will have an ongoing vulnerability to suffering further trauma. Even with good treatment, we may continue to sometimes feel threatened, triggered and unsafe in the world. Trauma hollows us out, often leaving us feeling of less value than others. As a consequence, we can expect bad treatment and then expect to see it everywhere. An experience of deficit so easily colours our experience of life.

Attitude shift

To support a traumatized person an attitudinal shift may be necessary, to look beyond 'bad behaviour' – that can be part of trauma's vocabulary – to search for meaning and spacious understanding. I believe that we need less condemnation and more tolerance, less averting of gazes and more seriousness about the emotional weight of what happens to ourselves and others. Adversity leaves us humans with particular challenges and struggles. Our best chance of building resilience after adversity is through the quality of relationship – through kindness, which we first need to show to ourselves.

Resilience step 3: Noticing triggers and finding a safe space
Using beauty to find space through cosmic wonder

We cannot face painful truths until we feel safe. Building safety will allow recovery from too much stress – trauma. Taking the foot off the stress pedal is the first stage, if only for moments at first. As already stated, when we step back we can begin to think. In addition, many individuals cited in the book found that post-trauma regulation *often takes active work*. Finding a psychologically safe space is integral to changing trauma patterns and expanding the green-zone Window of Tolerance. Finding an actual physical space where we can attend to our minds and bodies, allowing our beleaguered nervous systems to feel soothed, can be a real help. I heard the phrase 'cosmic wonder' and think this term expresses an important post-trauma superpower.[11] We might have a favourite chair, or a shed at the bottom of the garden, a favourite tree, anywhere that nurtures or anchors us. The natural world has simplicity, spaciousness and continuity that can hold all our inner ripples, our fears and our griefs, expressed beautifully in the poem 'The Peace of Wild Things' by Wendell Berry.[12] Someone I worked with said she remembers how much better she felt as a child, looking at a large sky and feeling small. Even a tiny awareness of beauty can heal us. In our safe places, we can feel life returning to our dried and cracked inner crevices once more.

Internal safe spaces

The next stage is to create a safe space for ourselves *in our minds*. Going to a safe place in our imagination can be done even if there is no external safety, as was explored by Victor Frankl in his seminal book written about the holocaust: *Man's Search for Meaning* (1946).[13] The ability to do this takes courage, practice, repetition, discipline, determination and patience. At first, our inner space may feel like balancing on a precarious ledge, not so easy to trust in. If we keep returning to a place of safety in our imagination, we will reach a tipping point where we feel safe more of the time and recover faster from our triggers – *practising repeatedly returning to a calmer place of curiosity and safety is an antidote to trauma*. The meditations and exercises in this book foster the developing of what Roger Robinson calls a 'portable paradise', a place inside of beauty and wonder.[14]

When we feel on safe ground, we are more likely to be able to understand what is happening to us, calm down and think properly. From a scaffolding of safety, we can have a wider perspective to understand ourselves and see other points of view than our fixed

11   These words were spoken by novelist, journalist and publisher Tom Stacey who died in 2022. He used this phrase in a talk called Exploring Faith – Our Spiritual Lacuna, in Holland Park on 17 October 2022, http://hollandparkbenefice.org/sermon-blog/2022/10/17/exploring-faith-2022-tom-stacey-our-spiritual-lacuna.

12   Berry, W. (2009). 'The Peace of Wild Things.' In *The Selected Poems of Wendell Berry*. New York, NY: Counterpoint Press.

13   Frankl, V. (1963, originally published 1946). *Man's Search for Meaning*. New York, NY: Washington Square Press.

14   Roger Robinson is the winner of the 2020 TS Eliot prize. His poem *A Portable Paradise* is published by Peepal Press (2019).

trauma beliefs. From an inner safe place, we build recovery and we build resilience.

Investigating our triggering means acknowledging the truth of our experience slowly and honestly

In a safe space, *truth can emerge and be acknowledged, if only as occasional glimmers to begin with.* Sometimes, facing our emotional truth can feel too much, but a little acknowledgement goes a long way. At the right time and with the right person, a truthful framing of what is going on for a traumatized person can feel like an oasis to a parched body. A part of trauma work necessitates us developing a habit of enquiry. Giving ourselves time and the space to notice, we can dare to ask ourselves penetrating questions such as *what is my deep trouble? What is my emotional truth? How might I acknowledge and find ways to deepen my acceptance of this truth, however scary? What do I know about the meaning of what is going on?* When the individuals featured in this book faced their painful truth with compassion, a bit at a time, many of them changed their trauma story.

Compassion means meeting pain with love and understanding

For so many, being stuck in trauma is like being stuck in concrete without being able to move, yet saying what is true at the right time is like weight training, giving us the beginnings of freedom and strength. We are less in thrall to our trauma processes when we meet our pain with active understanding – *compassion*. Doing this takes an imaginative leap – being stuck in trauma survival does not leave much space for compassion.

How to foster compassion

If I am in relationship with a traumatized person, can I imagine they might feel like they are stuck in concrete? Can I ask them what they feel like? Might knowing it give me more empathy? Can I take time to listen to their story, and maybe disregard any perplexing behaviour that I might want to judge because I do not understand it? Might I try to hear the music beyond their words? Might I learn to patiently and repeatedly ask, *what might help you right now?*

Building safety means noticing where we feel safe and with whom

We can also find safe people who feel like home.[15] The individuals portrayed in the stories in this book often found a trusted other, such as Pete with his brother in Chapter 6. Breathing the same air with trusted others regulates our stressed nervous systems and calms us, allowing us to accept ourselves and surrender in safety. Next time you are with a deeply trusted person, imagine taking a plumb line to your heart and listen to what you feel inside. It can feel as if you are laying emotional slabs at the bottom of yourself. If you are trusted like this by a lonely individual, you may mean more to them than they let you know.

Getting to be experts in our own triggers

From a place of greater honesty about ourselves, we can get to know our triggers. Like Joe, our mountaineer in Chapter 3 (and so many others), triggering can take us down a river, but if we get to the bank, notice what is there and gather the fearful debris in an 'awareness dam', we may then choose not to respond from our triggers, but be thoughtful about their emotional underbelly. Once it is identified and understood, we can allow our trigger 'log' to float down the river.

Awareness is a post-trauma power

We should not be surprised when our triggers keep coming. Trauma recovery can be discouraging – when we are triggered, our pack of cards can easily collapse all over again. Awareness of our triggers will help speed up our recovery. The more awareness we develop of all that flows through our Window of Tolerance, the less power our triggers will have. Trauma's urgency may necessitate us to change tack. We may need to set strong limits for ourselves or change something fundamental – a proper reboot. A virtuous cycle can be built from the foundations of our personal safe space. From here, we can begin to notice shards of good that we can appreciate and take in. This is our hard-work, post-trauma weight training.

---

15 These words feature in Mackesy, C. (2019). *The Boy, The Mole, The Fox and The Horse*. London: Ebury Press. It is a beautiful and meditative story. The animated version can be found on YouTube.

Resilience step 4: Body awareness
Focus on our bodies and send them 'top down' messages of safety

Finding a place of safety helps our bodies relax. We are embodied – this where we hold our experience. Therefore, we need to treat our bodies with respect; if they hold trauma they are also part of us finding our path through it. We can become whole by allowing our bodies to tell us what they hold, to 'speak' their emotional truth and then release it and let go.

How do we do this? A first job may be to use our minds to focus on our bodies, like a hovering helicopter. We can find ways to help our bodies feel safe. We can support our backs and root our feet to the floor, then notice the difference inside. We may need to pull our shoulders back, lengthen our backbone, open our chest, and become aware of the weight and ease our bodies when we feel safe in our own skin. At other times, we may need to tune into and respect our bodies' messages and invite them to tell their story.

Our bodies give messages – sometimes protective, sometimes not about now

They give us signs that something is wrong. For example, we might stop properly breathing in shock, brace ourselves, feel like giving up, feel a weird buzzing, or find ourselves ploughing through with our shoulders hunched to just keep going with a necessary narrow focus. A number of individuals in the book found a way through trauma by learning to trust in and follow the lead of their bodies. Wilmer, in Chapter 12, listens to his body, which gives him an important protective message. He understands this message, then he lets the activation go. Sometimes these messages are anachronisms, no longer needed in our current lives. In the same chapter, Julian learns to respect his body's cowering – an old fearful message. He understands its meaning as it shows up in his close relationship, and he releases the power of his trauma fizz, letting the emotional charge go through repeated out-breaths. With repetition, this practice helps Julian begin to love the skin he is in.

Our bodies can help us through releasing trauma

At other times, our bodies can help take us out of trauma. Research shows that physical activity can stimulate the growth of new neuronal connections in the brain.[16] Freya, in Chapter 2, finds a way to move through her repetitive and consuming trauma fear by allowing her body to remind her that she can skate. Moving her body helps her heal, soothes her anxious thoughts and allows her to restore balance in her life. She is literally 'doing something' with her pain. There are numerous ways we can find to release the pain when our bodies are frozen or constricted with trauma, such as exercising to raise our heart rate, sweating, taking ourselves to an edge through sex, releasing adrenalin in fairground rides, yelling, singing, performing, singing, dancing, being creative, watching an activity or sport, touching, immersing ourselves in nature, doing martial arts. These are just examples – there are so many ways to express ourselves and release the pain of trauma.

Self-soothing and coming into 'now'

Our bodies are great barometers. They sometimes need us to pay attention and calibrate them. Even if we are actually safe right now, we can still carry body messages that tell us we are not. I heard about someone who would wake up in panic but found applying a cold flannel to his face brought his mind and body to 'now'. This profoundly soothed his body, giving it the powerful message: 'You're safe here, now.' Another way is to place a soothing hand on the part of our body that holds any fearful activation. In so doing, we acknowledge the fearful tension held in our muscles with compassion, then let the emotional charge go on an out-breath, imagining it flowing like a ripple down our bodies and out through the bottom of our feet. A longer exhalation each time will activate our parasympathetic nervous system, allowing us to move from activation into deep rest. When we repeat this practice, we may notice an increase in bodily peace, as we learn to surrender and let go. Massage or experimenting with self-touch can be so restorative and renewing.[17] These are ways that we learn to be calm and safe in the present moment.

---

16   Sherman, C. (2019). The quest to cure PTSD. *Psychology Today*, October. This article examines the research of neuroscientist Ronald Duman on this subject.

17   Developed by US neuroscientist Dr Ronald Ruden, the Havening Technique uses gentle self-touch to soothe, such as, with crossed arms, gently stroking from shoulders to elbows, gently touching the face and lips in repeated ways. www. healthline.com/health/mental-health/havening, accessed 28/01/24.

How seeking out pleasure works at a bodily level

I already mentioned that trauma often cuts us off from pleasure. Sometimes, if our bodies feel unsafe, it might help to shift posture. Simply opening up our chest may allow us to become more receptive to good things, such as the intricate beauty of a flower or a shaft of light sending its beam through a cloud. As we allow in what gives us pleasure, we might notice our breathing drop in the relief of safety, as we lean into the fullness of life once more. Post trauma, some people report that the simple act of lying on the ground holds their distress at a deep level. We can ask ourselves repeatedly: what feels good? What do I need to do right now? Then do it! As we build pleasurable moments, one good thing cascades into another. We move from only seeing one trauma colour, to seeing a post-trauma rainbow. Allowing our senses to take in the sound of gentle singing, the crash of waves on a beach, the fresh aroma of air after heavy rain, or the hug of a friend, a piece of art or the touch of a pet, might soothe, restore and expand our horizons. We can experiment with hope. What makes us feel alive is personal to us. It may be delicate and as varied as we are. What are gifts and signs of life that we can take into our minds, spirits and bodies, helping us grow and giving us vitality and peace?

Resilience step 5: Befriending our fear

Fear tells big stories that may need to be heard. We have a society that dislikes fear and can see it as a weakness, so it is often counter-cultural to look over the precipice of our fear and learn its landscape. As a consequence, it is very common to blame ourselves when we are afraid, or react to it in other ways by running from, fixing or avoiding things (Chapter 5), or spring into defence or judgement by attacking or hating others (Chapter 4).

Don't partner with fear! Work out whether fear is present or past

One way to begin to see our own trauma processes is to develop dual awareness with the help of our noticing minds (see Chapter 14). Listening out for our body fear from a more mindful place, we are far more likely to be able to tolerate our fear without reacting to it. When pausing, we may notice a tightening or ball in the chest. Can we allow a sensation that we hold to 'speak' or express itself? For example, if we listen, a fearful scrunch or flip in the belly might want to say 'No, no, no!' when it feels threatened. 'I need to protect you from harm!' fear often says. We can ask ourselves: is this an old fear that needs to be released or a message pertinent to now?

It is a paradox, but noticing fear often diminishes it. Fear can easily grow, becoming the only show in town, convincing us of its conclusions. As an American colleague of mine says to her clients: 'Don't partner with fear!' It is a subtle distinction to be able to hear and acknowledge (befriend) our fear, without allowing it to dominate our thoughts and actions (partnering with it). A good question: is my fear realistic, or might it be an old story that I continue to carry?

Fear can be camouflaged

Taking a long hard look at fear processes requires courage and perseverance. Fear frequently can operate inside, in camouflage, so hearing it within ourselves may take much attentive listening. It is so much easier to focus on the things that frighten us rather than the fear itself. Outside is easier to bear than painful and scary things inside. When we do manage to acknowledge what we carry inside, it can be a relief to let the snakeskin of fear go, and become softer and calmer, if only for a short time to begin with. This may lead us to feel out of control and vulnerable, so we may need someone to help us. Remember Benita and Caleb in Chapter 10 who learned to *linger* with feelings together and found over time that their relationship revived?

Resilience step 6: Find someone to entrust your feelings to
Finding good people

According to Meg Jay, 'Good people are everywhere. We should find someone to tell our secrets to... If they say the wrong thing, find someone else...soon.'[18]

---

18 Jay, M. (2017). *Supernormal: Stories of Adversity, Resilience and Growth*. Family Action Network, accessed 27/01/24, www.youtube.com/watch?v=kFunEkA72MI.

Think of Finella's painful pressure to make something better long ago in the childhood home (Chapter 4) and the tears of relief she shed when speaking this truth with her friend. It can feel wonderful to have someone else properly see who we really are. Being unseen is at the heart of many traumas and also perpetuates them, as explored in Chapter 17. Kerri ni Dochartaigh's journey began when an empathic doctor told her that she did not deserve to feel the way she did and she had done well to survive.[19] It had taken her a long time to risk telling her inner story.

To practise saying what we know is true to ourselves and someone else can feel as destabilizing and scary as descending a rickety lift shaft, but speaking our truth can also become a vital and relieving discipline to do regularly. It is wonderful to find 'our people', our community, where who we are is accepted, where we find our place, where we build resilience with the support of others. Someone I worked with who always felt unseen – an 'added extra' in a troubled family life – described feeling overlooked as being 'a cherry on the cake'. When he found an Al-Anon group, he was amazed and joyful to discover others who felt as excluded and overlooked as he did.[20] In an environment of safety, he spoke about he felt to like-minded others who listened and gave space to the practice of understanding. To be taken seriously felt like a balm. When he shared his drips of truth, he was healed with joyful relief. He said the group members often felt similar things – the room was like a bowl of cherries! I believe that the potential for change in belonging and sharing goes beyond words: over time, drips of water can carve rock.

How to help someone who does not trust easily

Trauma separates us from others and it can be hard to trust others post trauma. Trauma teaches us that we are on our own, and that we therefore need to survive in a solo capacity. If you want to support a traumatized person, they will need your trauma-informed under-standing so they can dare to develop trust in you. You may need to understand that they have a 'need to forget and a wish to remember'

---

19 ni Dochartaigh, K. (2022). *Thin Places*. Edinburgh: Canongate Books, p.179.
20 Al-Anon is a worldwide organization set up to support the family and friends of alcoholics.

what has happened to them.[21] It may be important to honour and respect both of these at different times. A traumatized person will need special treatment of active consistency and love, demonstrated in many stories in this book. It is important to weigh the weight of their experience in your mind, with imagination and without judgement. When we humans are lost, our need is to be repeatedly found. Someone who is traumatized needs others to stick around and keep offering a non-dominating presence without agenda and 'maximum contact' care. They need to be offered an 'invisible string' that connects them to others inside.[22] If it is too much, trust that the traumatized person will say so, and carefully follow their lead. Many people do this for others all the time.

The power of empathy to mitigate fear

Chantal's post-trauma work began with receiving a bullseye of empathy (see Chapter 19). Empathy is a powerful commodity. In a polarized world, it can sometimes feel as though empathy has died. We need to hold on to it, while recognizing that it can be demanding to offer a hurting person safety and loving care on a daily basis. If we are a carer, we need empathy too and to develop our own plentiful inner resources to draw on in order to keep going. Can we repeatedly offer empathy to ourselves, especially when the going gets tough?

If you are supporting a traumatized person, they may need you to believe in them when they cannot. You may need to offer to help with maybe simple practical tasks that their trauma renders them unable to do. Kay in Chapter 8 gratefully accepts the help of her friend's 'auxiliary brain' when she is overwhelmed by catastrophic loss. Many of the trauma sufferers featured in this book are helped by the quality of consistent care that never gives up on them. Finding someone who believes in us is gold dust: it is a major indicator of hope for post-traumatic growth.

Fear tells us to banish painful feelings, dismiss them, avoid them, make them smaller than they are. Empathy mitigates fear. What we

---

21 Woodcock, J. (2022). *Families and Individuals Living with Trauma*. London: Palgrave, p.114.

22 Karst, P. (2018). *The Invisible String*. New York, NY: Little, Brown. This is a picture book about the unbreakable connections between humans.

most need is someone to open their minds and imaginations up enough to grasp what we have suffered. If they do this, it gives us the message that our feelings matter, that we matter, even with all this 'stuff'. If we receive this message and believe it ourselves, we can carry on. We can be ourselves. We can transform our trauma with care.

Resilience step 7: Finding meaningful things to connect with
Expanding into a sense of purpose and possibility...

Individuals who find their way to post-trauma growth often do so through finding a sense of purpose. Joe, in Chapter 3, after an encounter with a listening tattoo artist, dedicates himself to helping others through difficult life experiences. It is possible for trauma's charge to be redirected to something that makes meaning out of meaninglessness. The fearful contraction of trauma responses will often lead us to say 'Yes, but...' to ourselves and others and to life itself. This *but* leads us down the same old path. A post-traumatic position will understand the pull to 'Yes, but...' and with determination and awareness accept the truth of trauma and then determinedly ask what life might lead us to next. Like an improvisational comedian, in order to build trauma resilience, we can ask ourselves: 'Yes...and...? What can I do now?'

Whatever next is will be as varied as we are. We might think of individuals whose loved one suffers a miscarriage of justice. Springing from an experience of deep trauma and loss, so many determindly keep faith with something that is worth fighting for. They do this by operating from love for the one who is hurt or lost and the pursuit of love's instrument – justice. We may be inspired by such stories of individuals who find post-trauma meaning, following where love for another takes them, proving that, ultimately, 'love is as strong as death'.[23]

---

23 Song of Solomon, Chapter 8: 6, 7.

Information gathering can bring a sense of power

Children's author Michael Rosen writes about his son Eddie's death from meningitis.[24] What helps him find meaning in the aftermath is discovering all he can about meningitis and speaking to others who have had similar experiences. Information gathering can be part of post-trauma growth. In the face of terrifying events and out-of-control situations, information soothes us. Figuring out what has happened is our brain's way of not being swallowed up by trauma and gives us an important sense of post-trauma mastery.

Finding some devotion

Another person may find meaning in following a spiritual practice. After trauma, we can find comfort in a repeated engagement with something that fits with our values and what is most important to us, where 'discipline can move to devotion'. Following a practice of some sort can bring purpose, solace and renewed direction to our lives.[25] Jase, in Chapter 15, finds solace and self-expression through practising art. We might find meaning through going on long walks in remote areas, alone or with others, or finding a liminal place of beauty or developing another kind of practice, such as playing the piano or joining a martial arts or yoga community.

Resilience step 8: Developing a scaffolding of support
Do we need therapy or not?

Throughout the book, through the trauma stories and resources, I have offered ideas about how to find and weave pathways back to ourselves and others. There are as many routes through as there are people and one size does not fit all. We can be creative in finding ways to discharge or mitigate the chilli powder of overwhelm that is trauma. Specialized therapeutic support is not always necessary, but therapy can help if emotions are overpowering or debilitating or if

---

24   Rosen, M. (2023). *Getting Better*. London: Ebury Press. This outlines how the author faces unbearable losses in a variety of ways, including the sudden trauma of finding his son suddenly dead from meningitis one morning.

25   Fannen, L. (2021). *Warp and Weft: Psycho-Emotional Health Politics and Experiences*. Bristol: Active Distribution Publishing, Section 104 on Practice.

it is right to take the courageous step of dissipating trauma's charge with a skilled helper. Becoming open to scary feelings in a therapy room is not easy. It needs to be done at the right time and when a person has sufficient support. A strong scaffolding of care will be necessary to help us manage any painful feelings that are unearthed in the excavation of a trauma therapy process.

Examples of post-trauma growth are as varied as we are

Another person may not wish to be introspective or reflective about their experience in this way and may find other routes through trauma that suit them. There is no compunction for anyone to have therapy or process their trauma if they do not wish to or are not ready to. There are many routes to creativity, meaning-making and recovery. A person might write a novel, take up golf with a passion or become a gardener. Someone I heard of made a study of the four-mile radius around their house, walking as though they were kissing the land, slowly and with attention, exploring the land and changes in seasons with a kind of reverence – a ritual that brought healing and a profound sense of being grounded.

Remember that it is never too late to make changes

I realize that we left Nikko rather high and dry in Chapter 5 with his painful past and his addiction to gaming and fast food. Though Nikko's trauma struggles were real through much of his life, he ultimately found meaning and peace through enjoying the appreciation of his technical skills in his small team at work and through making jam from the plum tree he adored in his garden. In these ways, even though his addiction and isolation were severe, he found a path to grow and find something new post trauma.

We are more connected than we think

I often observe how much we humans enjoy coincidences – it often thrills us when we meet someone who knows someone we know, reminding us how connected we are. Developing connections – both outside and inside – is a post-trauma superpower. We are stitching together the threads of our own tapestry. Connections can move us from feeling out of control to feeling as if we are in charge of who we are. There are many ways to achieve this, through meditation, through seeking out and having regular contact with others who support our thinking and meaning-making. More on this in step 9.

Resilience step 9: Believe in ourselves and look after each other
The way we treat ourselves matters – gently weaving in forgiveness

The process of coming to understand ourselves can be hard yet ultimately can bring us more fullness and freedom. Trauma destroys joy, yet being open to bear discomfort and face what is painful for the sake of truth is an act of faith and hope – hope that we can find peace and joy again. Can we weave a thread of forgiveness into ourselves and soften our self-judgement through understanding? Rather like throwing a boulder into a pond, the ripple effect is potentially far-reaching.

Our wounds show us what really matters

Our tears and what causes them matter. Our wounds inside us need to be honoured, seen, gently leaned into, weighed and expressed – so that what grows around them can become strong and beautiful. When this happens, trauma gives us the *gift of perspective* – teaching us what is most important in the gift of life itself. I recently heard someone interviewed, whose child had been tragically killed, and they said, 'Look after each other, look after what you have.' He also became an activist, raising the awareness of knife crime in Parliament and setting up projects to support young people struggling with drugs and violence. Through finding words, being honest, reaching out, giving space and stating our limits, trusting ourselves, pondering what is most important now, being determined to make change, we honour our wounds. Through learning to trust our feelings as barometers and through letting goodness and nurturing in, we learn to feel properly safe. Our feelings matter and so do our experiences. Trusting in all this helps us develop post-trauma resilience.

Resilience step 10: Growth through accepting fragility and loving kindness
Honouring the invisible and working with it

So much of this book has been about moving in, in order to move on. In our attempts to survive trauma, we forget and we cover up. As a consequence, we cover up the treasures that we hold within us and lose the potential of who we might be in the world. The glory of our own and the world's goodness gets eclipsed.

We need to work towards greater visibility of the things that are hidden and broken. The Japanese art of Kintsugi has been developed over centuries as a way of repairing a broken vessel by highlighting the breaks in the pottery and applying gold. The philosophy behind this is that we should try to repair things because sometimes in doing so we ultimately create objects of even more beauty and worth. Paying attention to the fractures is time consuming, but it allows an artist to appreciate the vessel in a completely different way. This is the essence of resilience and traumatic growth: the superpower found in discovering a new relationship to our pain and our fears and the power and gifts we find through going through fire and coming out the other side.

We can find ways to cope with traumatic events through learning how our experiences form us, by taking the best from them and knowing that it is exactly these experiences that make each person unique and precious. Our experiences do not mean we are less than others. Kintsugi is difficult. This is often the case in facing painful experiences and feelings inside. In fact, it may feel as though we are looking over a precipice when we truly look inside for the first time. Can we bear it? Or can we bear not to, and carry on in the same way?

The journey matters

To embark on this process of becoming whole can be like beginning a long journey with no clear route or destination. We may need the help of a skilled other to be a good mirror, to help us learn who we are and who we could be. Or we may not. Whatever our route to finding our voice, may we face our wounds with honesty and realize our enormous capacity for regeneration and adaptability.

Doing the work of discovering our layers is humbling. Understanding what lies inside and beyond the obvious may lead us to treating ourselves with more kindness and accepting ourselves, right to our roots. If we rehabilitate the hated, fearful and painful parts inside and learn to treat ourselves with compassion, we may find we are able to live in a place of greater cohesiveness and coherence inside. We can live in loving freedom.

Seeking out goodness

Kindness has the potential to unlock creativity. If we are at ease and honest with ourselves, touching base with our truth, moment by moment, the person we can be is able to emerge. Then we are more likely to view others with tolerance and understanding, seeing their wounds and struggles. We might discover that using our imaginations to commit to discovering the good and the gift in our lives is a bold and liberating choice.

Trauma is powerful. It changes us but can also bring strength – strength that is forged through trusting that our broken threads can be reconnected even as we struggle in the dark. In doing so, without realizing it, we are going further, we are erecting a scaffolding of gold that fuses around our wounds, building our resilience. We can use trauma's power to make us more determined to live openly and courageously, being determined to notice where goodness is found for us and for others. We begin to live in ways that help break loose from all that binds us, becoming expectant and hopeful about what life has to offer us.

We begin to live trusting that our future will be bigger than our past. This is my sincere hope for all who read this book – that you will find the gold within you.

These are the words written for everyone mentioned in this book:

Trauma survivor know your roots
You are allowed
To be who you are
In your roots
(painful though)

Under the ground our
Capacity is legion
Intricate delicate threads
Connecting experiences
Memories, feelings

Love rooting in its own time
It is in each other interweaving
Like an entanglement of trees
That our freedom comes

You can find a short video that highlights some points from this chapter at https://www.youtube.com/watch?v=hjn7MGXJrwo or by scanning the QR code.

Appendix 1

Needs audit: then and now

The headings below might help you focus and reflect on needs, both then and now. Take space and time for this and return to it, if it is helpful. This kind of exercise is particularly useful for those with trauma from long ago.

	Needs that are not met	Needs that were/are met
Child's needs		
Needs now		

Appendix 2

Jar meditation on post-traumatic space

The picture below is a metaphor for post-trauma growth in three different sized jars. In each jar, there is a tennis ball which is the same size. The tennis ball is the trauma activation.

In the jar on the right, the tennis ball completely fills the space. This is us when we are captured by trauma activation, when trauma is ruling the roost and dominating our lives.

In the second sized jar, the tennis ball still takes up most of the space, but there is also a little space in our minds to notice, think about or dissipate trauma's power.

In the larger jar, we still have our trauma, but there is so much space and other life-giving activity around in our lives that trauma's power is minimized. Our trauma experience is integrated into the warp and weft of our lives and, in the space, we hold some important lessons from our trauma. In the space, we hold our resilience and our hard-won superpowers.

Which jar is us, now? Maybe this changes from day to day. Let us reflect on what the things are that help bring spaciousness and increase our ability to notice the good. How might we continue to build our post-trauma resilience?